Modern Comparative Politics Series
edited by
Peter H. Merkl
University of California,
Santa Barbara

THE BENELUX NATIONS

0   100
miles

N

North Sea

BRITAIN

Channel

FRANCE

GERMANY

NETHERLANDS

Groningen
Friesland
Drenthe
Noord Holland
Amsterdam
Overijssel
Zuid Holland
The Hague
Rotterdam
Utrecht
Gelderland
Zeeland
Noord Brabant
Limburg

Antwerp
Oost Vlanderen
Antwerpen
Limburg
West Vlanderen
Brussels
Hainaut
Brabant
Liège
BELGIUM
Namur
Luxembourg

LUXEMBOURG
Luxembourg

KEY

– – – National Border
– – – Provincial Border
——— Language Border—Belgium
       Flemish North of Line
       French South of Line
– – – German East of Line
● National Capital
○ Major City

THE BENELUX NATIONS

The politics of small-country democracies

Gordon L. Weil

HOLT, RINEHART AND WINSTON, INC.
New York   Chicago   San Francisco   Atlanta
Dallas   Montreal   Toronto   London   Sydney

To Roberta, Anne, and Richard

Copyright © 1970 by Gordon L. Weil

Library of Congress Catalog Card Number: 76–96137

SBN: 03–079755–1

Printed in the United States of America

9 8 7 6 5 4 3 2 1

FOREWORD TO THE SERIES

This new series in comparative politics was undertaken in response to the special needs of students, teachers, and scholars that have arisen in the last few years, needs that are no longer being satisfied by most of the materials now available. In an age when our students seem to be getting brighter and more politically aware, the teaching of comparative politics should present a greater challenge than ever before. We have seen the field come of age with numerous comparative monographs and case studies breaking new ground, and the Committee on Comparative Politics of the Social Science Research Council can look back proudly on nearly a decade of important spade work. But teaching materials have lagged behind these changing approaches to the field. Most comparative government series are either too little coordinated to make systematic use of any common methodology or too conventional in approach. Others are so restricted in scope and space as to make little more than a programmatic statement about what should be studied, thus suggesting a new scholasticism of systems theory that omits the idiosyncratic richness of the material available and tends to ignore important elements of a system for fear of being regarded too traditional in approach.

In contrast to these two extremes, the Modern Comparative Politics Series attempts to find a happy combination of rigorous, systematic methodology and the rich sources of data available to area and country specialists. The series consists of a core volume, *Modern Comparative Politics,* by Peter H. Merkl, country volumes covering one or more nations, and comparative topical volumes.

Rather than narrowing the approach to only one "right" method, the core volume leaves it to the teacher to choose any of several approaches he may prefer. The authors of the country volumes are partly bound by a framework common to these volumes and the core volume, and are partly free to tailor their approaches to the idiosyncrasies of their respective countries. The emphasis in the common framework is on achieving a balance between such elements as theory and application, as well as among developmental perspectives, sociocultural aspects, the group processes, and the decision-making processes of government. It is hoped that the resulting tension between comparative approaches and politicocultural realities will enrich the teaching of comparative politics and provoke discussion at all levels from undergraduate to graduate.

The group of country volumes is supplemented by a group of analytical comparative studies. Each of these comparative volumes takes an important topic and explores it cross-nationally. Some of these topics are covered in a more limited way in the country volumes, but many find their first expanded treatment in the comparative volumes—and all can be expected to break new scholarly ground.

The ideas embodied in the series owe much to the many persons whose names are cited in the footnotes of the core volume. Although they are far too numerous to mention here, a special debt of spiritual paternity is acknowledged to Harry Eckstein, Gabriel A. Almond, Carl J. Friedrich, Sidney Verba, Lucian W. Pye, Erik H. Erikson, Eric C. Bellquist, R. Taylor Cole, Otto Kirchheimer, Seymour M. Lipset, Joseph La Palombara, Samuel P. Huntington, Cyril E. Black, and many others, most of whom are probably quite unaware of their contribution.

P. H. M.

Santa Barbara, California

PREFACE

This book, about three small nations of western Europe, is intended to serve two purposes. First we shall investigate how these countries, and the Netherlands in particular, have developed a variety of mechanisms, some outstandingly successful and others clear failures, for dealing with the major problem of Western political society—the relation of the individual to his political culture. Models of political stability on the European continent, they are often overlooked—yet their experience is relevant to virtually all Western countries.

This book includes many case studies, and each is illustrated by one of the Benelux nations. The Netherlands represents a society that has achieved a remarkable degree of internal harmony and one of the most democratic political systems. Belgium is a nation grappling with a social and political question—the language dispute between French- and Flemish-speaking Belgians—in the framework of a political society that is threatened by the violence of the struggle. In a sense, Belgium is seeking the kind of domestic political consensus that the Netherlands has found. Finally, Luxembourg is a "ministate" that has succeeded against great odds in maintaining its political integrity and in creating a society of plenty.

A second function of this book is to probe the motivations and policies of small nations in international politics and, in particular, in the European integration movement. It is almost self-evident that small nations should seek to band together to face common problems in a world dominated by countries spanning continents and with hundreds of millions of inhabitants. In examining the political development of the Benelux nations, we can understand more clearly the need for this kind of joint action. At the same time, the Benelux experience indicates the extent to which small nations may enhance their influence by joining with other states in international organizations.

It is common belief that France plays a dominant role in the European Community. Yet the history of the Community reveals the strong and often effective action taken by the Benelux nations, led by the Netherlands, in resisting French demands. While France has indeed been successful in blocking moves toward greater political integration, it has been prevented from transforming the European Community (and the North Atlantic Treaty Organization) into a French-dominated organization. This is largely due to the policies of the Benelux nations. As shall be seen, these policies are firmly rooted in the domestic political realities of the three countries.

During the almost five years that I lived in Belgium and came to know the Benelux countries, a great many people helped me understand the politics of these nations. It would be impossible to name all those who took the time to discuss Benelux politics with me, and it would be unfair to mention some but not all of these politicians, professors, journalists, and government officials. I hope my thanks is expressed in my attempt to understand all points of view and to render a fair and balanced account of them.

Three officials, however, merit special thanks. Ch. Philippe de Schoutheete de Tarvarent and M. van der Epst of the Belgian Ministry of Foreign Affairs were continually available with answers to almost any conceivable question about Belgian affairs and policy. They were unfailingly helpful and outstandingly courteous. Mr. P. J. H. Jonkman of the Netherlands Embassy in Brussels and Delegation to the European Community demonstrated the utmost speed and effectiveness in obtaining information for me and in arranging contacts in the Netherlands. His devotion to his duty as an information officer was remarkable.

I must also acknowledge my debt of gratitude to the students of the Spring 1968 session of the Drew University Semester on the European Economic Community. They prepared papers on the Benelux nations that allowed me to gauge the nature and depth of undergraduate interest in these countries. Some of them did excellent research work that was a great help to me. They, in turn, came to learn about the nations in which they lived and worked for several months.

Finally, to my wife, Roberta M. Weil, I express my profound appreciation for her encouragement and collaboration in this work.

Naturally, none of the above-mentioned is in any way responsible for any errors in the text.

G. L. W.

New York City
November 1969

CONTENTS

INTRODUCTION

Hardly a week passes for the careful newspaper reader without his seeing *Benelux* in articles on European affairs. To some the word simply means the three small countries—Belgium, the Netherlands, and Luxembourg—that occupy one corner of the jigsaw map of Europe. To others, it represents an economic grouping, somewhat of the order of the European Common Market, though on a smaller scale.

These conceptions fail to give a complete picture. The Benelux states, despite their tiny area and small populations, have shared a common history; they have been world powers and they were leaders in cultural and intellectual enlightenment at the end of the Middle Ages. Though they now occupy a much more modest place in a world dominated by superpowers, they exercise an influence far out of proportion to their size. They have given up their positions of political dominance for a less dramatic, but equally effective, role as economic powers. As they pool their efforts, they achieve even greater strength on the world scene.

At one time, the Benelux nations were united; but as the Reformation and Counter-Reformation split Protestants from Catholics, the Netherlands was separated from Belgium and Luxembourg. Though they were joined briefly at the beginning of the nineteenth century, it was not until 1944 that they began voluntarily to draw together more closely. Faced with the common challenge of the Nazi occupation, they realized that only by working together could they help prevent the regrowth of European rivalries, which had repeatedly plunged the Continent into war.

The centuries of separation had given to each of the three a different national character and indeed a different set of problems. Yet they could agree that on the major issue of the postwar period—the creation of a peaceful order in Europe—they shared a common interest and common problems. Differences of religion, culture, economy, and even of the basic political system remained, but all three states were firmly wedded to the concept of democratic government.

The most obvious reason for their common interest is their size. Each had found, usually through the painful process of foreign occupation, that by itself it was unable to protect its national territory from outside aggression. Yet repeated incursions by the major European powers into the national life of these small nations strengthened their determination to preserve their national identity. Before World War II, each tried its own formula for self-preservation. Sometimes neutrality was the key; at other times the small states would seek to play the major powers off against one another. But the political collapse of Europe in 1939 proved all these efforts vain. Before the war, when any such gesture was doomed to failure, the Benelux nations began to push for the creation of an entente among the smaller powers of Europe to counteract the policies of the major powers. This move was badly timed and conceived. It was too late, of course, and also it sought a common position among such varied states as the Scandinavian nations, Switzerland, and the Benelux countries. The failure of this attempt to bring the smaller states together provided solid proof that while size was an important factor in determining common interest, smallness was not enough.

A second factor uniting the three Benelux nations and distinguishing them from other small countries was their economic position. As early as the seventeenth century they had become leaders among the trading nations of the world. Without relative freedom in international trade, their economies would be stifled.

The three states, recognizing their diminished political influence and their dependence on trade, sought new strength through trade groupings. The first, for which the foundations were laid by the three governments-in-exile in London in 1944, was Benelux. Originally conceived of as a customs union to remove all tariff barriers among the three nations and adopt a common external tariff, Benelux was later transformed into a plan for an economic union, the creation of a single economy common to the three.

But Benelux was clearly not enough. If it promised to give the three states new economic power, it nonetheless left them a relatively small unit. They subsequently became firm supporters of a larger European economic grouping. They were among the six original members of the European Community (the coal and steel pool in 1952 and Euratom and the Common Market in 1958), and they came to place greater emphasis on this broader economic grouping than on their own cooperative efforts. They became staunch partisans of expanding the European Community to include other European states, thus creating a large European customs union.

The demand for the enlargement of the European Community was not based solely on economic considerations. These three nations share a firm attachment to the democratic form of government. Two of the other Common Market members, West Germany and Italy, had known periods in recent decades when their people had been stripped of the effective power to control their governments. In France, political chaos did give way to greater stability after 1958, but under a personal form of government repugnant to the Benelux nations. Other states still outside the European Community had a historical attachment to democratic government, which the Benelux nations felt was a necessary guarantee for the European Community as a whole. For this reason, the three smallest members of the European Community championed the cause of the enlargement of the Common Market.

Our purpose here is to examine what this democratic rule in the Benelux countries—paradoxically, all constitutional monarchies—has come to mean and how it has persevered on a continent where democratic government has suffered many reverses and where the small nations are generally at the mercy of the big nations.

A subsidiary consideration will be the ways in which states can cooperate effectively once they shed the belief that they are great enough to go it alone. In a world dominated by superstates only a few nations are not, in fact, small nations. The Benelux states are content to accept their position of relative weakness as a given factor and are thus ready to shed the inhibitions of sovereignty in an effort to achieve a greater political stability.

Because of the evolution of the European Community, in which an intransigent France has continued to block the enlargement of the Common Market and most progress toward a true unification of the economies of the Six, Benelux has once again come to have a real meaning. The three states have renewed their own efforts to create an economic union among themselves, based on consent, and have begun to coordinate their own efforts in the European Community in order to play a greater role there.

The first chapter presents Benelux political development in its historical context. The second chapter examines the nature of the Belgian and Dutch societies and their relation to politics. The contrast between the two is sharp: Dutch political society is based on a substantial agreement on the form of the nation's political system and on a strong legislature; Belgian political society is characterized by a high degree of strife and by a strong cabinet and party system. The fourth chapter reviews the parties themselves in the Netherlands and Belgium, after a brief examination of the role of local government and politics in these small, centralized states.

The fifth and sixth chapters analyze the distinctive political decision-making patterns in the Netherlands and Belgium. These indicate a strong attachment to democratic processes in both countries, but a substantial difference in approach. The legal system, which in both countries is relatively distinct from the main current of political life, is surveyed in Chapter 8.

Chapter 9 treats the Luxembourg political system as a whole separately from Belgium and the Netherlands.

As noted above, small nations such as these have come to play an important role in international affairs. The final chapter discusses the bases of their foreign policies and activities in four selected areas.

A word on terminology is necessary. In this book, the *cabinet* means the governing coalition composed of ministers and junior ministers (equivalent to the American term *Administration* and the usual European term *Government*). By *government* is meant the entire mechanism of political decision making and execution (equivalent to the American term *government*). The term *administration* means the entire civil service structure.

ONE
THE EUROPEAN
PIVOT

A brief developmental history of the Benelux nations

Tourist guidebooks speak of Belgium, the Netherlands, and Luxembourg as the "low countries," and there is much truth to this appellation. Indeed, the Netherlands, which in fact means "low countries," is largely below sea level, with its farmlands protected from the North Sea by the legendary dikes. In Belgium, the broad plain of Flanders extends over more than half the country. Only in the east and throughout Luxembourg does one leave the flatlands for the Ardennes, a low range of hills and small mountains.

GEOGRAPHY

The character of both the Dutch and the Belgians has been strongly influenced by their geographical situation. The long struggle with the sea has prompted a sentiment of stubborn determination among the Dutch, who have vowed not only to hold their own against the periodic inundations, but to reclaim land from the sea and thus enlarge the nation. This is virtually the only case in history where a country is gradually but substantially increasing its territory, not through a contest with other nations, but through a centuries-long battle with nature. Even with modern technology, the cost is great and success is uncertain. As recently as 1953, the Dutch suffered a major setback when the sea invaded large parts of the southern provinces. Yet the sea has done much to give the nation a feeling of unity; for whatever the political points of view, all Dutchmen are united in their desire to push back the sea.

Belgium has not been as severely challenged by incursions of the sea. Indeed Belgians have often seen their access to it cut off when major rivers such as the Zwin silted over or when the vicissitudes of world politics denied them free passage to it. Yet the Belgians have been conditioned by their geography, for the Flemish plain offers no obstacle to the chill winds and steady rains that originate over the Atlantic. The typical Belgian peasant, seasoned by years of contact with the harsh winter weather, has himself become tough and solid in his physique and his opinions.

The Benelux nations lie at the crossroads of western Europe—an advantage for them as trading states but a hazard when foreign invaders were on the move. Brussels, the Belgian capital, is centrally located between Paris, London, The Hague, and the major cities of Germany. The Benelux countries are linked with one another and with neighboring nations by an intensive network of rail connections. Each of the three has a national airline linking it with principal centers in Europe and the world. Two of the world's largest ports, Rotterdam and Antwerp, make the Benelux countries the principal gateway to western Europe.

Indeed the two principal resources of the Benelux states are their location and their people. The people strive to take maximum advantage of the location and may fairly be called "a community of traders." Almost half of the gross national product of these states is a direct result of their trading prowess.

With the exception of the rich Dutch countryside, home of a highly efficient agricultural economy, and the raw materials for steel production found in Belgium and Luxembourg, the Benelux states are poor in natural resources. Like Switzerland, they succeed as viable economies because their people are industrious and highly skilled. They buy the vast bulk of their raw materials on the world market and turn out high-quality manufactured goods for export. But the future may yet reveal that these nations have hidden natural resources. Twenty years ago, few would have thought that the Netherlands would become one of the principal producers of natural gas in Europe. Yet discoveries under the North Sea, adjacent to Holland, have made the Dutch gas fields a kind of second Klondike.

Of the three countries, the Netherlands is the largest, both in size and population. It covers some 15,800 square miles and has a population of 12.4 million people. Though the vast majority of the territory is given over to agriculture, the population is concentrated in a highly urbanized area—the Randstad or rim city—located in the triangle between Amsterdam, Rotterdam, and The Hague. Amsterdam, the nation's largest city, is the royal capital, but The Hague is the center of government. Dutch is the official language, though Frisian, a regional dialect, is still spoken in one part of the country. About 40 percent of the population is Roman Catholic, almost 40 percent belongs to one of the Protestant denominations, and the remainder belong to other religions or to none.

Belgium covers some 11,781 square miles with a total population of 9.5 million. As opposed to the Netherlands, the population is spread relatively evenly over the national territory, though it is sparse in the extreme eastern area. French and Flemish (which differs from Dutch in about the same way American differs from English) are the two main national langues. About 5.3 million Belgians live in the Flemish region and 3.1 million in the French-speaking region, also known as Wallonia. Brussels, the capital, has a population of 1.1 million and is theoretically bilingual, though a majority of the population speaks French in preference to Flemish. There is a small area in the eastern part of the country where German is the official language and where about 60,000 Belgians live. According to official statistics, over 90 percent of the population is Roman Catholic, though in fact there is a high percentage of "freethinkers" who are not affiliated with the Church. There is also a small Protestant population.

Luxembourg is tiny, its 333,000 residents living in an area of 999 square miles. Surprisingly, the capital city, also known as Luxembourg, has only some 77,000 inhabitants. Thus the country has no real urban area, and it gives the impression of a rolling countryside punctuated by a concentration of steel mills. The nation's official language is French, but everybody's first language is, in fact, a local dialect of German. German is also widely spoken, and any of the three languages may be used in the national parliament. The country is overwhelmingly Roman Catholic.

HISTORY OF THE BENELUX NATIONS TO 1815

The modern history of these three distinct countries has a common starting point. In the fifteenth century, the dukes of Burgundy unified the lands lying within the zone limited by the Scheldt, the Meuse, and the Rhine rivers, forming the nation then known as the Netherlands. This Burgundian territory managed to maintain its independence from French encroachment.

In 1543, Charles V succeeded in unifying virtually all of what is now the Benelux area with the exception of the county of Liège, now in Belgium. Although Charles V was also the king of Spain and the head of the Holy Roman Empire, he devoted most of his attention to the seventeen provinces that formed the Netherlands.

Had it not been for the Reformation, this unified state might well have expanded to include adjacent areas and would thus have become one of the greatest European states. But the waves of reform swept into the Netherlands, and Charles took steps to stem the tide. Repression of what was considered Protestant heresy was particularly cruel and implacable under Philip II, his successor, and the division of the Netherlands became inevitable.

Thus ended the golden period of Dutch and Belgian history. Under Charles, who himself had been born at Ghent, culture flourished and the political independence of the area was assured. To appreciate the atmosphere of the times, one must merely recall that this was the period of Erasmus, the leading philosopher of humanism, and of Mercator, mapmaker of the world. Among the musicians were Josquin des Prés and Orlando de Lassus, and among the artists were the van Eycks and Pieter Breughel. But even more important was the foundation of the University of Louvain, which served as a training school for the administrators of the Netherlands state.

Philip II did not have the same attachment to the Netherlands as did his father, and he thought of himself more as the king of Spain. As a defender of the faith, he felt it his duty to show no tolerance to the Protestants. Finally the northern provinces began active resistance under the leadership of William of Orange-Nassau, who succeeded in enlisting the support of other Protestant powers. A final effort was made in the Pacification of Ghent in 1576 to bring the seventeen provinces into union once again, but eventually the northern or Protestant provinces went their own way. The destruction of the Spanish Armada and the struggle against Henry IV of France, a tolerant king, drew Spanish strength away from the effort to maintain the unity of the Netherlands. By 1579 the split was complete.

At this point the history of Belgium and Luxembourg on the one hand and of the Netherlands on the other take their separate courses, though the three states were destined to be reunited briefly at the beginning of the nineteenth century. But in 1579, when the Union of Utrecht was concluded, only the Netherlands had achieved a degree of political independence from foreign domination.

The growth of Dutch power

William of Orange-Nassau, also known as William the Silent, became the head of the new Dutch Republic formed of the seven northern provinces. He came to this position through his appointment as *stadtholder,* representative of Charles V, in three of the most important provinces of the northern Netherlands. Though he was assassinated by order of Philip II in 1584, his young republic was already able to stand on its feet and resist the Spanish attempts to reassert control. The Treaty of Westphalia in 1648 marked the formal recognition of the independence of the Protestant Republic of the Seven United Netherlands.

The golden era of the seventeen provinces had come under Burgundian rule, and the southern provinces led the way. Now, once the northern provinces attained their independence, the Netherlands began to assume a role as a major world power. The Dutch became what may well have been the world's greatest trading people. For example, at the end of the sixteenth century, 25,000 Dutch ships plied the waters between Holland and the Iberian peninsula. Like Columbus before him, Henry Hudson, an Englishman in the service of the Dutch, tried to find a new trade route to the East by sailing west. Finally, Dutch sailors mastered the trip around the Cape of Good Hope, and in 1602 the East India Company was formed. This unique institution was given a monopoly on all trade east of the cape. A similar concern was later formed for the West Indies. The very fact that these were companies rather than governmental agencies indicates that the Dutch did not seek to establish colonies but rather to open new areas to their traders. They did, however, create one of the world's greatest colonial networks, including the Dutch East Indies (later Indonesia), parts of Brazil, New Netherlands (later New York), and the Cape of Good Hope (later part of South Africa).

The Netherlands thus became the principal maritime power of the world—but it was continually challenged. Forced into balance-of-power politics in order to maintain its freedom of the seas, the Netherlands faced England in three separate wars in the seventeenth century. In the second of these, a Dutch admiral, de Ruyter, sailed up the Thames and threatened London. A high point in Dutch history, this exploit is commemorated in numerous canvases by the great artists of the period.

In the third quarter of the seventeenth century, life was running so smoothly for the Dutch Republic that no statdholder was named. The Republic was governed by high administrators and the merchants. Major land-reclamation projects were begun and science flourished. But the seeds of trouble had already been sown, and the end of the Republic approached as the strength of France increased.

Louis XIV, the "Sun King," married a Spanish princess and began to demand a share of her inheritance, including a major portion of the southern or nonindependent Netherlands. This in turn menaced the Republic, particularly when it became clear that England was ready to challenge French claims to the Netherlands. The Dutch administrators were pushed aside and William III, the young prince of Orange, was placed in charge of the Republic. He led his country into its third encounter with the English and its first with France. The Dutch fleet, having lost none of its strength, staved off both the great powers, thus ensuring the Republic's continued independence and making William the arbiter of the European balance of power.

When the English king James II converted to Catholicism, the Parliament at Westminster invited William and his consort Mary, daughter of James II, to assume the throne of England. Thus William was both king of England and stadtholder of the Dutch Republic. In effect, the Republic was not equal to the new role cast upon it as defender of Protestantism on the European continent and by the time of William's death, in 1702, England was supreme on the sea, France on land. But for much of the eighteenth century France was preoccupied elsewhere, and England was linked with the Netherlands, thus removing any cause for concern, and an adequate balance of power existed in Scandinavia. The Dutch settled down to living the good life and devoted themselves to preserving what had already been won— essentially the opportunity to carry on a booming trade.

Decline of the Dutch Republic

The Republic had in fact been governed by an oligarchy, a benevolent dictatorship of the enlightened and industrious merchants. During the period of relative calm, the government became less benevolent and lapsed into abuses of the people's rights. At the same time the navy—which had been the chief source of Dutch strength and which had assured the freedom of the seas for Dutch shipping—began to decline. By the end of the eighteenth century the Dutch Republic found itself once again at war with England. This time, with other continental powers, it fought to maintain access to the sea, which the English, in connection with their war with the newborn American republic, had tried to cut off. But a new force was arising on the Continent. After 1789, France was infused with a revolutionary zeal, and under Napoleon's leadership it undertook to place the entire European continent under its domination. The Netherlands, now considerably weaker than at the beginning of the century, was needed as a subject territory in the war against England. In 1795, French revolutionary troops entered the Dutch Republic, forcing the last stadtholder, William V, to flee to England. The French proclaimed the creation of a subject state, the Batavian Republic.

As in many other cases, the French occupation brought a fundamental change in the system of government in the Netherlands. The confederation of provinces where each had stressed its independent powers, though all had admitted that the province of Holland was the leader, was transformed into a unitary state. One of the most democratic regimes that Europe had known in the eighteenth century was thus ended. The Batavian Republic's Constitution was modeled on the French constitution and followed each modification made in Paris, as the First French Republic was gradually transformed into the Napoleonic Empire. Just as the Constitution became French, so did the administration. There was increased centralization of authority and use of the Napoleonic code of laws. Even now, reminders of the period remain in the Netherlands where the military police are still officially called by their French name, the *Maréchausée*.

The Dutch grew restive as French control became tighter. The Batavian Republic gave way to the Kingdom of Holland under Louis Napoleon, brother of the Emperor. Continued protests against French decrees led to the direct annexation of the Netherlands as part of the French Empire in 1810. But Napoleon's defeats on the battlefields of Russia gave the Dutch the opportunity to reassert their independence. In 1813, the son of the last stadtholder landed at Scheveningen, near The Hague, and was proclaimed William I, king of the Netherlands. Thus, the French occupation had transformed the Netherlands into a kingdom, but the ruler, who continued to be a member of the House of Orange-Nassau, was no longer prince but king.

The Congress of Vienna in 1815, redrawing the map of Europe after the upheavals of the Napoleonic period, rejoined the southern Netherlands to the kingdom, creating a buffer state among the great powers. Thus, by the stroke of a pen, the Netherlands were reunified. Yet the 250 years of separation had worked fundamental changes in both parts, and the union was not to endure. A review of the course of Belgian and Luxembourg history since 1579 will reveal the causes of the split.

Belgium and Luxembourg under Spain and Austria

Although the period from the breakup of the Netherlands until the Treaty of Westphalia in 1648 was an era of national consolidation for the northern provinces, it included "the years of misfortune" for the South. The southern provinces remained a part of the Spanish Empire.

Albert and Isabel, the Austrian monarchs, ruled from Brussels, not Vienna, and fought to secure economic advantages for their country, often at the cost of prolonged battles with the Dutch. In 1621, upon the death of Albert, the territories reverted to Spanish control, there being no child to assume the throne. Thus ended a brief, relatively happy period, during which the artist Peter Paul Rubens reached the height of his achievement and other thinkers carried forward important scientific research.

In the ensuing years, Belgium and Luxembourg became a battlefield in the wars between the Spanish Hapsburgs and the Bourbons of France. The Treaty of Westphalia fixed Belgium's northern boundary and cut the country off from access to the sea through the port of Antwerp, when both banks of the Scheldt were ceded to the Dutch. But Spain and France had been unable to come to terms in 1648, and war raged for another eleven years. Then Philip IV, king of Spain and successor of Albert, ceded the southern part of Luxembourg to the French, clearly the victors in the war.

The French continued to press their attack during the reign of Charles II, who acceded to the throne in 1665 at the age of four. In 1684, Louis XIV succeeded in occupying the whole of Luxembourg, which was made an integral part of the French kingdom. Yet the French domination was not to last long, for in 1697 Dutch troops forced the French out of Luxembourg and returned it to Spanish rule. Though Belgium was never completely swallowed up, it suffered in the invasion and the counterattack of the two sides.

When Charles II, the last of the Spanish Hapsburgs, died in 1700, the Spanish Netherlands became once again the battlefield of Europe and the prime stake in the War of the Spanish

Succession. As a result of this conflict, which pitted an Anglo-Dutch force against French troops, the Treaty of Utrecht in 1713 gave possession of the territory to the Austrian emperor. Austrian rule lasted until the French Revolution.

The Austrian emperor Charles VI introduced a period of relative calm in the wartorn area. At last the agricultural potential of the region began to be realized. The frontiers of Belgium were defined by the completion of the southern border with France. The northern border was still a cause of concern, as Belgium continued to be blocked from the sea by the Dutch. Charles tried to circumvent this blockade by creating the Ostend Company, which, with its base on the Belgian coast, sent trips on the same trading routes used by the Dutch. The competition from Ostend proved so sharp that the English and the Dutch forced the Emperor to disband the Ostend Company.

The death in 1740 of Charles, the last of the male Austrian Hapsburgs, opened the way for the War of the Austrian Succession (1740–1748). Empress Maria-Theresa, Charles's successor, salvaged the Austrian Netherlands from this conflict and from the Seven Years' War, and she ruled her northern territories benevolently. They continued to be directly supervised by governors appointed in Vienna. Although the governors acted to increase public education and promote commerce, they were not required to consult the people themselves in any way. Joseph II succeeded to the throne in 1780 and pushed reforms, including religious toleration for non-Catholics, with vigor if not with complete effectiveness. In 1787 the Austrian regime introduced a sweeping administrative reform, abolishing former provincial units and replacing them by administrative districts allowing for even greater direct control. At the same time, the territory was equipped with a more modern judicial system instead of the seigneurial system.

This reform was the first step in a chain of events that was to give Belgium and Luxembourg their independence from Spanish and Austrian domination. In October of 1789, just after the storming of the Bastille in Paris, the Brabantine Revolution broke out in Belgium. Austrian troops were driven out of much of the country, and early the following year the United Belgian States was established—the first independent government of

Belgium. It was made subject to a "Sovereign Congress" holding the executive power and to an Estates General. Yet the government, in which Luxembourg had not taken part, did not even last one year, for it was weakened by a dispute between Catholics and liberals. In late 1790 Austrian troops retook the areas under the control of the Republic of the United Belgian States. The Austrian emperor, Leopold II, restored the former administrative system of the country. He was succeeded in 1792 by the young emperor Francis II.

Thereafter the French became increasingly aggressive, proclaiming that the states surrounding France were a threat to their revolutionary existence. In April of 1792 the French Assembly declared war on the German and Austrian emperors. By October 1, 1795, French conquest of Belgium and Luxembourg enabled their formal annexation. The French occupation of Belgium was greeted as a liberation from foreign rule and provided an impetus for the closer unification of the Belgian provinces. Yet both Belgium and Luxembourg continued to be ruled by decree and public ordinance. The situation improved somewhat after 1799 when Napoleon took the post of first consul of the French Republic. Coupled with his policy of conciliation, the efforts to reform the administrative structure of the territories made this French regime generally popular in the former Austrian Netherlands. But they suffered from the almost continuous war effort mounted by Napoleon, and they, like the Netherlands to the north, began to pull away from the French Empire as Napoleon met serious setbacks in Russia. Finally, at Waterloo in Belgium, Napoleon suffered his final defeat at the hands of the allies.

THE NETHERLANDS, 1815–1830

The Congress of Vienna met in 1815 not merely to reestablish the *status quo ante bellum* but to redraw the map of Europe. Among the prizes to be divided were the territories of the former Austrian Netherlands (Belgium and Luxembourg) and the Dutch Republic. The Congress decided that William of Orange-Nassau, sovereign prince of the United Provinces, should be made king of the Netherlands and that Belgium and Luxembourg should be placed under his control. The Belgians were not trusted by the statesmen at the Congress of Vienna, who believed that the leading Belgians, either reactionary or revolutionary, had supported France too warmly to be trusted to maintain their nation's integrity were Belgium made an independent state. Thus Belgium was returned to a direct union with the northern Netherlands and became an integral part of the Kingdom of the Netherlands. At the same time the eastern Belgian cantons of Eupen, Malmédy, and Saint Vith were ceded to Prussia. Luxembourg was in a somewhat different position and was made into a grand duchy with William of Orange acting as the grand duke in addition to his functions as king of the Netherlands. William did not respect the autonomy of Luxembourg and administered it as a part of his kingdom, though legally Luxembourg was a member of the German Confederation.

Thus in 1815 the three parts of the Benelux region were once again reunited under Dutch leadership. The Dutch had the longest traditon of political independence, having once been one of the most powerful nations in Europe. They had been able to develop their own administrative and governmental standards and indeed their own economy. The Belgians and Luxembourgers had not yet proven their ability to govern themselves, and their countries remained pawns in the dealings of the European powers. The Netherlands had, however, an international standing of its own. In addition, the victorious allies sought to reward William for his help in bringing an end to the Napoleonic regime, and thus it seemed logical that all of the Low Countries should be transferred to him.

This state of affairs does much to explain the political situation of these countries a century and a half later. The Dutch have a sureness of their political history, a feeling of continuity with a long period of independence and strength.[1] Belgium, on the other hand, at the beginning of the last century had not begun its own political history. This late start, together with the country's internal disputes—mainly over language—explains

---

[1] This is, perhaps, what led Charles de Gaulle to characterize the Netherlands and France as the only true nations of the European Common Market.

why in many respects Belgium lags behind other European nations in the formation of a national consciousness. The situation is different for Luxembourg, which for many years had the status of a distinct dukedom, maintaining this legal position even after the Napoleonic period. Even more important was the national sentiment in favor of keeping the tiny state a distinct entity. No such defensive feeling had yet become widespread in Belgium.

On paper the Kingdom of the Netherlands seemed a splendid idea. But practice proved that there was more to divide than to unite the three component parts. William I was a "divine right" monarch (as indeed were all of his successors on the Dutch throne), and he sought not only to reign but to rule. The country's Constitution guaranteed individual rights and freedoms, and the legislative power was vested in the States General, of which one chamber was elected. This chamber had 110 seats, equally divided between Belgium and Holland. But the Constitution also gave considerable powers to the king. William has been called "too liberal to be a king, and too much a king to be really liberal." [2] He undertook energetic action to promote the economic welfare of his kingdom, though the economic union of the two parts was not complete.

Politically, William was supported by the liberals. These were "liberal" in the European sense of the word—stressing individual rights and liberties and favoring free enterprise. Thus they were oppposed to official relations between the church and state and to any governmental control over the economy. At the outset, William was opposed by the Catholics, mainly those in Belgium, who argued that the rule of religious toleration that had become a customary part of the Dutch regime was no longer acceptable. The Catholics gradually modified their position and by 1827 were willing to accept much the same kind of individual rights that the liberals favored. The union of these two elements marked the beginning of the end of the kingdom of William I.

The Belgians, though full partners in the kingdom, began to protest, sometimes with considerable exaggeration, the alleged abuses of the Orangeist regime. The linguistic system, which

[2] André Mast, *Les Pays du Benelux* (Paris: Pichon et Durand-Auzias, 1960), p. 12.

dictated that the Dutch language should be used in the Flemish part of Belgium, also aroused opposition in the South. In addition, the Belgians disliked the liberal use of royal prerogatives by the King. The King obviously did make clumsy errors, and the Belgians began to feel the hot wind of rebellion blowing from Paris, where the Restoration was about to give way to the regime of Louis Philippe. The French and the English opposed the oppressive rule of the Holy Alliance, and 1830 was a year of revolution in Europe. The Poles, the Greeks, and finally the Belgians lashed out at the old regime. After a brief skirmish in Brussels, the Dutch troops withdrew, leaving the way clear for the creation of an independent Belgium, which was duly proclaimed on October 4, 1830.

Britain took the lead in assuring the Belgians of their continued independence. The English saw in Belgium a buffer state on the Continent that would keep the great powers apart and over which the British government might exercise some influence. Also it represented a more liberal regime—for the Constitution of 1831, which survives, emphasized individual rights as well as restraints on the exercise of governmental powers. On July 21, 1831, the German prince Leopold I entered Brussels, having been chosen by the national Congress as the first king of the Belgians. When the Dutch army responded by a fresh invasion of Belgium, the French army moved in to assure the continued independence of the young state. The London Conference in 1831 quickly imposed a cessation of hostilities and drew the frontiers between Belgium and the Netherlands. Despite Belgian demands, Luxembourg and parts of the southern Netherlands were not turned over to its control. Thus the Belgians failed to gain unfettered access to the Scheldt, although the way was opened for the development of the port of Antwerp.

THE NETHERLANDS AFTER BELGIAN INDEPENDENCE

The Dutch king did not accept this settlement until 1838, since he continued to hope for a return of Belgium to the United Kingdom of the Netherlands. Finally he was forced to accept the existing situation, and on April 19, 1839 the Treaty of London was signed, formally recognizing Belgium. This treaty turned over almost half of Luxembourg to Belgium in compensation for its losses in the southern Netherlands. The great European powers guaranteed both Belgian and Luxemburg their national independence and integrity and declared them to be perpetually neutral states. Thus began the history of the three modern states of Benelux.

The Netherlands had been affected by the events in the South, and pressure grew there for greater liberalism and an end of the personal rule of the king. The upheavals of 1848, when a liberal wave swept Europe, "made William I into a liberal overnight"—as the adage has it in the Netherlands. A new Dutch constitution introduced the principle of ministerial responsibility. This meant that the cabinet ruled and was to be held responsible for its acts; the king reigned and could not be held accountable for measures undertaken in his name by the cabinet. William became the "first citizen" of the kingdom, reverting to a certain extent to the position occupied by the princes of Orange as stadtholders.

The representatives of the people were elected by a limited suffrage, and the rights of the Chambers of the States General were extended. The rights of the agricultural areas were assured and provision made for local government. This Constitution, the work of J. R. Thorbecke, is the basis of the present-day Dutch Constitution. It was modified over the years until in 1917 universal suffrage for men was adopted, followed two years later by a similar measure for women.

During the nineteenth century the effect of religion on politics came to be particularly marked. One cause was the so-called Réveil, or Awakening Movement, in the Protestant churches, opposing many of the liberal trends that characterized Dutch society and that were represented by Thorbecke in the States General. The 1849 Constitution aided the churches by banning state interference in any of their internal regulations, including the naming of bishops. A struggle also began over the creation of denominational schools, which had been prohibited before 1848. For the first time the Catholic and Protestant churches joined together in demanding state subsidies for these schools.

By 1920 they had won this battle, although the state was given the power to check on teachers' qualifications.

Throughout this period various "tendencies" were represented in the States General, although there were no political parties until late in the century. The existing groups were the Conservatives and Liberals (neither having any connection with any church), the Roman Catholics, and the Anti-Revolutionaries (linked with Protestantism). With the rising political awareness of the working class and the gradual extension of the right to vote, the Social Democrats began to play a political role at the end of the nineteenth century.

Dutch economic and political strength

Perhaps the most significant development in Dutch life in the nineteenth and twentieth centuries has been the formation of giant corporations such as Royal Dutch Petroleum, Unilever, and Philips, an outgrowth of the events of two centuries earlier, when the Netherlands first emerged as a major commercial power. Perhaps because of its very size, the Netherlands understood the importance of large-scale enterprises earlier than many other European states. Companies were created that provided work for vast numbers of the population and gave the Netherlands a real influence in the world. Even in the mid-twentieth century, Royal Dutch Shell and Unilever, now Anglo-Dutch firms, are the largest in the world outside the United States. Another indication of Dutch economic dynamism was the creation of the Dutch airlines KLM, the first airline company in the world.

Technical advances since the creation of the Kingdom of the Netherlands have also allowed the nation to push back the sea and reclaim sizeable areas. The famous Zuyder Zee was closed off and made into a lake, from which have risen large new agricultural areas called polders. In recent years, under the Delta Plan, a massive operation has been closing off many of the estuaries on the south coast. These activities, representing a major portion of governmental expenditure, are above political controversy in a nation united in its struggle against the sea.

Finally a word should be said about the development of a

new international role for the Netherlands. Drawing upon its status as a neutral nation, the Netherlands built up during the nineteenth century a reputation as a nation committed to peace. The peace conferences of 1899 and 1907, which laid the groundwork for such later organizations as the League of Nations and the United Nations, were held in The Hague. T. M. V. Asser won the Nobel Peace Prize in 1913 for his work in the codification of law, and the World Court was established in The Hague after World War I.

The neutrality of the Netherlands was respected by the Germans during World War I and the country was spared the long years of trench warfare. It became a center of efforts to end the war, and it was here that the Kaiser took refuge as his empire collapsed. Thus, like Switzerland, the Netherlands developed a reputation as a neutral nation whose neutrality could serve a useful purpose in international relations. But as a small nation it could have no great influence on the course of world events and was forced to follow the tide.

The setback of the war

In the interwar period, the Netherlands saw the gradual decay of the European political situation without being able to influence it greatly. Together with other small nations, it attempted to find a way out of the spiral of disaster leading to World War II. But its suggestions were ignored by the great powers—and the Dutch, their neutrality ignored by Hitler, were subjected to brutal aggression. The bombing of Rotterdam, when almost 90 percent of the center of this metropolis was destroyed in a matter of minutes, led to the formation of a strong resistance movement against the occupying force. The cabinet and Queen fled to Britain. When the war ended, they returned to a devastated country. The large Jewish population, which had enjoyed a high degree of tolerance, had been decimated; their plight became known through the diary of a young girl, Anne Frank, who had been deported by the Nazis.

Internally the nation faced a major task of reconstruction. The Constitution remained basically the same, as did the fundamental political system. The royal family, by reason of their leadership in the resistance, enjoyed an even higher popular esteem. In international affairs, the Dutch were more convinced than ever of the efficacy of international cooperation as a means of preventing the reoccurrence of international conflict. Thus the Netherlands has become one of the chief proponents of the use of international organizations.

The development of the Netherlands since 1815 shows an initial period of semiautocratic rule giving way in 1848 to a liberal regime, which throughout the years gave the nation a period of sustained internal development and the international posture of a peacemaker. The chief domestic conflict concerned the role of the church, which has had a strong effect on the nation's political life. But there was a general agreement that some accommodation should be found among the various positions, and this prevented the religious question from ever threatening to tear the country apart.

A nation's character, if indeed it exists at all, is difficult to define. The development of the Dutch nation seems to have allowed for the creation of a harmonious attitude among all parts of the population. Politically, all divergent elements have been willing to play by the rules of the game rather than to call them into question. Although the Constitution of 1848 was modified many times, this reflected a concern for political perfection, the desire to keep tinkering with the mechanism in hopes of improving it, rather than an underlying dissatisfaction with it. In terms of society rather than politics, the Dutch have accepted many of the same liberal values, and all elements have been willing to work together for their preservation. This has given the nation an internal coherence that could not fail to affect its relations with other states.

BELGIUM SINCE 1830

Belgium, which in many ways has had a parallel development to the Netherlands, nonetheless shows numerous contrasts. The Constitution adopted in 1831 has survived with only minor changes to allow for increased suffrage. The first of these in 1893 created plural voting while it increased the number of male voters. This meant that the privileged classes, who alone had been authorized to vote in the past, still maintained a certain advantage over the workingmen.[3] The second revision in 1921 made male suffrage universal, although the vote was not extended to women until 1948.

The Constitution provided from the outset that the king would reign but not rule. Thus the principle of ministerial responsibility, which was not established in the Netherlands until 1849, was included in the Belgian system from the very outset. Indeed, even in legal myth, the Belgian king has never been sovereign. Instead, in accordance with republican principles, it is the people, represented in the Parliament, who embody the nation's sovereignty.

The framers of the Belgian Constitution were much influenced by the principles of the French Revolution and the philosophy behind it. Thus, in theory at least, they stressed the need for separation of powers among the cabinet, the Parliament, and the judiciary. In fact, the preponderance of power was given to the Parliament. At the same time, the concept underlying the Declaration of the Rights of Man influenced the early Belgian political leaders to emphasize the rights of the individual. Once again this obviated any need for reforms in 1848, when the liberal wave swept Europe.

Belgian society

The Belgian political and social system came to represent the enthronement of the bourgeoise. Like the July Monarchy in France that brought Louis Philippe to the throne in 1830, the Belgian monarch and government found their greatest support in the bourgeoisie, which was already a flourishing class, thanks to the early arrival of the Industrial Revolution in the country. The system embodied their middle-class values, establishing these values as the goal for which all Belgians should strive. Although this may have seemed an oligarchy, it was open to newcomers,

[3] See Val Lorwin, "Belgium: Religion, Class and Language in National Politics," in Robert A. Dahl, *Political Oppositions in Western Democracies* (New Haven, Conn.: Yale University Press, 1966), pp. 156–157. Voting was open to men over twenty-five—additional votes, to a maximum of three, being awarded heads of families over thirty-five, property owners, and men with advanced education. In 1894, 850,000 men had one vote, 290,000 had two, and 220,000 had three.

and the king even accorded titles of nobility to businessmen who had arisen from humble beginnings to wealth. Yet such a system was essentially paternalistic, with the ruling classes acting on behalf of the poor without taking the trouble to consult them.

There was much less religious strife in Belgium than in the Netherlands, for a far greater part of the population supported a single church, the Roman Catholic. The problem of state support for education in church schools did, however, arise, and it was not settled until 1958. In the nineteenth century politics were dominated by members of the Catholic and Liberal parties, who were not associated with the Church. As in the Netherlands, the latter part of the century saw the growth of the workers' movement as the franchise was extended. The Liberals were the most penalized by this development, and there was relatively little slippage from the ranks of the Catholic group to the Socialists—who, like the Liberals, were not associated with the Church. In fact, the Liberals were saved from almost complete extinction by the introduction of proportional representation.

Nor did the linguistic division of the country cause political difficulties during the nineteenth century. Clearly the French-speaking part of the population dominated the nation's affairs both in politics and business. When Flemish businessmen rose to positions of importance, they almost invariably adopted the French language.[4] However, as the century drew to a close, a revival of Flemish culture was well under way, and this was to awaken the political aspirations of the Dutch-speaking part of the population.

The economic face of the country was reflected in the domination of the French-speaking elements. Although the plain of Flanders was mainly agricultural, Wallonia was the home of important coal mines, which led to the creation of a large steel industry in that part of the country. A major portion of the nation's wealth came from these steel mills.

The role of the king

Paradoxically, though the kings of Belgium did not actually rule, they exercised the effective leadership in the nation and pro-

---

[4] Lorwin, p. 158, cites the adage applied to wealthy Flemings arisen from the masses: "French in the parlor, Flemish in the kitchen."

moted its rapid development. Leopold I sought to gain international acceptance for his new state, and his position was strengthened—at least temporarily—through his marriage with the daughter of Louis Philippe. Leopold promoted "unionism" in the early years of the kingdom, discouraging partisan politics, but this policy gave way to factionalism after 1848. Belgium was suffering from a severe economic crisis when the 1848 wave of revolt swept across Europe. With relatively few internal political problems at this moment, Leopold was able to take advantage of the situation and strengthen his country's position. Belgium, patterning itself on Britain, its international patron, adopted the free-trading system and was thus ready to benefit from the period of European economic growth after 1850. In 1863 the Belgians negotiated with the Dutch the end of the tolls for the use of the Scheldt, and the way was finally clear for the full development of the port of Antwerp.

The opening of Antwerp stimulated Belgium to industrialize at a far greater rate than its neighbor to the north and many other European countries. One of the first trips ever made by steam locomotive took place between Brussels and Malines, leading the way to the creation of the most extensive rail network in Europe. At the same time Belgium became known as a supplier of high-quality, low-cost manufactured goods.

As the Netherlands gained renown as an advocate of peace, Belgian fame spread through the work of men who provided industrial and financial assistance to enterprises in other countries. Contacts were established with Africa and China, particularly in the field of railway and mining engineering. Among the countries benefitting from Belgian assistance were China (where 1800 miles of railroads were built), Egypt, Turkey, Mexico, Argentina, and Russia (where most of the public utilities were organized by Belgians). The effect of a single scientific discovery—the development of soda ash by Ernest Solvay—further extended Belgian renown.

An important outlet for Belgian energies was provided by the second king, Leopold II, who in 1885 became the personal sovereign of the Independent Congo State. This territory was to become a Belgian colony.

Thus the nineteenth century was a period of increased

democratization at home and commercial expansion abroad. The king exerted a considerable influence on the development of his country and won the respect of his people. The constitution was not opened for any major revision, beyond the extension of suffrage, mainly for fear that the linguistic question might find its way into any such amendment.

Like his predecessors, King Albert did much to weld national unity. In 1914, Belgian neutrality, guaranteed by what the Germans derided as "a piece of paper," was violated, and troops of the German Empire invaded the country. They succeeded in occupying most of the Belgian territory, but Albert led the national resistance to the invaders. At the war's end, the German territories—Eupen, Malmédy, and Saint Vith—were returned to Belgium. Albert had achieved a general esteem among the population that brought patriotic spirit to its high point. Yet Belgian efforts, like those of the Netherlands, to prevent a second relapse into war through the concerted action of the small powers were doomed to failure.

The "royal question"

King Leopold III came to the throne as the war clouds gathered in the thirties. At the suggestion of his young minister of foreign affairs, Paul-Henri Spaak, he once again proclaimed the neutrality of his country. As a result of this move, the nation was insufficiently prepared for the German invasion in 1940.

When it became clear that the Germans were going to seize all of Belgian territory, the cabinet decided, after some hesitation, to withdraw to London. They asked the King to accompany them into exile. Unlike the Dutch Queen and the Grand Duchess of Luxembourg, he refused to go, claiming that the Constitution made him the commander-in-chief of the armed forces, and that he could not desert them. He interpreted the Constitution to assign this role as chief of the army as a personal power, not one affected by the concept of ministerial responsibility. This decision drove a wedge between the King and Spaak, one of the leaders of the Socialist party. During the war, the King, whose consort had been killed in an accident several years earlier, married a Belgian commoner. This too aroused opposition, for his first wife had been quite popular and many thought it inappropriate for the King to remarry during the war. In addition, the King claimed that by staying behind, he could intercede with the Germans on behalf of his people. There is no way of knowing how effective his efforts were, but some considered that he had in fact collaborated with the enemy.

As the Allies began to retake the Continent, Leopold was moved to Austria. After the war his brother Charles was made regent in his absence, for there was much opposition to Leopold's return. Finally, in 1950, a referendum on the return of Leopold saw 58 percent of the population vote in his favor. Yet shortly after his return violence broke out, and one of the leaders of the opposition was Spaak. Seeing the situation turn sour, Leopold announced that he would abdicate in favor of his son Baudouin, who assumed the throne on his twenty-first birthday in 1951.

This so-called royal question was probably the most serious internal crisis the Belgian nation has ever faced. It threw into sharp focus the divisions in the country. The King's supporters included many of the Flemings, who generally could be considered the adherents of the Christian Social (formerly Catholic) party and members of the Catholic Church. They appreciated Leopold's gestures toward the Flemish culture and argued that he had acted correctly during the war. In the opposition were many of the Walloons, freethinkers (nonreligious), and supporters of the Socialist party. They were highly critical of Leopold's alleged collaboration with the enemy.

The "royal question" brought to an end the considerable influence of the king on Belgian affairs. The monarch could continue to exercise the limited powers given him under the constitution, but the people were unwilling to see him extend them, even in the national interest.

In the period that followed, Belgium joined with the Netherlands in promoting international cooperation and developing its national economy. The linguistic question played an increasingly important role in the nation's political evolution, even threatening to alter the basic structure of the state. This issue prevented Belgium from achieving the same kind of internal coherence as the Netherlands, and thus it weakened the position of the government internally and of the nation in world affairs.

LUXEMBOURG DEVELOPMENT

Luxembourg, the third of the Benelux countries, followed a somewhat different course from its two larger neighbors. The Grand Duchy remained under the sovereignty of the king of the Netherlands until 1890, when there were no male heirs of his line of the house of Nassau. From that time onward, Luxembourg had as its sovereign a monarch distinct from the royal line in the Netherlands, though later women were allowed to reign. These sovereigns lived in the Grand Duchy, unlike the Dutch kings.

Until 1867 Luxembourg was a member of the German Confederation, and Prussian troops were stationed in its capital. But in that year the Treaty of London made Luxembourg fully independent politically. At the same time, the great powers guaranteed the neutrality of the Grand Duchy in the same way they had for Belgium. This status of neutrality disappeared when the Germans invaded the little state at the beginning of World War I. The end of this war brought the end of Luxemburg's participation in the economic union with Germany that had grown out of the nineteenth-century *Zollverein,* or customs union. In 1921, the small nation joined an economic union with Belgium after its request for a similar arrangement was rejected by the French.

Internally the country accepted increased democratization under its Constitution and a generally benevolent reign by the grand dukes. In 1919 the young grand duchess Marie Adelaide abdicated in favor of her sister Charlotte, after charges were raised that she had not put up sufficient resistance against German occupation.[5]

The main problem facing the nation until the end of World War II was its very right to survival. A state this size in Europe had traditionally been a pawn in the power struggles of the larger nations. But the Luxembourgers were tenacious in their self-defense, putting up stiff resistance to the German occupation and staving off annexation by the Third Reich. Grand Duchess Charlotte went into exile during the war and bent her efforts to convincing the Allies of the need to maintain Luxembourg as a

[5] See Chap. 9.

separate and independent state. When this was accomplished after the war, it was clear that the age-old battle had been won.

The Benelux states are trading nations, and the importance of economic affairs in their political development cannot be overemphasized. A nation's strength is based largely upon the value of its production and raw materials. In a continental nation endowed with natural resources, such as the United States, the national policy reflects this economic power. The Benelux states, on the other hand, must sell a great part of their production abroad, and they must have easy access to raw materials from abroad. This, too, has an influence on the national policy, not only in the field of foreign policy but also internally. It does, obviously, make these states more sensitive to the changing winds of international relations, and indeed it prevents their exercising full control over national economic policy.

THE ECONOMY OF THE NETHERLANDS

The Dutch economy had been shattered by World War II, and the total destruction of Germany meant the loss of one of its major markets. At the same time, the Dutch East Indies, a major dollar earner, slipped from the control of the Netherlands. The Dutch recovery required a long-term effort and a period of austerity.

A major program for industrial investment was a key part of the recovery. The industries selected for investment were to serve as earners of foreign exchange through their exports. In order to maintain a competitive position, the Dutch government instituted a policy of strict control on wage and price increases. Indeed, the low price-wage structure was to remain the chief characteristic of the economy for about twenty years after the war.

The government extended tax advantages to industry and even took a direct share in several large corporations when insufficient risk capital was available. Assistance was also given for the reconstruction of Rotterdam, much of which had been devastated during the war. As the principal outlet for Dutch trade and a large share of German trade, Rotterdam's recovery was vital for the entire area, and at the same time the port stood to benefit from the general return to prosperity. This investment has proven to be worthwhile: Rotterdam has become the world's largest port in terms of tonnage. As a complement to the industrial investment policy, the Dutch government also offered special incentives to encourage the development of the country's more backward areas.

The metals industry, which is the largest industrial group, produces about 40 percent of the income from exports. Other major industrial sectors, together accounting for over 40 percent of industrial sales abroad, are food, drink, tobacco, and chemicals. It should be noted that industrial exports make up some 62 percent of total sales abroad.

A major effort was also made after the war to restore Dutch agriculture. Much of the farm production is efficient; it can be made available on foreign markets at competitive prices. The key to the Dutch success was an emphasis on high productivity. For example, a cow in the Netherlands produces 50 percent more milk than one in the United States. One problem was the size of farms, many being too small to permit the use of modern equipment. Land redistribution is, however, possible because of the gradually declining farm population and the development of cooperatives.

Of all important nations in the world, the Netherlands is the most dependent on its foreign trade. Expressed as a percentage of gross national product (the value of all goods and services produced) foreign trade represents 75 percent. In other terms, about 30 percent of national income is a direct result of the export of goods and services. The chief export markets are the Belgium-Luxembourg Economic Union (BLEU) and West Germany. Major suppliers of imports are these two and the United States. A large share of Dutch imports is crude petroleum, for the Netherlands has become a major refining center.

The growth of the gross national product in the decade between 1950 and 1960 averaged 4.9 percent annually, a tribute to the effective incomes policy that kept wages at an artificially low level. But the pull of the Common Market and natural demands for increased freedom along with greater prosperity led, in 1964, to the end of controls. The economy appeared able to absorb this change without any major shock, possibly because of serious overemployment. When wages were increased, there was no rash of unemployment.

A word should be said about the monetary strength of the Dutch florin. It is one of the rare currencies that has been re-valued in the postwar period. In other words, after 1961 the dollar could buy fewer florins. The ending of wage and price controls amounted to another revaluation. With a generally favorable trade balance, the Netherlands has been able to build up sizeable reserves of gold and dollars. This has made the Netherlands one of the dozen most important monetary powers in the world, and perhaps it is the best indication of how small states can play powerful roles in a world where not all disputes are settled by force.

The Dutch economy has become one of the soundest in the world, though it is largely dependent on foreign trade.[6] In a way, the devastation of the war was beneficial, for it forced a com-plete economic renewal that gave the Netherlands a modern industrial structure. The contribution of an industrious people, who accepted the government's wage and price controls for an extended period, cannot be underestimated.

THE BELGIAN ECONOMY

Belgium found itself in a much different position at the end of the war. It had been spared the brunt of the German attack, and much of its industrial structure was undamaged. In addition, the Congo, which had remained in Belgian hands, provided the state with a considerable income in hard currencies. Finally—with the exception of the eastern part of the country, which was the scene of the Battle of the Bulge—Belgium was liberated in 1944 and had a head start on its reconstruction.

A large part of the credit for the speedy Belgian recovery, which took advantage of the existing economic structure, must go to Camille Gutt, a banker and government official. His policy stressed a restoration of individual purchasing power rather than accelerated investment in industry. High consumption would

---

[6] Thus, when West Germany suffered a recession in 1967, the Dutch economy was also hurt by the loss of markets.

stimulate increased production and productivity. Thus the Belgian National Bank kept credit under tight control and took measures to safeguard the solidity of the Belgian franc. This was achieved by a drastic reduction of the amount of money in circulation. Thus the initial shortage of goods was met by a shortage of money, with the result that inflation was impeded. The strength of the Belgian franc allowed the country to become one of the few European nations that gave others aid when the Marshall Plan was established.

Belgium resumed selling to its traditional markets and was able to reactivate its steel industry. By 1948 the Belgian economy had returned to stability, owing mainly to the high prices that its exports brought in a world hungry for most industrial goods.

Belgium (or more properly the Belgium-Luxembourg Economic Union) is almost as dependent on trade as the Netherlands. Farm exports make up only a small portion of total sales abroad. Among its major exports are steel (18 percent), mechanical equipment (23 percent), and textiles (14 percent). The high percentage of foreign sales resulting from steel was first the strength and later the weakness of the national economy. At first, Belgian steel, though relatively expensive, could find a ready market. But as the 1950s drew to a close, world steel production came to outstrip demand. This meant that relatively less efficient producers, particularly those such as Belgium that depended on expensive coal, would suffer from the competition. Belgium did follow the trend, establishing a modern mill on the coast that could receive raw materials at low transportation cost and ship the finished product easily. But much production was inefficient and in a long-term decline, and not too much could be done about it.

This economic development had a direct political impact because it coincided with the language problem. The formerly rich inland area, populated by the French-speaking population, was saddled with the more outmoded means of production. Flanders, situated along the coast, came to benefit not only from the new steel mill, but from the development of a major industrial center at the port of Antwerp, principally in the petrochemicals sector. In addition, with the gradual abandonment of the farm and the larger natural increase in the Flemish population, there was a ready supply of workers for new industry.

But even this economic revival, which saved the country from a prolonged decline after the immediate postwar period, would not have been possible without considerable foreign investment. All Common Market countries benefitted from industrial investment after the creation of the European Community in 1958, because many firms, mainly American, wanted to get inside the customs wall of the six countries. Belgium more than any other of the Six made an effort to attract this investment, and because of a generally favorable attitude toward Americans and a central location was able to attract hundreds of American firms. To this influx Belgium owes much of its economic growth —which nonetheless, has been slow, averaging less than 3 percent annually.

In order to attract both foreign and domestic investment, the Belgian government in 1959 and 1966 passed laws establishing certain regions in which considerable tax and investment aids were available. These laws were the cause of internal disputes, for the Walloons believed that too much aid was being offered in Flemish areas. The main growth came, however, in Flemish regions not covered by either law—for example, near Antwerp.

Despite these efforts, Belgium has consistently had a relatively high rate of unemployment, which official figures show to run at about 5 percent. This contrasts sharply with the Netherlands and Luxembourg, where unemployment has been negligible. The Belgian government maintains a continual effort to aid these unemployed, mainly found in Wallonia, but must temper its efforts in order to balance the national budget. This creates one of the major domestic political issues in Belgium.

Monetarily, Belgium ranks alongside the Netherlands in terms of reserves. The Belgian National Bank also serves Luxembourg.

THE LUXEMBOURG ECONOMY

The Luxembourg economy reveals an almost complete reliance on steel. At the beginning of the 1950s, Luxembourg ranked sixth in the world according to per capita national wealth. But the outlook for the small country darkened as traditional markets in Europe came to be served by other producers and the general world market for steel deteriorated. The domestic market in Luxembourg is exceedingly small: some 80 percent of production (94 percent for steel) is exported. This means that the government can do little to influence the development of the economy. This situation is accentuated by the existence of the economic union with Belgium, for Luxembourg receives a fixed percentage of the tariff revenues of the two countries, no matter what actual performance may be in a given year.

The major government effort has been to attract foreign firms, outside the steel industry, into the country to provide for adequate diversification. At the same time, Luxembourg agriculture, least efficient of the three Benelux nations, is being radically reformed. Since 1962 the industrial picture has improved with the arrival of American firms. By the end of the 1960s the effects of agricultural modernization should be evident. The increase in gross national product has hovered around 2 percent annually, following a period of 4 percent increases. It may be expected to improve as the economic situation in neighboring nations strengthens.

A unique element of the Luxembourg economy is the money market that has grown up in the capital. It is the major money market on the Continent for international issues and thus takes its place beside London. Local legislation also makes it easy for corporations to establish their headquarters there.

As we shall see later, the 1960s revealed an increasing willingness of these three nations to pool their economic efforts, both in Benelux and the Common Market, in an attempt to improve their relative position in the world by carrying greater weight in world trade. This desire had a major influence on their foreign policies. Community of interest, although generally accepted domestically, did not completely eliminate rivalry. Thus, for example, competition continued for American investment, as did competition between Rotterdam and Antwerp.

TWO

TWO SEABOARD DEMOCRACIES

**Political socialization
and culture**

The basic political unit of any democratic system is the individual. The government acts in his name, as part of a greater collectivity, and it supposedly acts for his benefit. His political attitudes are shaped by a variety of influences, the total of which result in a man who, on the one hand, may ignore and despise politics or, on the other, may have a brilliant political career. But even as a simple voter, the individual plays a vital role in the political process, for he embodies a part of the nation's values. We shall look first at the ways in which the political man is created in Belgium and in the Netherlands; then we shall examine the underlying political values of the nation.

DUTCH SOCIETY AND POLITICS

The Netherlands is a nation with a high degree of built-in harmony, or "consensus." [1] This does not mean, however, that all is

[1] Arend Lijphart (*The Politics of Accommodation* [Berkeley and Los Angeles: University of California Press, 1968]) believes that *consensus* overstates the extent of agreement existing among the Dutch. He prefers *accommodation.* Yet the extent of the Dutch commitment to their political system, together with the lack of major disputes that

dull uniformity. On the contrary, one finds an amazing variety of groups and opinions which must be welded together to create the national consensus.

Family

The family is an especially strong unit in the Netherlands, with less than 10 percent of the population living alone or in larger social groups. Dutchmen reputedly treasure family life and private amusement rather than public, and statistics show fewer cafés and lower attendance at movie theaters in the Netherlands than elsewhere.

Not surprisingly, one of the chief elements binding families together is religion. Religious homogeneity in families is relatively high; intermarriage between individuals of differing religions is far below the rate in other European countries. Over the years, most churches have had the same percentage of adherents, and any secularization has been gradual. These factors secure an important place for religion in family life. Indeed, December 5, Saint Nicholas' Day, is a family and religious holiday of the first order, far surpassing the American observance of Christmas in its emphasis on both family and religious values. By "keeping the faith" in the family, this social group attains considerable political importance. As we shall see, the relationship of religion to political affiliation is rather clearly drawn in the Netherlands.

A subsidiary factor in the transmission of political values is the role of the Dutch father as head of the family and consequently as arbiter of its opinions. In a society characterized by small farms and businesses, the family remained intact throughout the workday, and the father's necessary authority was not questioned; it extended far beyond the day's labors. But in the present century the breakdown of the family for occupational purposes has undermined the father's position and made for greater democratization of the family. Nonetheless, indications of paternal authority remain.

---

threaten the fabric of society, justifies, I believe, the word *consensus*. The differences that exist are more apparent than real, though they certainly are of some importance.

Class

Class allegiance is strong in the Netherlands and is relevant to people's political attitudes. The income gap between classes is pronounced, and this is reflected in social relations among Dutchmen. Though actual class discrimination is extremely rare, people of differing classes do not normally associate, mainly because of the acute awareness many Dutch have of their relative position on the social ladder. This is naturally reflected in participation in politics, where individuals may seek to join others of their class in party activity. The influence of class on party participation extends beyond the obvious examples of the Socialists and Liberals. The religious parties also exercise a subtle social selection. Even when party activities are not involved, class does affect the voting habits of many Dutchmen.[2] Paradoxically, among the nation's political leaders, class distinctions are often considered irrelevant, and all politicians may be said to enjoy the same relatively high standing.

Education

Many Dutch children go to religious schools, sometimes from primary school through university, and these institutions tend to reinforce religious values taught at home. At the primary level almost three fourths of the students attend religious schools. Although in secular and parochial schools there is a common curriculum designed to promote national unity, after the first six years of school, religious differences relating to such subjects as history do become evident. But the further a person pursues his education, especially if he goes to the university, the less likely he is to remain within his own religion's institutions. At the level of higher education, there is the greatest chance for the individual to move from one political group to another.

All children must attend school until age fifteen. There is relatively little discrimination by class or religion against any who are willing and able to continue beyond this age and perhaps to go to the university. Roman Catholics have been relatively underrepresented at the university level, but this distinction is fading rapidly.

[2] See the subsequent discussion of religion.

At the university level, there are the "right" schools for an individual who has decided upon a political career or on one in the national administration. The University of Leyden, for example, is generally considered the appropriate institution for budding diplomats. Crown Princess Beatrix studied there. On the other hand, a person of socialist stock may prefer to study at the University of Amsterdam.

Professions

Once the individual has finished his education, he enters a profession. This also will have an effect on his political attitudes. Conversely, a person's social and political views will help determine the nature of his job. A study has identified six classes of occupations: professionals, civil servants, teachers (3 percent of the population); managerial and executive employees (8 percent); shopkeepers, artisans, medium-scale farmers (20 percent); skilled manual workers (34 percent); semiskilled workers (27 percent); and unskilled manual laborers (8 percent).[3] A very high percentage of the population is, therefore, skilled, and this portion is expanding, while the semi- and unskilled groups are shrinking. In political terms, a large part of the population thus has a vested interest in maintaining the fabric of a society that allows them to live well and get ahead. It creates some difficulties for the traditional workers' parties, which must alter their programs or else run the risk of losing their supporters to more conservative groups. But it should be noted that, even as a person becomes wealthier, the likelihood of his passing from a religious party to a nonreligious party is not high.

The sector in which a man works is not likely to force him to make a choice among political options because of his work. There are three major labor unions—Socialist, Roman Catholic, and Protestant—making it possible for each worker to find a union in line with his political and religious convictions. A similar framework exists for the employers' organizations.

Beyond any doubt, the most prestigious position in the Netherlands is that of university professor. This creates a hier-

[3] Johan Goudsblom, *Dutch Society* (New York: Random House, 1967), pp. 67–68.

archy of education rather than of wealth. But more importantly it allows professors to be called upon to play key political roles as "experts" on the basis of their advanced knowledge of a given subject. A great deal of mobility exists between the political and professional ranks. University teachers are thus encouraged to maintain a certain degree of political detachment, the reward for which may be the right to take part in political decision making. Professors may be appointed as government ministers, they may serve as "prestige" candidates on party electoral tickets, and they may be called upon as experts. To cite one example, Jelle Zijlstra, a man with excellent academic credentials as an economist, was called upon to serve as a "technocrat" prime minister while awaiting new national elections and proved to be an extremely popular and effective chief of government. But he insisted on leaving his governmental post to accept a previously promised position as the governor of the Netherlands' central bank.

Religion

The major factor determining the political orientation of individuals is religious belief. There are four religious groups [4] in the Netherlands. The Roman Catholics are the descendants of the part of the Dutch population, mainly living in the south, that did not accept the Reformation. From the outset, Protestantism was divided into two parts: a doctrinaire Calvinism—so often identified with the Dutch Church—and a more liberal and tolerant Protestantism. Finally with the nineteenth century there appeared the movement toward secularization that produced a group of people unaffiliated with any church. In 1960, the population was divided among the various religious groups as shown by Table 2–1.

Dutch sociology has come up with a term, *verzuiling*, or "pillarization," representing the four religious "pillars," which extend into institutions of a nonreligious character. In politics, it would be totally inaccurate to say that there is a political party for each religious group. Yet the general tendency is for Catho-

---

[4] The traditional Dutch term is *zuilen*, or "pillars," meaning vertical social groups. These groups are based mainly on religion.

Table 2–1   Religious groups as of 1960

	Percent
Roman Catholic	40.4
Dutch Reformed (liberal)	28.3
Reformed (more strict)	9.3
Others (other Protestants, Jews)	3.6
None	18.4

lics to support the Catholic party, members of the Reformed Church to support the Anti-Revolutionary party, members of the Dutch Reformed Church to support the Christian-Historical Union, and nonbelievers or "humanists" to support either the Liberals or the Socialists. Thus, once a person is born into a given church, he is likely to adhere almost automatically to a given political party. Economic factors play a primary role in determining whether a "humanist" would support the Liberals, identified in the public eye as the party of business, or the Socialists, the party of labor.

The link between religion and party is of general importance only, having relatively little to do with specific issues. Indeed, on many issues there may be no difference at all between the stands of two given parties, but voters will continue to adhere to the one they have traditionally supported. In some cases a party may even take a stand contrary to the interests of many of its members, but they will continue to support it for they feel they "belong" to it. As one observer has put it: "It is not so much a question of issues; one is just more comfortable with a certain group of people." [5] This notion of being "comfortable" indicates that the great religious disputes of the past have lost much of their importance, and thus a person does not support the party of a certain religion because it must defend that religion's interests in a major struggle.

The direct involvement of the churches in the nation's political life has been diminishing. Formerly, priests or ministers could be seen among the members of the States General; this is no longer the case. And, as will be seen later, the churches,

[5] This was the comment by one leader of the Anti-Revolutionary party to the author.

speaking through their clergy, no longer attempt to intervene on national political issues.

One example may illustrate the effect of religion on politics. In 1953, when Joseph Luns was called upon to assume the portfolio of minister of foreign affairs, he was serving as a diplomat. He was thus an administrator rather than a political figure. But he soon found that he would need to enter politics and run for the States General if he wanted to retain his post. Luns, a Catholic, quickly became an active member of the Catholic party, a move considered entirely logical. Though he had been chosen as an "expert" in the field of foreign affairs, he had been selected by a government with Catholic participation. Subsequently, Luns was to become the party's best vote getter.

Randstad and country

Among the other factors that divide society and that might be expected to affect political attitudes is the division of the country into two parts—the Randstad, or rim city, and the rest of the country. This may be seen in simplest terms as a split between the urban area and the countryside. But in many ways it also represents a division between the Establishment and the outsiders. The concentration of population in the Amsterdam-Rotterdam-The Hague-Utrecht area, where more than half the Dutch populace lives, helps create a common feeling that these people are running the nation's affairs. The government is there, trade is there, business and industry are there. For those living outside the Randstad, mainly on farms in much less densely populated areas, a real concern exists that government may overlook their needs. Thus living outside the Randstad may help promote more radical political opinions—in a conservative sense. People there tend to demand the same kind of social services as in the cities, but they adhere to more fundamentalist ways of thinking. Indeed the rural inhabitants provide the main source of support for the right-wing Protestant parties.

Political parties themselves attempt to train individuals to become effective citizens, oriented to the parties' own positions. The parties attempt to throw their doors open to mass membership, particularly the Catholics and the Socialists. They sponsor youth organizations and finance political research centers. The actual effect on individuals is not possible to measure, but it is certain that individuals with a political bent are given the opportunity to play a role, however minor, at a relatively early age.

Youth

In recent years the attitude of youth to political life in the Netherlands has become the most important single pressure for change in the Dutch political system. Mere membership in the "under thirty" age group gives one the right and virtually the duty to push for a reform of the existing political structure.

The acceptance of the national consensus has meant that the young people have had to accept a given place in society. There are five categories in Dutch society: children (to age 14), youth (15–24), younger adults (25–39), adults (40–64), and the aged (above 65).[6] This stratification means that young people must wait many years before they are admitted as full participants in the decision making that affects society. The young adult, though he may head his own family, is not considered ready to assume certain positions in society. This situation is bound to cause a certain amount of unrest.

Another factor stimulating youth's involvement in politics is the general economic well-being of the Netherlands. As in other countries, youth has begun to question the purpose of a society that seems content to provide itself with as much comfort as possible. They believe that society should have a heightened sense of social obligation to the world as a whole. Thus in a period where ideology has come to play a minor role in politics, youth has been seeking a meaning for society.

Young people are generally becoming more politically aware at the university level than was true in the past. This is probably due to new methods of choosing student leaders, a modification demanded by the students. Traditional student societies have given way to political organizations, which have extended their activities to the universities. They propose candidates for student offices, and an increasing number of students participate in the elections. As might be expected, student political organizations tend to correspond with the traditional political parties.

[6] Goudsblom, *Dutch Society*, p. 43.

Thus, students are encouraged to make up their minds about politics during their university years, rather than using their university education as background for later political choice.

The initial reaction by youth against the traditional values of Dutch society came from the "provos," or "provocateurs," centered in Amsterdam. Seen as an anarchistic group, they opposed the existing power structure without proposing an alternative with any chance of acceptance outside their own, relatively small group. They tried to act by example, and their famous white bicycles, freely usable by any person, became their symbol in Amsterdam. They did win a few seats on municipal councils, but their movement appears to have lost force because of the general public disapproval of "hippies" and because some of their activities degenerated into mere hooliganism.

But the reaction of youth did not end with the provos, who, in any case, survive. The young adult group, rather than the youth, have been most effective in their efforts to transform society into what they consider to be more modern forms. These young adults actually formed a new political party, Democrats '66, thus trying to change the system from within. They received surprising support from the electorate in 1967, indicating the extent of dissatisfaction among young adults. Their chief political demand was for greater democracy and hence a greater say for the young people. Only in the Netherlands has the youth revolution had a direct political result.

One case will illustrate the political impact of the movement. A leader of the Socialist party, member of parliament, and professional party worker rose to his current position by the age of thirty-four. He achieved this success through leadership in the youth wing of the party and then in a local constituency. Despite his phenomenal success, he admits that, if he had it all to do over again, he might have preferred to join Democrats '66.

Women in the Netherlands occupy much the same "disenfranchised" position as young adults. This results from the status of the man as head of the family and the woman's role as homemaker. A far smaller percentage of Dutch women work than in many other industrialized countries. Though there has been some emancipation of women—the first woman government minister was appointed in 1956—their best hope for greater opportunity may come through such groups as Democrats '66. In fact this party has numerous female members.

The news media

Both the newspaper industry and radio-television are organized to reflect the "pillars" of Dutch society, and so they might be expected to reinforce the divisions of opinion that exist on religious grounds. This is true for the press, less so for radio-television.

Twelve newspapers are circulated throughout the country as a whole; there are also some seventy-eight provincial or local papers (2,000,000 total circulation), some of which may exceed in circulation some of the smaller national papers. Of the twelve national papers (1,550,000 total circulation), two are Socialist, two are Catholic, one is Protestant, three are Liberal, two are independent, and one is Communist. Similar affiliations exist for the provincial papers, which, quite naturally, focus on local issues and events. Over 95 percent of all newspapers are delivered to the home by subscription, with only a relative few sold at newsstands. The highest classes in society tend to read two of the national Liberal papers (*Algemeen Handelsblad* and *De Nieuwe Rotterdamsche Courant*); the middle classes prefer the other national newspapers; and in general, the provincial papers appeal to the lower levels of society. But none of these papers is "sensational" by American standards.

Broadcasting licenses have been granted by the government to five companies: Socialist, Catholic, orthodox Protestant, liberal Protestant, and "general." These companies share broadcast time, and it is understood that they are also to represent the "pillars" of Dutch society. But unlike the newspapers, the radio and television stations seek to appeal to a broad spectrum among the population and thus actually counteract the cleavages in the Dutch population. As in other European countries, television has gained tremendous popularity in the Netherlands.

Toward greater participation

Until the present, as in most developed societies, the net effect of these various influences has been to allow politics to remain in the hands of the few. However, four factors are bringing more individuals into political life. First, presence at a polling place on election day—and thus, in fact, voting—is compulsory. Failure to vote may be punished with a fine. Citizens are required to take a minimum interest in politics. Second, there are the activities of the so-called peoples' parties, notably the Catholics and the Socialists, which try to include as many people as possible in their internal, democratic decision making. Third, people may become politically involved even to the extent of membership in the States General on a part-time basis, and consequently politics becomes a "hobby" for some. Finally, the situation caused by Democrats '66 has stimulated many to a greater interest in political life. But for the majority, the sum of political participation comes once every few years, when a vote is cast.

DUTCH POLITICAL CULTURE

One leading observer has noted: "In general it can be said that for the past century Dutch society has shown an *increasing national integration of social structure* and, along with this, an *increasing acceptance of a common national culture* by all its members." [7] This has been the direct result of recognition by the whole of the population of the importance of scale in modern society. Thus a feeling of national identity results, when all Dutchmen come to believe that only through a political, social, and economic unit the size of their country (or larger) [8] can they satisfy their needs and draw the greatest benefit from modern technology.

The nation

Because of these attitudes and the common history shared by all of the Netherlands, the country has been welded into a nation, which can rely on the support of its citizens. In many respects, the resulting society seems to be similar to the traditional Anglo-

---

[7] Goudsblom, *Dutch Society,* p. 28 (italics in the original).

[8] Lijphart believes that Dutch interest in European integration is a reflection of the lack of sufficient elements to create a strong national consciousness. Many Dutch, however, appear to have made a rational decision to reject what they consider the outmoded concept of nationalism in favor of European integration.

American concept of society. It is a society in which virtually all members accept "the system" (which includes a provision for its own reform but only through gradual evolution and certainly not through abrupt change). This acceptance implies a sense of trust among the Dutch that no group will seek to denature the system and that the underlying agreement will remain that gives every group the hope of seeing the changes it wants made at some time in the future.

Two factors have done much to enhance the sense of cooperation in the population. First, there is the continual struggle against the sea. It is virtually impossible to wax overly poetic on this subject, for it is a matter of the highest priority for the Dutch. At the Brussels World's Fair of 1958, for example, the chief exhibit in the Netherlands pavilion was a wave-making machine, which gave the Dutch the chance to show all that they were doing to combat the sea. This factor of national unity has, however, begun to lose some of its force in the major cities, which now seem far removed from the struggle with the sea.

A second factor that did much to build a spirit of cooperation among the Dutch was World War II and the Nazi occupation of their country. To a significant and often lasting extent, religious, social, and political differences were ignored in the common effort to resist the occupation. Many of the cooperative institutions that appeared on the Dutch scene in the late forties were a direct result of this wartime cooperation.

Authority

The Dutch are often reputed to have a respect for authority based upon the Germanic origins of their culture. Certainly there is a recognition of the authority of the father as the head of the family, of the teacher, of church leaders, and of the "boss" (the very word is of Dutch origin). But all of this, including church authority, has been undergoing considerable change in recent decades.

In particular, a change in the leadership role of the church leaders and of employers is of some political importance. Churches, with the possible exception of the Reformed Church, have become more receptive to the pressures of democratization. In part this may be due to the growing numbers who are leaving any formal religious organization, which may encourage churches to make a greater effort to attract them to remain in the fold. As for the employers, there can be no doubt that a considerable change has occurred, owing partly to the strength of the labor unions and the Socialist party, which gave the workers the strength to demand a say in the management enterprises. This in turn altered the attitude of the individual worker to his "boss." In addition the war did much to draw them together.

Modernization

The conflict between the traditional and the modern has been resolved largely in favor of the latter because of the need to compete in a modern world. But some traditional elements have not wholly disappeared. The provinces have maintained the residue of their particularism, dating from the period of the Dutch Republic. For example, the Frisian language is still spoken in the area north of Amsterdam. From this same historical development comes the dominance of the province of Holland. Indeed it is customary to speak of the Netherlands as Holland, a reflection of the importance of this province. Both the preeminence of Holland and the regional variations of the other provinces are disappearing with modern communications, but they are not entirely gone. Another traditional characteristic that is disappearing is control by the merchant elite, owing in part to the creation of a general mercantile society and in part to the extension of democracy in the late nineteenth and early twentieth centuries.

Finally, there is the religious sector, in which the country has been known for both its strong Calvinism and religious diversity. Calvinism remains in certain parts of the Protestant Church, but it has been directed toward new ends. Thus "Christian witness" means to some an essentially Socialist view of society, involving sacrifices by the middle class for the poorer and weaker elements. This contrasts sharply with another, more conservative, view that each must earn his own well-being. Numerous denominations still exist, but one finds less conflict between them, particularly as the ecumenical movement gains ground.

The elements that have contributed to a victory of the

modern over the traditional have been characterized as industrialization, bureaucratization, centralization, urbanization, and
democratization. In general they tend to force people to live and
work together in larger groups, which breaks down the traditional divisions that have characterized the Netherlands.

The economy

In a country where the economy plays such an important role, it
is not surprising that the major political issues have been economic. On the issues that have confronted the nation in the
postwar period one finds a growing consensus.

On the question of public ownership or nationalization of
the means of production there is, in general, a wide area of
agreement in favor of the status quo. On the left, some elements
favor increased nationalization, while the conservatives would
prefer to turn some government operations over to private industry. But this is not a hotly contested question. Economic
planning, too, was once an impassioned issue, but no longer. In
general, a favorable attitude exists toward the government's
guiding and stimulating the development of the economy. Yet
there is a gap between the left, which favors major public expenditures, and the rest of the political spectrum, which prefers
an increase in private spending.

Other issues also show a growing similarity of views. There
is no basic difference of opinion on social security; the only disputes concern the way in which the system will be extended.
Interest has shifted to the question of the distribution of income
among the working population: should differences between high
and low incomes be ignored? Here the tide is running in favor of
the Socialist view that the differences should be made smaller
through the tax system. Only the conservative business community embodies a majority opposed to this trend, but few advocate
an increase in the income gap. In terms of property, the situation
is a bit different, with the Socialists calling for a redistribution of
large property holdings and the remainder proposing means to
ensure small holdings to all. Still another area in which similarities can be noticed is the matter of worker participation in industrial decision making. In general, all elements agree that workers

should be given a greater say, though the Socialists make the most extreme demands.

On this range of socioeconomic questions, one can detect a growing unanimity in the Netherlands. Yet on matters such as the distribution of income and property, wide gaps remain between the Socialists and the business community, with the rest of the population ranged somewhere between the two extremes. It should be noted that the differences, where they do exist, prevail between the rank and file of the various political parties and are less pronounced among the political leaders. This is due both to the necessity of compromising stands in order to arrive at a governing coalition and to the recognition that these are questions of principle, to be settled by a gradual evolution rather than by head-on conflict. Yet such issues can become burning questions unexpectedly. There is little doubt that the recent success of the Boerenpartij, the farmers' party, has been due to discontent with paying taxes and not receiving what was considered to be an adequate return. The reaction is similar to the Poujadist explosion in France in the 1950s.

Religious controversy

In discussing the influence of various factors on the political formation of the Dutchman, we noted the predominant role of religion. This could then be expected to make religious questions the primary theme of political debate. Indeed they are so described in this passage by a leading Dutch political scientist:

> The great debate is that between the religious and non-religious parties, the one group denying the other's *raison d'être*. The Liberals (economic conservatives) and the Partij van de Arbeid (the Labor or Socialist party) argue that members of different religious communions may perfectly well share the same political opinions, that while an individual's religious and political convictions may be closely related, no such relation is necessary in the nation at large, and that, indeed, a relation between religion and politics at the national level is detrimental to both because it exposes religion to the vagaries of ephemeral political passions while it confuses political issues by introducing irrelevant religious considerations.

The religious parties, on the other hand, claim that politics is not something separate and purely temporal but something to be subordinated to eternal values. Religious parties, they claim, are natural and rightful parties, and any political differences there may be should be settled by discussion and compromise *within* religious positions.[9]

All of this is true, yet it has become less and less relevant to the Dutch political scene. This is in large measure due to the disappearance of issues on which a religious stand is of primary importance. Thus, in 1916, the question of state aid to confessional schools was settled in favor of full public assistance. This was an issue where the religious parties, both Catholic and Protestant, had adopted a common position. But since that time, the struggle between the "humanists" and the believers has had little occasion to manifest itself on any major doctrinal issue.

Another problem is the way in which the argument of the confessional parties, as outlined previously, can be put into practice. Exactly how does a voter or politician relate his religious creed to the problem of the Common Market agricultural policy or the decision to build a new road? Admittedly it can influence a legislator on the question of aid to developing countries, but the nonreligious parties may take an equally benevolent view, and usually do. Finally, the differences between the parties, confessional or not, tends to be blurred when each knows that it may soon be either in the cabinet or opposition and that, if in the cabinet, it will be forced to compromise its stand in the interests of the coalition.

Thus one finds the most paradoxical of situations. Religious belief is the chief determining factor in the individual's choice of a political party, either to join it or to support it, but this has little practical effect when it comes to political action.

The harmonious society

The underlying theme of the Dutch political system is, then, one of harmony and cooperation. There is a general agreement on the need to improve society, and the chief political disputes are

[9] Hans Daalder, "Parties and Politics in the Netherlands," *Political Studies,* 3 (1955), 6–7 (italics in the original).

on the ways by which the commonly accepted goals may be achieved. This is a society of consensus, much like the system that has gained considerable fame for Sweden. In some ways it works better than in that Nordic country, for in the postwar period the willingness to accept restraint on individual demands on the economy has been especially marked. In addition, neutrality has not kept the nation from participating in whatever international arrangements seem propitious for achieving the national goals.

At all levels of government, and in interest groups, there is a general recognition of this consensus. As a result of the general consensus and the religious factor in politics, there is relatively little political turbulence or shifting from party to party. Small and often militant political parties do exist, based on a particular point of interest, but they choose to work within the system, rather than seek to promote revolution or fundamental structural changes. The smallness of the country allows for a rapid transmission of new ideas, and they may be fairly evaluated and eventually acted upon in one way or another. Thus the Netherlands represents a homogeneous and stable political society, reflecting the consent of virtually the entire population.

BELGIAN SOCIETY AND POLITICS

Belgium differs strikingly from the Netherlands on almost all points of comparison. Belgian society is characterized by deeper cleavage among groups, with the language dispute dominating all of national life.

Family, education, and work

The family is a strong social unit in Belgium. Politics are passed down, for a child is exposed to opinions, generally shared by both parents, that are not subjected to much critical debate. He thus begins by measuring other opinions against those he has learned at home and for which he probably has a good deal of respect.

Unless the child goes to a confessional school, which is expected to reinforce the opinions given him at home, the next major step in his political evolution will come at the university.

For children who do not go to the university, the political choice is even more likely to be that of the parents, because, in this case, the child probably comes from a working-class background and accepts the same kind of job as his father and many of his opinions. At the university, the student is thrown into an atmosphere of political ferment, particularly at the two nonstate institutions, the Free University of Brussels and the Catholic University of Louvain. Chances are that the student will move to the left during this period, though this shift will have a lasting effect for only a few of the students. In any case, he will be exposed to a wide variety of opinions, which will undoubtedly help influence his later thinking. The Free University of Brussels is, for example, a breeding ground for intellectual Socialists—people with little direct contact with the problems of the working class.

The job will be less an influence on political views than a manifestation of social class and hence of political views already held. If, however, a person has kept his political opinions to himself or has not yet completely formed them, then when he is appointed to a position in the nation's larger economic institutions, or when he begins working as a lawyer or banker, he may find it convenient and logical to join either the conservative wing of the center party or the more conservative political party, the Party for Liberty and Progress. Certainly the political views he holds will be of utmost importance if he seeks appointment to a governmental administrative post. Here the "spoils system" is at a peak of refinement, and jobs go to the party faithful.

Labor unions also will not have much of an influence on political beliefs. Like the political parties, they are a manifestation of the beliefs already held, not a forum for shaping political opinion. There are three major labor unions, one for each of the major political tendencies in the country.

If we look, however, at the ways in which Belgian society is divided, we find a series of overlapping influences that are of the greatest importance in shaping political views. Belgian society is split in several ways.[10]

---

[10] These divisions are called *zuilen,* as in the Netherlands, but are not based to the same extent upon religion.

Religion and class

Historically, the Catholic and the Liberal "spiritual families" confronted each other in the nineteenth century. Thus the religious factor was the source of political orientations. The two elements joined together to participate in the Belgian state in order to defend certain rights, but their views of these rights differed considerably. The Catholics saw in the state a way of ensuring their freedom of belief, but also a way of promoting the rights of the Church. The Liberals, on the other hand, were more concerned with the rights of the individual—and in particular his right not to be forced into a confessional framework. They favored greater secularization of education and the separation of church and state.[11]

The forces of industrialization added a third element to the basic Belgian "cleavage." With them came the growth of the working class, which demanded that the state and industry provide them with a fairer share of the profits of their labors and far greater social benefits. The response of the Catholics to this new element was ambivalent. In part they supported these views in hopes of preventing widespread disaffection from the Church by workers. On the other hand, conservative elements tended to line up with the Liberals, who opposed the Socialists on almost all social and economic questions. Only on the demand for increased secularization did the Liberals and Socialists agree.

This three-way split has continued to exist in Belgium, although it has attenuated. The nation is still divided into two basic classes. The working class represents the majority of the population. The bourgeoisie, composed of typical Belgian burghers, enjoys a middle-class existence. Almost all workers want to climb to this status. It has become politically impossible for the bourgeoisie to oppose this social evolution—and thus the Catholics, for example, have become increasingly favorable to improving the social conditions of the worker. But the middle-class philosophy still remains: by hard work a man should be able to pull himself up without much help from the state.

[11] For a fuller discussion, see Val R. Lorwin, "Belgium: Religion, Class and Language in National Politics," in Robert A. Dahl, *Political Oppositions in Western Democracies* (New Haven, Conn.: Yale University Press, 1966).

Language

Superimposed on this religious-class cleavage is the split that has come to play the greatest political role in Belgium—the language split. Though it has existed from the outset of modern Belgian history, it has become more acute in recent years.

The Belgian people are not of two different origins, although they speak two different languages. In the northern part of the country, which shares a border with the Netherlands, the people speak Flemish, which is similar to Dutch. The people to the south, known as Walloons, speak French. Because history was to give French a more important place as an international language, the upper classes in Belgium, whatever their origin, took to using this language. In Brussels, the nation's political capital, French became the principal language, although the city is situated in Flemish territory.

The conflict between the two language groups heightened as the Flemings became more aware of themselves as a cultural entity and as a political force. This was due partly to the Flemish cultural movement at the end of the nineteenth century and partly to the fact that with increased democratization the Flemings found their greater numbers giving them real political power. The conflict has been fought in three major areas: economic, cultural, and political.[12]

The economic power of Belgium was for the first 120 years (1830–1950) of Belgian history clearly in the hands of the French-speaking population. The economic leaders of the nation, even in the Flemish part of the country, chose the French language because it represented an international "elite" language. This in turn stemmed from the fact that the traditional economic leadership came from Wallonia, where the first industrial development took place. Here was found the coal that led to the creation of the Belgian steel industry.

After 1950, this situation was altered by economic developments unrelated to the language question and by the increased political power of the Flemings. Increased industrialization occurred in Flanders because of the growth in the port of Ant-

[12] See *The Language Problem in Belgium* (Brussels: Belgian Information and Documentation Institute, 1967). Mimeo.

werp, the proximity of the region to the sea, and the ready availability of labor—all of which combined to attract both Belgian and foreign investment to the area. At the same time, Wallonia went into a period of economic decline owing to the inefficiency of the coal mines in comparison with those in other countries and the worldwide oversupply of steel. Politically, both sides entered into a continuous struggle for the public works expenditures and tax incentives to investment doled out by the national government. Recently the government has tried to meet the demands of both sides, at least to a limited extent, but the monopoly on economic discontent has passed from the Flemings to the Walloons.

In the cultural area, both sides demand greater autonomy, but the most serious problem is the teaching of the "second" language. Most Flemings choose to learn French as their second language, thus making them eligible for many administrative posts in the national government open to bilingual Belgians. Most of the French-speaking population is opposed to bilingualism, claiming that Dutch is only marginally important as an international language.[13] Another problem, only recently settled at the primary and secondary school level, is the language of instruction. A linguistic border has been drawn between the two parts of the country, with all instruction to be in Dutch north of the line and in French south of it. An exception is made for bilingual Brussels. Problems arise when a pocket of people of one language is found on the "wrong" side of the line. When six communes were transferred from south to north several years ago, a national controversy arose. At the university level, where there has been no legislative requirement for linguistic homogeneity, a struggle has broken out over the University of Louvain, a bilingual institution located in Flemish territory. Ultimately the French-language section of this university will be transferred to Wallonia.

Brussels is also the scene of cultural conflict. Many Flemings who move to Brussels choose to educate their children primarily in French, which they continue to believe is needed to

---

[13] This is in marked contrast to Switzerland, another country with more than one national language, where bilingualism or even multilingualism is the accepted practice.

"get ahead." French-speaking leaders stress that the father of the family should be allowed to choose freely the language in which his child is educated, for they see this as a way of increasing the strength of the French-speaking population. Flemish leaders argue that fathers will choose French because educational facilities in Dutch in Brussels are inadequate. They want an improvement of these facilities and the obligation for the child to be educated in the language of his parents.[14]

Political aspects of the language dispute

Finally, political issues divide the two language groups. A series of civil rights laws has been passed, assuring the Flemings fair treatment by the administration, schools, army, and courts. The most important guarantee was the creation of the linguistic border in 1962–1963. The main problems growing out of this measure are the previously mentioned case of the transfer of six communes to the Dutch-speaking area and the lack, according to many Flemings, of adequate sanctions for failure to respect the right to use the Dutch language.

The political question can be seen as a struggle for territory. The Flemings fear that the French-speaking population wants to expand the limits of legally bilingual Brussels until contact is made with Wallonia. A junction of the two would gradually increase the strength of the French-speaking population in central Belgium. The Flemings also believe that the French position at Louvain could be used as a basis of expansion to bring an additional part of Flemish territory under control of the French speakers by gradually extending out from both Brussels and Louvain.

Another political problem, the fair representation in Parliament of the Flemings in line with their share of the population, has been settled. But at the same time the linguistic frontier was created, it was agreed that constitutional guarantees would be promulgated to ensure that the French-speaking members of Parliament could not be outvoted on certain categories of important questions. This constitutional revision, always on the parliamentary agenda, has not yet taken place.

[14] See Chap. 3.

The linguistic dispute has placed the very structure of the Belgian state in doubt. For, as members of both groups come to believe that they cannot gain full satisfaction of their demands in a structure encompassing the two language communities and show continual unwillingness to compromise those demands, a looser governmental framework becomes inevitable. Thus the trend in Belgium toward greater decentralization in the cultural and economic fields is undeniable. The major question for the future is whether the same development will take place in the political area, leading perhaps to federalism.

The division of the country along language lines is also related to the "cleavages" mentioned earlier. The greatest Socialist strength is clearly to be found in Wallonia, owing to the disaffection from the Catholic Church in the French-speaking part of the country. Incidentally, this development can also be seen as a factor in the relatively higher birthrate in the Flemish part of the country. Flanders remains the bastion of the Catholic "spiritual family" in Belgium. Finally, it is the French-speaking population of Brussels that is most clearly identified with the liberal stream of thought.

Thus divisions in Belgium by language, class, religion, and locality have a powerful impact on the political views of the individual and the politics of the nation as a whole. Though the mobility of Belgians from the countryside to Brussels or Antwerp does help to create more "national" views, it also removes many from their traditional political associations. Thus one finds the greatest manifestations of extremism on the language question—including the creation of linguistic parties—in these two cities.

The news media

The most basic division among the news media of Belgium is, of course, the language used. Within each language group among the newspapers, the various political views are also represented.

Some twenty-seven French-language (circulation 1,490,-000), fifteen Dutch-language (1,185,000), and one German-language (15,000) general-interest papers are published each day. The total circulation of the French-language papers exceeds that of the Dutch-language papers. This would indicate that, although Belgium has a Dutch-speaking majority, the vestiges of cultural domination by the French-speaking part of the population remain.

Among the French-language papers, there are ten Catholic or Social Christian, seven Liberal, six Socialist, and four "neutral" publications. The leading papers in French are the Catholic *La Libre Belgique* and the independent *Le Soir*. A survey of the Dutch-language press indicates that eleven are Catholic or Christian Democratic, two are Liberal, and two are Socialist. This distribution bears out the fact that there is a higher concentration of Socialists among the Walloons than among the Flemings. The leading Flemish papers are the Liberal *Het Laatste Nieuws* and the Catholic *De Standaard*.

Radio and television are operated by the government and are supposed to remain neutral on political questions. Three separate French-language and Dutch-language broadcasts are carried on the radio, and there is one television channel for each group. The three radio broadcasts appeal to the differing tastes of listeners, not to specific political, religious, or class groups. Nonetheless, the newscasting on the French-speaking broadcasts and telecasts does tend to favor the Socialist view on some occasions; this is a manifestation of the concentration of Socialist and Communist listeners among the Walloons. A similar tendency toward the Catholics on Flemish broadcasts is not as evident.

Parties, participation, and politicians

The political parties themselves do not represent additional elements of cleavage; they are merely reflections of the existing divisions in the population. In addition, their total membership is so small that they are not in a position to influence directly many people. One important trend, which does seem to have a certain intellectual appeal, indicates that an effort by the parties to play down the cleavages and stress elements of national unity, such as economic problems, may represent a "way out" for some Belgians.

In sharp contrast with the Netherlands, there is no reform movement among the young in Belgium. In fact, youth has been more restrained in Belgium than in most other European countries. One obvious factor is the strength of the family, which discourages the development of independence by the young. Belgian women, on the other hand, play a stronger role both in the family and in the nation's political life than in the Netherlands. Yet the general philosophy still relegates them to a place in the home or as helpers to their husbands at work, and this position they seem ready to accept.

As in the Netherlands, voting is compulsory. Thus the citizen is required to act out at least one phase of the democratic procedure. But he may be more active if he is particularly concerned with the language question. Then he may participate either in one of the linguistic extremist groups or within the major parties in trying to influence their approach to the issues of the day. He is less likely to be as involved when other, nonlinguistic issues are involved. In the economic sector, bankers and company executives are encouraged to play a role in politics, at a level commensurate with their position in business (presidents on the national level and junior executives in local politics), in hopes of influencing the trend of developments favorably. Thus certain institutions gain the reputation of having special access to the specific political parties. This tendency is, of course, self-perpetuating, and executives are often recruited with an eye to their political leanings and their willingness to play an active political role.

In terms of politicians themselves, a study carried out in Belgium reveals some of the paths they follow in their careers.[15] Six types have been analyzed. First is the "leader," who enters politics as an idealist. For him it is a mission or an art rather than a profession. He believes that he represents an ideology and is to defend the interests of the nation as a whole, not just one section. Rather doctrinaire, he believes in party discipline. A second type is the "wise man," or technician. He entered politics when the party, recognizing his expertise, invited him. He continues to work outside politics, and within his party he serves as an "intellectual," adviser, or lecturer. He, too, is most interested in the nation as a whole and has some disdain for "professional politicians." To be reelected, he counts on his personal

[15] F. Debuyst, *La Fonction Parlementaire en Belgique* (Brussels: CRISP, 1967).

prestige. The third category includes the man who has come from a social organization such as a labor union. He specializes in educational and social questions and is usually concerned with certain regional problems. Basing his political strength on his standing with the local party and his union, he believes that the national party should be responsive to local interests.

The fourth type of politician is the "good neighbor," who acquired a following through contacts in his own home area and his willingness to help find solutions to local problems. He is really not very interested in politics and has run for office, at the urging of his party, because he was already popular and had a ready-made political clientele. He is particularly interested in promoting the well-being of his electors and is thus more sensitive to local than to national issues.

Fifth, there is the "electoralist," or "born politician." He enjoys political activity and has been involved in it in many ways since his youth. He may hold an executive post in his commune in addition to his job as legislator. A bridge between the local and the national, he has a foot in each camp. He enjoys above all using his "charismatic" personality in contact with and on behalf of his electors. He depends less on the national party than on the voters.

Finally, there is the "contact man." For him politics is the atmosphere in which he has been plunged since childhood. He is often torn between the demands of his region and those of the national party, but tries to maintain a link between the two levels.

These are not the only political types in Belgium. There may be combinations, such as the regional "notable" or the "sectoral leader" (representing a class of society). In the language parties can be found "militants" and "political propagandists." For the Communists, a man must be a "worker" and a "party man."

Of the six basic types, the leaders or the wise men provide almost all the ministers of government. The men from the "social organizations" are most often Flemings and members of the Social Christian party, while the "contact men" are almost all Walloon and, for the most part, Socialist.

BELGIAN POLITICAL CULTURE

Belgian society is characterized by a sense of strife among the various groups mentioned earlier. In almost no case can any single group, be it religious, linguistic, or economic, hope to achieve its goals without requiring some other group to make a sacrifice. Thus there is a continual pulling and tugging. The government has taken the role of trying to provide an equitable solution. It is not the referee in these struggles; it is an active participant, for it comprises representatives of most of the conflicting forces. But it casts itself as an entity that has the responsibility of coming to a decision and therefore must find compromises that give some satisfaction to everybody. This proves increasingly difficult on the linguistic question as positions become more intransigent. Therefore the government seeks to avoid having to deal with linguistic issues, on which compromise is either exceedingly difficult or impossible, and devotes itself to trying to cushion the conflict among the competing groups.

Individual rights

Strife in Belgium is not merely a characteristic of the relations of the various groups. Even more fundamental is the spirit of conflict among individuals. This stems, in all probability, from the nineteenth century, when the function of government was seen by both the Catholics and the Liberals as a guarantor of individual rights. Whatever other groups and controversies have since arisen, Belgium has remained essentially a liberal state. The rights of the individual are given paramount importance. This may be contrasted with the Netherlands, where the good of society as a whole is understood to imply some sacrifice of absolute individual rights.

The effect of this insistence on individual rights can be seen in two cases of widely differing political importance. On linguistic questions, the example of Switzerland is often mentioned in Belgium. The Swiss do not permit the creation of schools of one language in a canton of another language on the grounds that this would impair the harmony of the nation and its linguistic peace. This example gets a cold reception from many

Belgians, who believe that the parent's right to decide the language in which his children will be educated should be given a higher priority than the harmony of the nation.

A second example is one that every Belgian meets daily. The code of the road prescribes that all vehicles coming from the right, no matter how small the road, have the right of way over other vehicles. The result is an astoundingly high accident rate, because drivers insist upon their right of way even when it is blatantly dangerous. This demonstrates the effect of an absolute insistence on individual rights.

The purpose of organized society is to provide a framework in which all can exercise their rights without doing damage to others. In Belgium the fabric of society is weakened by the extreme insistence on rights and the unwillingness to make sacrifices for the collectivity.

As might be expected, this attitude has its effect on the images of authority in the country. At home and in the schools, children are taught a respect for authority, but in practice they see their parents insisting in their contacts with others on an unmitigated recognition of their rights. However, in their contacts with government, people do tend to recognize its authority, probably because the state metes out benefits and the individual wants to receive his share with a minimum of difficulty. Within government, the sense of hierarchy is strong, owing probably to relatively high inefficiency (in turn due to the spoils system and the doling out of posts along linguistic lines), which induces many civil servants to try to pass responsibility to superiors.

The clash of tradition and modern needs

The conflict of tradition and modernism in Belgium is particularly sharp in the area of social and economic affairs. In this sector the real political debate in the nation is carried on, although it is often overshadowed by the linguistic question.

The more traditional view in the country maintains that the government should provide sufficient social benefits and aid to workers and the unemployed to improve their lot. The government is asked to support economically uncertain enterprises, not for their intrinsic value, but because their operation will provide needed jobs for the unemployed. Each class that expects certain benefits from the state (unemployed, widows, students, veterans, and so on) believes that aid should be increased regularly. This is essentially a "take from the rich and give to the poor" philosophy, which seeks to reduce income differences but accepts as a permanent part of the national structure the existence of the two chief economic classes—the working class and the bourgeoisie. Called by its opponents *le socialisme de papa,* because it is regarded as being out of date in its view of the class struggle, it usually results in an unbalanced national budget in order to meet the social welfare payments it promises.

The opposite view lays great stress on accelerating the economic development of the nation. This stems from the recognition that Belgium has not yet fully modernized its economic structure, because so much of its economy was spared during the war. In addition, much Belgian investment has gone abroad —for example, to the Congo—and the country has fallen behind technologically at just the wrong moment. Thus it is felt that maximum effort should be made to modernize and make competitive the best of Belgian industry so that the national income, so largely dependent on foreign trade, will continue to rise. The effects on the working class are seen as a kind of "economic fallout." Proponents argue that the gap between the two classes can be more effectively and more cheaply closed in this way, but it is admittedly difficult to sell the voter on the longer-run gains. He is, however, influenced by the balanced national budget that accompanies this philosophy.

These two points of view implicitly take into account the regional (or linguistic) split in the country. The more traditional view would allow for aid to be given to the weakest part of the country economically, through direct subsidies to industries needed to provide jobs and through social welfare payments. This approach recognizes the unwillingness of many Belgians to move from their homes to new areas where there are jobs. With the exception of the move to Brussels, which may signify a step up in the world, many Belgians are reluctant to move even within their own language region. The more modern approach treats the small nation as a whole and implies the need for workers to go where the most profitable economic activity can be established. It does not, however, mean that one region would be sacrificed for another.

Religious disputes

The religious question had, at one time, a great impact on Belgian political life, but this has subsided considerably in recent years. The conflict, largely a result of the struggle between the Catholics and the freethinking elements of the population, was manifest in the question of state and private schools. The dispute reached its climax in 1958 with the adoption of the Schools Pact by a commission representing the major political parties. While assuring state support for private (essentially Catholic) schools, it provided adequate financing for public schools as well. The pact has been called "an armistice drowned in subsidies," [16] for the amount of money to be spent satisfying the demands of both sides was considerable. But the pact put to rest the last remaining religious issue likely to have a major impact on politics. This reflected an evolution within the political parties themselves, for they had given signs since 1945 of increasing annoyance at being dragged into doctrinal disputes. The result was, after 1958, a subtle transformation of the parties away from close identification with doctrinaire positions on religious issues.[17]

The Belgian and his government

The individual in Belgium tends to feel a vague unhappiness with the political structure. For him, the outcome of any election seems inevitable, with each of the major parties retaining its relative position. The language question has, however, changed this situation somewhat, though it cannot be regarded as an encouraging sign. Nor does the individual have a very high respect for politicians. They are seen as people extracting financial rewards from their positions and more concerned with self-preservation than with public service. Clearly a career in business is considered more acceptable and worthwhile than one in politics.

The politicians themselves may have a more idealistic view

[16] J. Meynaud, *La Décision Politique en Belgique* (Paris: Armand Colin, 1965), p. 168.

[17] See Chap. 4.

of their roles than do the voters. Their greatest problem seems to be in reconciling their obligations to regional problems and the needs of a national political party. Depending on the desires of any given voter, their image will prosper if they succeed in reconciling these often conflicting demands.

The parties themselves are, in effect, instruments of government, for they represent a synthesis of regional views. In many respects they consider themselves more important than the Parliament as such, and a national party leader may have considerably more prestige than a cabinet minister. As might be expected, parties seem to act with greater responsibility when they are in the cabinet, with less when in opposition.

The social organizations and, in particular, the labor unions also consider themselves direct participants in the governmental process. They claim to represent coherent ideological positions, which they are not forced to compromise in cabinet coalitions. Yet the political allegiance of unions is of relatively little importance, owing to their common viewpoint on many issues.

National government must synthesize the nation's political will under extremely difficult circumstances. The majority parties play a major role in government decisions, and the opposition can be counted on to oppose under almost all circumstances. Local government, tied to the strong communes, tends to think of itself as the defender of Belgian virtues of individual independence and hence may find itself at odds with the desires of the national government.

Thus, in sharp contrast with the Netherlands, Belgium is a society in strife where any consensus on the purpose of government and the future course of the state is in doubt. Although most Belgians would admit that they must continue with the present framework, this is more an admission of frustration than of conviction that Belgium is following the right course.

THREE
THE DECLINE OF COMMUNE AND PROVINCE
Style and motives of local politics

Both Belgium and the Netherlands are centralized states; neither has a federal organization, and the national government has a monopoly of political responsibility. Yet in both countries there are administrative and political subunits, some with a tradition of considerable autonomy, and each retaining some prerogatives of its own.

THE DUTCH MUNICIPALITY

Local authorities developed in the Netherlands during the Middle Ages when a *drost,* or sheriff, was placed in charge of maintaining order in a given parish. This parish evolved into the town, with its own administrative powers and often under the control of corporations—representative bodies of the citizenry. By the time the Republic of the Seven United Netherlands, the towns had achieved extensive powers. Mainly because of their economic and political strength, the decentralized form of national government prevailed.[1]

Two events changed this situation radically. The first was the French occupation at the turn of the nineteenth century. As elsewhere, Napoleon established in the Netherlands a unitary

[1] See Chap. 1.

state with a centralized government. This followed the French pattern and allowed for easier control of the country. The unitary state remained after the French left. The second turning point was the adoption of the Constitution of 1848, which integrated the municipalities into the national administrative system. The local government structure of the Netherlands, based on that Constitution, still provides for some local autonomy and creates relations between the municipality and higher political authorities that are virtually unique.

The Netherlands is composed of more than 900 *Gemeente,* or municipalities, which, under the Constitution, are all governed in the same way. Thus there is only one form of local government in the Netherlands. There is a tendency to reduce the number of municipalities in order to create units easier to administer and to provide adequate social services at acceptable cost. As a result the total number of municipalities is shrinking rapidly. A considerable difference in size remains: Amsterdam, the largest, has 866,000 inhabitants, while the smallest has 261. All are administered in the same way, except that the size of the Municipal Council may vary in accordance with the size of the municipality and the province has certain added responsibilities with regard to the smaller municipalities.

Local institutions

The Municipal Council (Gemeenteraad), composed of from seven to forty-five members, is the highest authority in the municipality. Directly elected every four years, the council is composed of members chosen by proportional representation. The elections for the council do not take place at the same time as the selection of a new parliament. The council acts as a legislative body, adopting regulations for the administration of local affairs—including public order, morals, and health. Local officials, with the exception of the burgomaster, are appointed by the council, which also adopts the annual budget and controls all financial affairs of the muncipality. Certain of the functions assigned to the council are within its own power and discretion, but others—rules on building and housing and the sale of alcoholic beverages—are in accordance with laws adopted by a higher authority.

In addition to the council, the College of Burgomaster and Aldermen (Burgemeester en Wethouders) is part of local government. It is composed of from two to six members of the council, chosen for the same period as the council, plus the burgomaster. In larger municipalities, the post of alderman is a full-time, salaried activity. The college is responsible for the day-to-day administration of the municipality under the instructions of the council and in line with provincial and national rules. In more populated areas, the aldermen may divide among themselves the various departments of the local government, forming a kind of cabinet, but they are responsible to the council as a group for their actions.

Finally, in the local structure, there is the burgomaster, who has a preeminent role and occupies a unique position. He is appointed in theory by the Crown—in practice by the cabinet and usually the minister of the interior. The queen's commissioner in the province where the municipality is located makes the formal nomination. The burgomaster is often a career civil servant who has chosen local administration as his profession. As a young man, he may be appointed to a small municipality with the hope of being promoted to larger and more important towns if he is successful. For the largest cities of the country, the burgomaster may be a former national political leader. In making the appointment, the cabinet is careful to take into account the local political situation. Thus a Socialist will not be appointed burgomaster of a municipality that is predominantly Roman Catholic, nor the reverse. But the burgomaster may and usually does come from outside the municipality he will govern. It is possible hat he could have been elected a member of the council at the local elections, but this is rare. By appointing a man from outside the area, the cabinet assures itself of the loyalty of the person and of his objectivity in local affairs. Named for a six-year term, he can expect to be reappointed unless he is found manifestly unfit for his post.

The burgomaster chairs the meetings of the council, of which he is not a member, though he is a voting member of the college. He is, in effect, the chief executive of the municipality and supervises the local administration. He may, acting as representative of the national government, prevent, for up to thirty days, the execution of orders of the council or college if he believes it is contrary to the law or general interest. Within the thirty days, the cabinet may rescind the decision or let it pass. Although he is a representative of the central government, the burgomaster does not receive formal "instructions" from it, and his salary is paid out of the municipal budget.

In practical terms, the burgomaster is in direct charge of the police and fire departments. But in small municipalities that do not have their own police force he plays an advisory role to the national police authorities, which provide the police force. When there are extensive public disorders or a natural catastrophe, the burgomaster may issue police regulations with the force of law, subject to repeal by the council or by the queen's commissioner in the province.

The burgomaster and politics

The institution of the burgomaster in the Netherlands is unique and represents an imaginative balance between the requirements of local self-government and national unity. The post is one of considerable prestige, particularly for muncipalities of more than 50,000 inhabitants, where it is the cabinet as a whole that makes the appointment. As mentioned above, appointments are made in line with the general political and religious preference of the municipality. In addition, the cabinet attempts to keep a national balance of posts in line with the national distribution of political strength. The largest cities—Amsterdam, Rotterdam, and Utrecht—have Socialist burgomasters, thus making it improbable that the fourth—The Hague—would have one as well. Members of the States General may become burgomasters and the reverse, but the post is not usually considered a political stepping-stone. Thus a man who performs brilliantly in one of the major cities cannot expect, as a result, that he may become a cabinet minister.

Among the criticisms of the Dutch concept of burgomaster is the lack of democratic choice in his nomination. In practice, however, the burgomaster has come to be responsive to the will of the council and, from his position of strength as an expert in governmental affairs, may tactfully guide it. Conflicts can, of course, arise if the burgomaster is an innovator and has to face a conservative council, if he tries too openly to dominate it, or if he clashes politically with a majority of the council. In cases of serious dispute, where the cabinet must intervene, the council, as representative of the people, is likely to get its way. In his relations with the aldermen, the burgomaster is confronted with individuals having considerable experience in local government. This facilitates cooperation, but it may place the aldermen in a position to challenge the authority of the burgomaster. Because the municipal departments are under the aldermen, the burgomaster is provided with his own personal staff so that his administrative independence is assured. In practice the burgomaster often finds himself in agreement with the aldermen in defending local prerogatives against the central government.

One expert summarizes the character of the Dutch municipalities as determined by the basic applicable law:

> The Municipal Act of 1851 is a mixture of three main elements: the autonomous status of the cities under the Republic, the trend towards centralization and, in particular, standardization of the French and the post-French period, and the modern democratic concepts resulting from the revolutionary movements in many European countries during the 1840s.[2]

The Dutch municipalities must face two problems: finance and the limits that size places on ability to act. Some 90 percent of their income is channeled to them by the national government. The remainder comes from local taxes and income from municipal utilities and from town-owned property. Localities generally feel themselves overly dependent on the state because most of their income comes from this source, but there seems to be little likelihood that new independent revenues can be found for the municipalities.

The second problem concerns present legal limitations on joint action by municipalities. It remains difficult for them to create regional authorities to deal with common problems, especially because there is no legal provision for them to elect governing bodies for such authorities. The government increas-

[2] A. F. Leemans, "Local Government in the Netherlands," p. 3. Mimeo, a government publication.

ingly recognizes this problem, and a movement is under way to allow for regions, which would still remain smaller than the provinces. Some consider such regions as an intermediary stage on the way to new and larger municipalities.

THE PROVINCES IN THE NETHERLANDS

The Netherlands is divided into eleven provinces plus some of the land newly reclaimed from the former Zuyder Zee.[3] The provinces were the historical forerunners of the Dutch state. Under the Republic (1579–1795), seven provinces had considerable autonomy, and the area of what are now three others was administered by the central government. The eleventh province came from the division of Holland, the most powerful province, into two parts. After the French occupation, the rights of provinces were reduced in favor of the central authority. The king's (now queen's) commissioners acted in the sovereign's name. The 1848 Constitution accorded to each province a limited right to govern, thus allowing for differences among the eleven to be manifest politically.

Each province has a Provincial Council (Provinciale Staten) composed of from thirty-nine to eighty-three members, depending on population, who are elected every four years. The council adopts regulations for the province without approval of the government, except when they concern waterways and water control, public utilities, physical planning, and economic and cultural affairs.

In addition to the Provincial Council, there is a Provincial Executive (Gedeputeerde Staten) composed of the queen's commissioner and six members of the council elected for a four-year term. Its functions are similar to those of the Municipal College —the daily administration of provincial affairs. It also assures the execution of national laws. The executive has sole responsibility in the province for supervising the municipalities.

Finally, at the provincial level, the queen's commissioner

[3] The provinces are Zeeland, Utrecht, Overijssel, Gelderland, Groningen, Friesland, North Holland, South Holland, Drenthe, Brabant, and Limburg. The newly reclaimed land is administered directly by the national government.

(Commissaris der Koningin), appointed for an indefinite period and paid by the state, acts in much the same way as the burgomaster at the municipal level. He, too, is assigned a dual function, between the national government and the province. But the commissioner is more directly responsible to the national government, for he may be given formal "instructions" by it that he must carry out. In addition, he is required to visit all municipalities within the province at least once every four years and to report his findings to the Provincial Executive and to the Ministry of the Interior.

The provincial government, an intermediary level between the municipality and the national government, is relatively less important than the municipality. It does not, as in the United States, represent a state to which the locality is subject. Its funds come largely from the national government; only about one sixth are raised by a provincial tax. The total of budgets for the provinces is about 5 percent of the total of municipal budgets, indicating much about their relative importance and the scope of the activities directly under their respective jurisdictions.

A word should be said about the *waterschappen,* administrative districts for water control and having jurisdiction over dikes, canals, bridges, and roads. Subject to the Provincial Councils, they usually are supervised by a board, in charge of routine administration, which is elected by the landowners in the water control zone. They may lay down regulations, subject to approval of the Provincial Executive. At one time these waterschappen had considerable power and were a familiar part of the governmental framework.[4]

Links between local and national politics

The Dutch local government system clearly indicates the unitary character of the state. While there is a local consciousness, a country of the limited size of the Netherlands promotes an over-

---

[4] The waterschappen have diminished in importance mainly because of the growth of large cities whose inhabitants are not directly concerned with the struggle against the sea. But any authority concerned with water control, up to a major part of one ministry in the national government itself, continues to have an ample budget and considerable effect on the lives of the Dutch.

riding national awareness. There is no historical or cultural dividing line to maintain the distinction between the provinces, for religious differences find their political outlet through the national political parties rather than through regionalism. Where there is an important local interest—for example, the prerogatives of the port of Rotterdam—they may quickly be transformed into a matter of national interest.

Political parties have their foundations at the local level, and the smaller parties, which may have no success in the national parliamentary elections, do gain seats on Municipal and Provincial Councils. But in general, party politics are part of a single national system, and provincial or municipal officials do not build political careers by moving up the ladder of advancement from town hall to provincial palace to parliament. Even though the apportionment of municipal and provincial posts is in accordance with the national political alignment, there is no subsequent attempt by the national parties to bring political pressure to bear. Thus the office of burgomaster of Amsterdam may represent a political plum for the Socialists, but once in office, the burgomaster becomes more of a professional city administrator than a political official. Although the lines are somewhat blurred when a man is both burgomaster and member of the States General, there nonetheless remains a distinction between his administrative and political roles. Naturally, a burgomaster will be influenced by his political convictions in the actions he takes.

In the Netherlands, the national government dominates the province and municipality. The people insist on the right of self-government for local matters, but there is a general recognition that the number and importance of such matters is rapidly decreasing in an urbanized and modern world. Thus the belief in the prerogatives of the municipality, although still strong, is waning. Quite the reverse is true in Belgium.

THE TRADITION OF THE BELGIAN COMMUNE

The system of local government in Belgium is basically the same as in the Netherlands, but the myths surrounding the system are different. Local government is exalted in Belgium, probably more than in most other democratic countries. This is explained in part by Belgian history; some claim that the local authority known as the commune had its origins in Belgium.

A student of Belgian history finds that the equivalent of the Magna Carta or the Declaration of Independence was a document of the Middle Ages assuring that the rights of the communes would be respected. The foreign occupations of the country, from the mid-sixteenth cenutry until 1830, added to the importance of the local authorities. With the national government in the hands of the occupying power, the people turned to their local governments to protect their interests. Once again, from 1940 to 1944, communal administrations were headquarters for the resistance.

As in the Netherlands, the French occupation had a considerable influence on the organization of public authorities, creating a more centralized system and thus reducing the prerogatives of the communes. Once Belgium had become independent, the framers of the Constitution found it necessary to ensure that the primacy of the central government was made clear. The Constitution is relatively vague on the functions that communes and provinces are to perform, indicating merely that the communes are responsible for maintaining a separate administrative apparatus to record the vital statistics of the Belgian population.

A single system of government is applied to the more than 2600 communes (this is also the French name; in Dutch, Gemeente) that comprise Belgium. Because of the considerable importance attached in Belgian political mythology to the communes it has been virtually impossible to reduce their number to any significant degree. Two thirds of the existing communes have less than 2000 inhabitants. As one Belgian political scientist puts it: "There are too many communes in Belgium. It can be said that for the small communes, local autonomy is the liberty to do nothing." [5] The administrative costs for the smaller communes are, naturally, a higher percentage of the total budget. Legally, it is up to Parliament to make some change in this situation, but this might seem like an attack on local liber-

[5] André Mast, *Les Pays du Benelux* (Paris: Pichon et Durand-Auzias, 1960), p. 163.

ties. Thus it has been the cabinet that has taken the initiative in naming local officials authorized to serve in more than one commune—for example, the tax collector and the communal secretary.

Communal organization

As in the Dutch pattern, the commune is governed by a Communal Council, which varies in size according to the locality. All members are chosen by direct popular elections, which do not take place at the same time as the national elections. The council is essentially a legislative body, adopting regulations in accordance with national and provincial guidelines for communal affairs. As the Belgian political system has evolved, it has become increasingly difficult to pinpoint exactly what are communal affairs, for there has been a transfer of many powers to higher authorities. The commune has police powers, a fire department, and control over local roads and most public utilities and certain health standards. It also shares in the responsibility for education, particularly in the field of technical training.

The members of the Communal Council choose a smaller number, generally six, of their members to serve as aldermen (echevins; Dutch: Wethouders). The aldermen, together with the burgomaster (bourgmestre; Dutch: Burgemeester), are responsible for the daily administration of the commune's affairs. The communal administration is organized into several departments, and assignments are parceled out among the aldermen along the lines of a cabinet system. The burgomaster is also responsible for one or more departments.

These local boards are not under the control of the national government. The king and his cabinet cannot suspend or remove members of the communal councils from their posts, nor can the council itself be dissolved by the cabinet. Local officials can only be named by the communal authorities, not by the state. On the other hand, the burgomaster is appointed by the cabinet acting in the name of the king. But here the similarity with the Netherlands ends, for the cabinet almost invariably chooses a member of the Communal Council. In fact, the cabinet's choice merely ratifies the will of the council itself. The only exception to this rule is the choice of one person from among the voters of the commune, which is possible if the Provincial Executive gives its approval.

The burgomaster is a powerful political figure in the commune. He is not a link between the national administration and the locality; he clearly embodies the will of the commune. He cultivates his constituency as a source of political strength and protects its, and his, prerogatives from encroachment by higher authorities.

The chief importance of the posts of burgomaster and member of the Communal Council is in preparation for membership in Parliament. More than half of the members of Parliament are also elected communal officials, with an especially heavy concentration of the highest local magistrates of the largest communes. Former Prime Minister Paul Vanden Boeynants, for example, gave up his post as alderman of Brussels only with great reluctance when he became head of the Belgian government.

This dual function does much, of course, to strengthen the liaison between commune and national government. For the commune, it helps assure that a relatively high caliber of local administrators will be available, for they also aspire to higher posts. The autonomy of the communes is assured, Parliament being the only authority with the power to modify it. With such a high percentage of communal officials among its members, it is unlikely to make fundamental changes. On the other hand, this places virtually insurmountable obstacles before any improvements in the communal framework to serve modern industry, transportation, and health. In defending the liberties of the communes whenever a proposal for change is made, the members of Parliament who also hold local posts are protecting their jobs. There are benefits of the dual role for these members of Parliament. They gain direct experience with administering some of the laws that Parliament passes and are kept in relatively close contact with the voter. Each such official has a "clientele," and he can measure his influence and success by their reaction to his stands. Finally, he acquires some experience in government as an executive and not merely as a legislator, which would be the case were he only a member of Parliament.

The communes have come to be almost entirely dependent

on the national government for their finances. At one time, when the total tax burden was not so heavy, they had considerable latitude to levy taxes. But gradually the national government and the communes came to compete for tax revenue. In 1948, for example, communes were stripped of their right to tax wages and to levy many of the supplementary taxes that had been tacked on to national taxes. As a result the communes are financed by a common fund to which tax income is allocated and by a special assistance fund, also financed by the national Treasury. The remaining income results from interest on the commune's own holdings, payments for services, a minor stamp tax, a tax on automobiles, and a small percentage of the income tax. This loss of independent income did much, in fact, to undermine the autonomy of the communes.

Obstacles to communal cooperation

One observer writes: "The minister who decides to ask Parliament to reduce local rights, must, if he knows his job, begin by rendering a ringing homage to the communes. That is how profound the attachment is to the principles of local government." [6] But this attachment leads to a problem that is especially acute in Belgium—the urban area. Although in the Netherlands, too, there are obstacles to cooperative action by municipalities, the need there is somewhat less acute. The entire city of Amsterdam constitutes a single municipality, which allows for a centralized set of authorities for dealing with its problems. In Brussels, on the other hand, there is no centralized governing authority; the metropolitan area is divided into nineteen communes, only one of which is officially called Brussels.

The Constitution does not throw up an absolute obstacle to cooperation among local authorities. It provides that associations of communes are possible, but that Communal Councils cannot meet together. Councils, eager to protect their rights, have been reluctant even to use the limited powers given them by the Constitution. In Brussels, the water supply and public transportation are operated by intercommunal authorities.

But there is a great deal of waste and inefficiency. The distribution of gas and electricity in Brussels is divided among

[6] Mast, *Les Pays du Benelux*, p. 155.

several authorities. Road surfaces vary as a single street passes from commune to commune. Only a particularly dramatic killing prompted the police to create a single telephone number for the entire metropolitan area. One of the most difficult areas is social assistance (medical payments, relief), which remains under the control of each commune. These authorities seem to prefer mediocre local hospitals, for example, to centralized modern institutions. Local public assistance authorities simply refused in 1947 to obey a royal decree forcing them to cooperate. The decree was repealed.

The question of communal rights is not, however, the sole explanation of this situation. Some people resist the idea of Greater Brussels, because such a structure was imposed on the city during the Nazi occupation. Those Belgians who live outside the capital and who already fear the influence of this large city on the nation's affairs also oppose strengthening it too much. Finally, the language question underlies the debate. For those French-speaking people who hope to see the limits of the Brussels "agglomeration" extended, the creation of a single city would perhaps be a hindrance. The extension of Brussels beyond the nineteen communes could be accomplished, it is thought, by gradually drawing the peripheral communes under the same language laws as those within the metropolitan area. On the other hand, some Flemings press for the creation of a city of Brussels, with fixed boundaries, as a way of ending the threat of a gradual extension of the metropolitan area until it is linked with Wallonia.

The problem of Brussels, where only 20 percent of the population of the metropolitan area lives in the commune of Brussels itself, is one of the major national questions facing the country. The origin and much of the rationale of this issue is to be found in the deep Belgian attachment to the rights of the local authorities and fear of domination by greater Brussels, both of which may seem outmoded.

BELGIAN PROVINCES

Belgium is composed of nine provinces, with the same boundaries as the nine French departments they replaced after the Napoleonic forces withdrew in 1815.[7] These provinces do not have the same historical roots as those in the Netherlands, although there are some exceptions, notably Liège and Flanders.

The limited powers of the provinces include technical instruction, epidemic control, maintenance of local roads and small waterways, and the drying out of swamps (once of some importance, for Brussels was founded on the site of a swamp).

The chief legislative body of the province is the Provincial Council (Conseil provincial). In order to keep this body from becoming too independent, thus placing the unitary state in jeopardy, Parliament has limited the council's ordinary session to four weeks annually. Membership in the Provincial Council is often a reward for a national parliamentarian who is "being put out to pasture." As will be noted later, the council takes a part in the national election procedure. Besides the council there is a Provincial Executive (Députation permanente) presided over by the provincial governor and composed of six members elected from the council. With the exception of finances and official nominations, it exercises all the council's powers outside the four weeks when this body is in session. The Provincial Executive has certain jurisdictional functions and supervises the fulfillment of national administrative standards by the communes.

The governor, named for a virtual life tenure by the king upon nomination by the cabinet, prepares the work of the council and executive.[8] Even more importantly, he is in charge of the maintenance of public order in the province. He may receive instructions from the cabinet on the fulfillment of this function and has the national police at his disposal. The governor does not usually aspire to another appointment once he has been named to his post. Thus he becomes more the protector of the interests of his province than the representative of the government. This role may acquire a greater importance as the central government attributes greater economic and cultural authority to the regions.

[7] The Belgian provinces are West Flanders, East Flanders, Hainaut, Brabant, Antwerp, Limburg, Liège, Namur, and Luxembourg.

[8] In the bilingual province of Brabant, where Brussels is located, a deputy governor is also appointed from the one language group while the governor is from the other.

Links between local and national politics

In Belgium, the relation of local to national government is basically the same as in the Netherlands, but the public and its political leaders continue to refuse to accept the gradual passage of the glorious days of the commune into the history books. This perhaps reflects the individual's fear of being alienated from government, even in as small a country as Belgium. Politicians obviously remain attached to their local prerogatives, for a small fish in the national pool is often a big fish in the commune.

The intermeshing of national and local politics is particularly high because of the dual role of so many members of Parliament. The local political structure provides a field of activity for the local branches of the national parties. Local political action serves as a stepping-stone to higher positions, either in the party or in government or both. As in the Netherlands, the relatively small electorates in the communes allow parties unable to achieve a national standing to establish a foothold in local government.

The linguistic issue is not fought out at the communal level in general, although there are certain exceptional cases, including the Brussels area and six communes (the Fourons) that were transferred from the Walloon to the Flemish side of the language border. The battle lines on the language question seem to be drawn more in accordance with provinces—which are, with a single exception, fairly homogeneous linguistically. But even the provinces—four mainly French-speaking, four mainly Dutch-speaking, and one bilingual—do not seem to be the precursors of a federal state. They do not have distinct historical backgrounds, in many cases, and today they are not distinguishable from one another for any useful purpose. They may, nonetheless, provide the appropriate framework for the limited economic decentralization that seems inevitable in Belgium.

FOUR
MULTIPARTY SYSTEMS AND DEMOCRATIC STABILITY
The Netherlands and Belgium

The political parties in the Netherlands and Belgium are integral parts of the nations' political systems, serving not only as a means of offering candidates and programs, but also as active participants in the decision-making process. In multiparty systems, such as exist in these two countries, the political parties often become an adjunct of government and perform continuing political functions, vital to the system and distinct from the cabinet—even one in which the party is represented.

The operation of government is, in fact, the result of the confluence of the formal and informal rules relating to executive and legislative power and the action of the political parties. Of course, pressure groups exist and patterns of decision making do develop within the framework of the Constitution, if not identical with what the original framers had in mind. But in the Netherlands and Belgium, the parties help shape the actual decision-making process, and they subsume some of the functions of the pressure groups.

The situation is not, however, the same in both of these countries. Although there has been a certain parallel evolution of the political parties, the relationship of any one of them in the Netherlands to the total framework of government is markedly different from the relations of party and government in Belgium. In addition, the ideological underpinnings of the parties of the two countries differ, as the historical evolution of the Low Countries indicates, and this has a direct bearing on the structure, program, and method of operation of parties in the two countries.

DUTCH POLITICAL PARTIES

By general agreement, the most striking single characteristic of the Dutch political parties in their considerable number. Although the record dates from 1933, when fifty-four parties ran candidates in the national elections, the recent 1967 election had more than twenty-eight parties in the race for the 150 seats of the Second Chamber of the States General. This multiplicity of parties does not indicate a number of purely local parties or "one-man" parties. Virtually all parties have a national program, extending beyond one issue.

It may seem unusual to say that each party has its own "philosophy," in a system where there are so many parties. Indeed, it is often difficult for the outsider to distinguish among the parties. But most Dutch political parties are characterized by claims to uphold the correct philosophical approach to the solution of the nation's problems; almost every Dutch political party is founded on an ideology.

Before 1880 no formal political parties existed. Members of the States General might consider themselves Conservatives or Liberals, Catholics or Anti-Revolutionaries (Protestants), but they did not join together in formal groups. Indeed the dividing lines between the four groups were most unclear. The first formal groups that took the form of political parties were represented by the Liberals and the Conservatives. At first Catholics and Protestants tried to work through these existing parties, but they soon chose to pursue independent courses. This meant the end of the Conservatives, who were replaced by confessional (religious) parties. At the end of the nineteenth century the extension of the vote and the increasing awareness of the workers led to the creation of a Social Democratic current in Dutch politics. Later a few Communists made their appearance on the political scene. The end of World War II brought a reshuffle in these political groupings, yielding the current political party system. But throughout, the political parties remained faithful to their ideological bases.

Major trends in the party system

There are five major political parties in the Netherlands, and they represent four major trends of thought. All of the other parties that come into existence and then either fade or endure as permanent parts of the political system are related in some way to one of the four main currents. Most of the parties, both big and small, share the desire to attract a sizeable membership, although most fall short of this goal. The total number of members of the five major parties is 650,000, or about one tenth of the total electorate, and the Catholic People's party provides about half this number.

With the multiplicity of parties, it is virtually inevitable that any cabinet must be a coalition in which several of them are represented. Thus it is important for the elector to know which parties are likely to join with others in a coalition, although this represents a direct rejection of the cherished concept of ideological purity of the parties. The parties are realistic and recognize they must make some compromises in order to join in a coalition. They attempt to give the voter some idea in advance of those partners that would be acceptable and those that would not.

Coalition formation takes place only among the five major parties, whatever the strength of the other parties. It is conceivable that if one of the smaller groups gained sufficient seats in the Second Chamber to rival the smallest of the major parties, it would stand a chance of entering the cabinet, but this has not yet happened.

The four currents represented in the five major parties are Catholic centrism, Protestant centrism (two parties), the left (Socialists), and the right (Liberals). It might be possible to simplify further by eliminating the religious element from the picture, but this would no longer be a sufficiently accurate portrayal of the Dutch political scene. It should be stressed that this four-way breakdown does not correspond exactly to political parties. Many Liberals, for example, would dislike being considered on the right, and there are elements on both the right and the left in the three confessional parties.

Any coalition combination among these parties is theoretically possible, although a coalition of all five would seem to be out of the question except in time of extreme national peril. There has been no such coalition since World War II. The Socialists and the Liberals might be expected to refrain from joining in a coalition together, yet from 1948 to 1952 they both did take part in the cabinet. It has become somewhat less likely that they would do so again. It was also thought that after 1958 the two largest parties—the Catholics and the Socialists—would never join in a coalition again, but this was proved wrong in 1965–1966. This, too, is not likely to happen again in the near future. Finally, it should be noted that the Catholics have been in every cabinet since the war and have thus become a kind of pivot in the party system.

There are now no less than twelve parties with elected members of the States General. This includes the five major parties, four other important groups, and three fringe groups.

The Catholic party

The Catholic People's party (Katholieke Volkspartij—KVP), founded in 1945, is the largest of the Dutch political parties, both in terms of seats in the Second Chamber of the States General and because of its 325,000 dues-paying members. It is a party of the center both in its program and in the political role it plays.

Despite the word *catholic* in its name, the KVP is not formally linked with the Roman Catholic Church nor does that church, liberal in the Netherlands and a leader in the ecumenical movement, try to exercise control.[1] The KVP may, for example, take whatever stand it wishes on birth control. The word *peo-*

---

[1] The last attempt by the Church to exercise political control was in 1954, when a pastoral letter warned Catholics against joining the Socialist labor union and other contacts with socialism and threatened exclusion from the holy sacraments for failure to conform to this injunction.

ple's in the name is meant to signify that the KVP is a mass party, democratically governed. It is open to all, although the party leadership does not hope to gain many votes from non-Catholics. The KVP is on record as favoring the creation of a Christian Democratic party together with the two Protestant parties, but these two groups appear concerned about being swallowed up by the KVP in such an arrangement.

The KVP program is general and tries to steer a middle course between right and left. It favors an anti-inflationary policy, increased opportunities for workers to share in the management of enterprises, and greater scope for individual initiative. In the field of foreign policy the KVP, like other Dutch parties, seems idealistic. It wants reciprocal disarmament, European unification, and the allocation of 1 percent of national income for aid to developing countries.

Party decision making results from democratic action, with the membership organized on a hierarchical basis. The "division" at the municipal level is under the authority of a region, coterminous with one of the country's eighteen electoral regions. On the national level, a Party Council with about 350 members is the supreme political body. In addition, a Governing Council is in charge of organization. Routine control is exercised by a Central Committee, meeting monthly, and the Party Executive, meeting weekly. As in most Dutch parties, there is a youth organization, which is represented in all party organs.

The Labor party

The Labor party (Partij van de Arbeid—PvdA), also known as the Socialists, was founded in 1946 as a fusion of Social Democratic, Liberal, Christian Democratic, Protestant, Socialist, and Catholic elements plus some independents who had abstained from politics because it had been based on the religious-secular split. The Socialists thus attempted what they called a "breakthrough" in Dutch politics. They sought to weld into a single major political party all the varying points of view on religious questions. The PvdA now contains Catholic, Calvinist, and humanist groups who can agree on the major social issues.

But the breakthrough was of limited effect, and the PvdA did not succeed in attracting as many voters as it had hoped nor in transforming the Dutch political system.

The PvdA, with 145,000 members, considers itself a progressive mass party, run democratically. It favors the removal of religious barriers to political cooperation, but does not oppose the right of churches to express their views on how society should be organized. The PvdA, which supports restrictions on private ownership of property and proclaims itself the defender of the worker, advocates democratic socialism, which is defined as "a socioeconomic order without class distinctions, in which the community is responsible for the planned management of production and the fair distribution of wealth." In international affairs, it favors Dutch participation in international organizations, in NATO, and particularly in the European integration movement. The party would like to see as much as 2 percent of national income go for foreign aid.

Members are grouped in local branches. Every two years a Party Congress meets to determine the policy, organization, and finances of the PvdA and chooses the twenty-five members of the National Committee. Nine of these are responsible for the daily party activities as members of the Executive Committee. A Party Council, composed of regional representatives, meets several times yearly.

The Anti-Revolutionary party

The Anti-Revolutionary party (Anti-Revolutionaire Partij—ARP) is a Protestant party, based on Calvinist principles and having a total membership of 100,000. The oldest of the Dutch political parties, its name implies a rejection of the antireligious sentiments of the French Revolution. It is considered a well-organized party, drawing much of its support from members of the Reformed Church, the more orthodox of the major Protestant churches.

The ARP says that the state is subject to God and consequently there are limits on acceptable state action, particularly in its relations with individuals and interest groups. The result is a basically conservative stand on domestic issues, with considerable stress on individual initiative. But the ARP does support an increased role for labor in industrial decisions. As for religion, the party insists on the principle of free Protestant education with state financing on a par with public institutions. Before the ARP became a full-fledged party, this was virtually the only matter that concerned it. The party favors European unification, NATO, and increased assistance to developing countries.

The Christian-Historical Union

The Christian-Historical Union (Christelijk-Historische Unie—CHU) is also a Protestant party, an offshoot of the ARP. Yet its basic attitude resembles that of the ARP, and outsiders find it virtually impossible to determine why two different parties exist. Many of the CHU's 45,000 adherents are members of the Dutch Reformed Church, the nation's principal Protestant group. Perhaps the most compelling reason for the distinction between the two parties is tradition. In the nineteenth century the split was caused by rigidity in the ideological position of the ARP, which was composed of the "more vigorous and democratic layer" of Dutch Calvinism, while the CHU represented the "more tolerant and aristocratic layer." [2] In modern times, the ARP has placed greater stress on party discipline and a coherent political philosophy.

The CHU emphasizes that it is a union rather than a political party, but this in fact is meant to indicate the relatively little importance attached to finding a single "party" view on issues. In general, one may say that the members of each of these groups feel more "comfortable" with the other members, and for this reason they do not shift. In practice, they are almost always in the governing coalition together. The ARP has called repeatedly for a fusion of the two, but the CHU has been reluctant, fearing that, because of their bent for organization, the ARP would dominate the new Protestant party.

The CHU considers itself slightly more to the center than the ARP. It calls for a better distribution of the national wealth in the population, but emphasizes its attachment to private ownership. Taxes should not hit the upper income groups as hard as

[2] Hans Daalder, "Parties and Politics in the Netherlands," p. 4. Mimeo, a government publication.

they do, according to the CHU. At the same time, the party wants increased social benefits. On foreign policy issues the CHU takes much the same stand as other Dutch parties.

The Liberals

The People's Party for Freedom and Democracy (Volkspartij voor Vrijheid en Democratie—VVD), also known as the Liberals, is the fifth of the major Dutch parties. Despite the word *people* in its name, the VVD is also the smallest of the five major parties, having a membership of about 35,000. With its stress on the freedom of the individual, the VVD has become known as a conservative party, although it claims to be center-left.

The VVD argues that government is to provide conditions favoring the development of the potential of the individual. Thus it is opposed to inflationary measures and increased taxation. It says that both employer's and employee's rights should be protected. In foreign policy, the VVD favors the strengthening of the international rule of law and the rights of small nations.

The VVD party organization is also hierarchical with local branches, a General Assembly, a Central Committee, and an Executive Committee. A Party Council, which includes the VVD members of the States General, is to advise and stimulate party activities. But members of elective bodies are not to be bound by party orders.

Other parties

Besides the five major parties, seven other groups are represented in the Second Chamber of the States General. The party that has perhaps the most impact is Democrats '66 (Democraten '66— D '66). This party, composed mainly of younger educated people, claims that the Dutch political system needs reform and that the various ideological differences are either so blurred or so meaningless that the voter has no real choice. D '66 wants direct election of the prime minister on a predetermined platform, in order to prevent coalition formation after the elections from distorting the voter's views. D '66 also wants the single national constituency split into a number of smaller districts, from each of which two or three members of the Second Chamber would be chosen. This would result in a strengthening of ties between voter and elected. The party would like to see greater freedom for dissenting groups and for the entry of refugees into the Netherlands. Favoring a far broader national debate on foreign policy, D '66 emphasizes the need to push for an improvement of East-West relations, perhaps through an all-European security conference and the recognition of East Germany. On other foreign policy issues D '66 does not differ significantly from other parties.

The Communist party, which has been on the Dutch scene for several decades, supports a traditional Communist platform including extensive state planning and nationalization. It opposes any economic measures that might lead to unemployment, and it proposes the most sweeping measures for giving workers a say in running enterprises. The party draws most of its strength from the relatively poorly educated working class in urban areas, especially Amsterdam.

The Agrarian party (Boerenpartij) is gaining considerable strength in the Netherlands as a protest against much governmental action, even outside the farm sector. It opposes institutionalized cooperation of various elements in the economy [3] and wants drastic reduction in many kinds of taxes and the end of subsidies for much of farm production. The Agrarians represent an essentially negative reaction to government policy and, surprisingly, they have gained strength in towns more than among the farmers. A Poujadist party, it appeals to right-wing working-class people.

The Pacifist-Socialist party was formed in 1962 by dissident elements of the Labor party. Standing on the left of the Labor party, it favors disarmament, both nationally and internationally, and urges a high degree of public ownership of enterprises.

Besides these four groups, three others also are represented in the States General. The Calvinist Political party (Staatkundig Gereformeerde Partij—SGP) is a conservative political group believing that the other Protestant parties have strayed from the path and that the faith is not observed with sufficient strictness. The Calvinist Political Union (Gereformeerd Politiek Verbond—

[3] See Chap. 5, especially concerning labor-management and farm organizations.

GVP) differs only slightly from the SGP. It opposes most Dutch participation in international organizations and, like the SGP, favors increased support for the South African government, although this is not a major issue in the Netherlands. Finally, a group of three members of the KVP delegation in the Second Chamber split away from the main party in 1968 to form their own group, with a program somewhat to the left of the VVP and called "centrist radical." This group has not yet had a chance to face the electorate.

DUTCH ELECTIONS AND CABINET FORMATION

The basic national political campaign in the Netherlands occurs at the time of elections for the 150 members of the Second Chamber, or lower house, of the States General. These elections are held once every four years, although they may be held more often if the Second Chamber is dissolved by the queen before the regular election date, which normally falls in May.[4]

Campaigns and voting

The electoral campaign is relatively short, there being forty-three days between the date the names of the candidates are deposited and the elections. Parties are allotted time on radio and television, both of which are state controlled, for the presentation of their candidates and programs. Poster publicity for the leading candidates is also popular. Each of the major parties is linked with at least one principal newspaper, which carries extensive information on the party's position.[5] Candidates visit electoral meetings in the areas where their names appear on the party's list, with the traditional baby kissing and handshaking. Campaigning is extensively carried out by the leading candidates, such as Foreign Minister Luns, KVP parliamentary leader Schmelzer or

[4] The provincial legislatures are also elected every four years, but not at the same time as the Second Chamber. The members of the First Chamber of the States General, chosen for a six-year term with one-half of the Chamber replaced every three years, are elected by the provincial assemblies.

[5] See Arend Lijphart, *The Politics of Accommodation* (Berkeley and Los Angeles: University of California Press, 1968), pp. 40–47.

his liberal counterpart Toxopeus, whose names will make an impression with the voters. Others, chosen for their expert qualifications, may never make a single campaign speech nor solicit votes.

In general, the campaign effort is greeted with a mild response by others than the party faithful. Most voters will not be swayed from their traditional voting choice. The major departure from this pattern is the kind of enthusiasm that a new party like D '66 can arouse. Part of its success and the attention given to it derived from its unorthodox program and its overt appeal to youth.

The elections are held on the basis of proportional representation, with the Netherlands as a whole serving as the constituency. Thus the total number of voters is divided by 150 and this determines the electoral quotient—the number of votes a candidate needs to be elected. The country is, however, divided into eighteen election districts, and the parties may put up a different list in each district. In practice, they often do have more than one list in the country as a whole, while smaller parties may not have lists in all eighteen districts. Only twenty-five signatures are required for the submission of a list, although a financial guarantee must also be paid, which is forfeited if the list wins less than 75 percent of the electoral quotient. Thus the existence of the eighteen electoral districts helps candidates who are known in a given area—an aid both to the large parties, which can play their strongest card in each area, and to the small, who can gain a seat in parliament by winning the needed votes, about 42,000, in a single district. Votes cast for a given party in each electoral district, but which are insufficient to elect a candidate (that is, less than 42,000), are pooled at the national level and may result in a sufficient number being obtained to elect an additional member.

Voters include all Dutch men and women of at least twenty-one years of age who are in the country on election day. They vote according to names on the ballot; there is no indication of party. They may vote for any person on the list, but the vote is counted for the party. Obviously a strong candidate can attract a great number of votes, helping his party to gain additional seats beyond his own. Thus personality can play a role in swaying voters, but qualified observers believe that most votes are not for person but for party and that there is little prospect that personality will radically affect elections. Voting may be by machine, and the results are known the evening the elections end. The publication of votes, now processed by computer, is followed with much the same interest as in the United States.

The contemporary political scene in the Netherlands dates from the end of World War II. Since that time, the five traditional parties have been on the scene, thus making electoral results directly comparable (Table 4–1).

The most striking characteristic of these results is the stability of the strength of the parties. This is attributable to the voters' fidelity to parties expressing convictions, generally religious, in line with their own. But note that the two largest parties, the Catholics and the Socialists, have become relatively weaker as smaller parties have gained. The Liberals, on the other hand, have improved their position since the beginning of the period under review. This group was in general disarray after the war but regained its internal discipline. Although it has moved somewhat to the center, a growing number of voters of many persuasions find its program acceptable. As in other countries, the Communists who had been active in the resistance did well in the elections immediately after the war, but they later slacked off to a relatively weak position and show no signs of a new push. Finally, both Democrats '66 and the Agrarian party represent an attack on the existing political structure—one positive, the other negative. Their appearance lent some support to the claim that, although the system was outwardly stable, it failed to represent voter discontentment with the choice offered. These parties succeeded in gaining voter support where the major parties had not been able to dislodge each other's supporters.

Parties and cabinet

Once the elections are past, it is the job of the political parties to find a coalition capable of supporting a cabinet in office. In practice, this is an exercise involving the five major parties, which have (1) a vested interest in maintaining the system, (2) the habit of dealing with one another, and (3) enough votes to govern comfortably. In addition, the smaller parties either do not

Table 4–1 Second Chamber: percentage of votes by party and distribution of seats (in parentheses) [a]

Party	1946	1948	1952	1956 [b]	1959	1963	1967
Catholic (KVP)	31 (32)	31 (32)	29 (30)	32 (33) (49)	32 (49)	32 (50)	27 (42)
Labor (PvdA) Socialists	28 (29)	26 (27)	29 (30)	33 (34) (50)	30 (48)	28 (43)	24 (37)
Liberals (VVD)	6 (6)	8 (8)	9 (9)	9 (9) (13)	12 (19)	10 (16)	11 (17)
Anti-Revolutionary (ARP)	13 (13)	13 (13)	11 (12)	10 (10) (15)	9 (14)	9 (13)	10 (15)
Christian-Historical (CHU)	8 (8)	9 (9)	9 (9)	8 (8) (13)	8 (12)	9 (13)	8 (12)
Democrats '66							5 (7)
Communist	11 (10)	8 (8)	6 (6)	5 (4) (7)	2 (3)	3 (4)	4 (5)
Calvinist Political (SGP)	2 (2)	2 (2)	2 (2)	2 (2) (3)	2 (3)	2 (3)	2 (3)
Pacifist-Socialist					2 (2)	3 (4)	3 (4)
Agrarian					1 (0)	2 (3)	5 (7)
Catholic National (right)		1 (1)	3 (2)	1 (0)	1 (0)	1 (1)	1 (1)
Calvinist Political Union (GPV)			1 (0)	1 (0)	1 (0)	2 (0)	3 (0)
Other	1 (0)	2 (0)	1 (0)				

[a] Percentages may not add due to rounding.

[b] The Constitution was amended in 1956 to increase the number of seats from 100 to 150, thus requiring a change in the distribution of seats at that time.

seek to take part in the cabinet, but rather to act as a kind of pressure group on the major parties, or they are an unacceptable partner to almost any other party—for example, the Communists.

The cabinet crises, during which a new coalition is sought, are usually quite lengthy, although infrequent. Once a coalition is made, it stands, as Table 4–2 indicates. A number of explanations have been suggested concerning the relationship of the parties to the creation and maintenance of a cabinet.

Table 4–2   Party coalitions in cabinets, 1945–1968

Dates in office	Prime minister	Parties
1945–1946	Schermerhorn-Drees	PvdA, KVP
1946–1948	Beel	KVP, PvdA
1948–1951	Drees	KVP, PvdA, CHU, VVD
1951–1952	Drees	KVP, PvdA, CHU, VVD
1952–1956	Drees	KVP, PvdA, CHU, ARP
1956–1958	Drees	KVP, PvdA, CHU, ARP
1959–1963	De Quay	KVP, VVD, ARP, CHU
1963–1965	Marijnen	KVP, VVD, ARP, CHU
1965–1966	Cals	KVP, PvdA, ARP
1966–1967	Zijlstra	KVP, ARP
1967–	de Jong	KVP, VVD, ARP, CHU

The rigid positions of the parties prevent the maneuvering from becoming simply a question of personalities. In addition, it is parties that are elected, not people, and the egalitarian atmosphere of the Second Chamber reduces the chances that there will be obvious candidates for the cabinet. Finally, private interests have little opportunity to intervene in government crises, where the parties are already dealing from fixed positions.

Party influence of the cabinet is reduced, because they have made their compromises to form a cabinet and cannot sustain the great debate on principles over the years they are in office. As we shall see later, there is also a certain dualism between cabinet and parliament in the Netherlands. Indeed, it is one of the chief characteristics of the Dutch political system. To a certain extent, the Second Chamber does not judge the members of the cabinet as much as their policies. Cabinet ministers are not members of parliament. Indeed, prime ministers often do not come from the States General. In any case, dark horses can be chosen from party ranks to serve in a cabinet, both because of their personal (if not electoral) qualities and as a way of finding a compromise when the maneuvering among parties becomes particularly difficult.

The cabinet and parliament are in a delicate relationship, partly because each is sensitive to the problems of the other. In addition, the parties have had to compromise in accepting the coalition; they do not, however, want to forego their basic principles, and they continually criticize cabinet tendencies to wander too far afield. But on details of policy the parties are at a disadvantage, unless it is a matter in which they are greatly interested, for the cabinet can avail itself of the expertise of the national administration, many times larger than the staffs of the parties or parliament. Dissolution of parliament and a call for new elections is not a threat the cabinet can use easily, for elections are not fought solely on the cabinet's record. But a given minister may threaten to resign, which may have an undesirable effect on his own party, in which case he may be allowed to win the day. On the other hand, the party in the Second Chamber can choose to force the cabinet's hand—as in 1966, when the parliamentary Catholics opposed the cabinet led by a Catholic, leading to its fall.

Much of what has been said in the foregoing analysis of cabinet-party relations applies to the dialogue between cabinet and parliament. Yet both are composed of representatives of the nation's political parties, although, naturally, all are not in the cabinet. The parties are of vital importance to the political system and subsume many of the roles played by other groups in other nations because of their multiplicity. They try to reflect all of the major nuances of Dutch political opinion and, barring a direct call to modify the system itself, they appear to succeed quite well. Yet there is a distinction between the party as a whole, the party in parliament, and the party in the cabinet. The first is the upholder of the purity of party philosophy. The second must try to protect this philosophy, while at the same time getting on with the business of decision making. The party in the cabinet must try to preserve its identity, but must concede much in the interests of governing. This system may work as well as it does because on many of the fundamental issues facing the nation, there is fundamental agreement in fact, if not in theory, among the major parties. This will become clearer as we examine the decision-making process itself.

Hans Daalder, a leading Dutch political scientist and the originator of many of the theories discussed earlier, offers this explanation:

> On the whole, the most remarkable paradox of the Netherlands has been that its often extreme sectarianism has not prevented practical cooperation. This perhaps points not so much to any strong national feeling or to a particularly clear desire for toleration, as to a businesslike determination that the job should not be allowed to suffer. One even wonders whether the very rigidity and separateness of its groups may not have contributed to this feeling. If anything, these factors have tended to a centralization of political life as well as to an increasing reliance of political leaders on expertise. This may explain why the Netherlands can have party disputes that are almost theological in nature and yet have sound administration, and why there can be such great disagreement over politics and yet, in some ways, alarmingly little over policy.[6]

BELGIAN POLITICAL PARTIES

The Belgian political party structure is more similar to the general European pattern than to the rather special framework that exists in the Netherlands. Seven parties are represented in the Belgian Parliament, but they do not each represent an ideological trend in the population. Instead, the pattern of major parties, surrounded by smaller, special-interest groups, mostly is based on the national language question. Thus there are "single issue" parties, abstaining from taking a stand on many major political questions, although there are none based on the personality of a single political leader.

[6] Daalder, "Parties and Politics in the Netherlands," p. 17.

Left, right, and center

The Belgian parties are the result of an evolution beginning with the foundation of the kingdom. At that time, ideological bases could be found for the distinction between parties. The two prevailing views, early in Belgian history, revolved about the religious question, although there was never much doubt about the separation of church and state. The Catholics followed a confessional policy, attached to the maintenance of their own school system, but also were supporters of private enterprise and the rights of the localities and regions. The Liberals, on the other hand, pressed for a clearer separation of the church and state and favored a more centralized government. Thus, in effect, they were on the left and the Catholics on the right. By 1847, King Leopold I had succeeded in creating a sentiment of national union between the "reasonable Liberals" and the "moderate Catholics." These two groups were the originators of the party system, as they developed their own programs and clienteles.

As in the Netherlands, the extension of suffrage and the growing workers' movement led, at the end of the nineteenth century, to the growth of a Socialist political movement. This group drew considerable support away from the Liberals, as it made the same nonreligious appeal, but attracted the support of a wider number of voters. Subsequently the Communist party appeared on the scene, partly through the efforts of Camille Huysman, a Belgian collaborator of Lenin. Finally, after World War II, the political party system was almost entirely restructured, although the process took some fifteen years. The result is the modern Belgian party system.

At the heart of this system are the three national or "traditional" parties, as they are called in Belgium. They can be said to represent the left, the center, and conservatism. It is among these three parties that the coalitions are formed, although with only two at a single time. In almost all cases the center or Christian Social party is a coalition partner, together with either the Socialists or the Liberals. The result is that the changing orientation of the government is due mainly to the partner of the center party, and this party orients itself to the situation arising from the needs of the coalition. Obviously, within this center party there are elements more willing to cooperate with one potential partner or the other, and they come to the fore depending on the coalition arrangement that is most workable after the national elections. It is also possible for the Socialists and Liberals to form a coalition without the center party, but this is not likely in normal times, for their economic and social programs differ too significantly for a happy partnership to endure. They did form a government in the period from 1954 to 1958, but this reflected a single major issue, the schools controversy, pitting the Catholics against the freethinkers, and on this point the two parties were in basic agreement.

The Liberals, it will have been noticed, are characterized as conservative, not "right." This is because of the presence throughout much of this century of "rights" parties, most predominantly those connected with the language issue. Although they are essentially concerned only with this issue, their political reflexes are ultraconservative, and they usually differ widely from the Liberals.

With the exception of the linguistic extremist parties, Belgian parties have a vested interest in the maintenance of the political system. They benefit from its operation and stand a reasonable chance of taking part in a cabinet at fairly regular intervals. These are parties of "orientation" rather than ideology. Thus each has considerable flexibility in adjusting its position to meet the needs of an existing situation. One might argue that the Liberals and the Socialists find it in their best interests to differ, for they provide the real element of choice to the electors. The center appeals to the Belgian's traditional attachment to calm and stability. The Communist party is, of course, essentially an ideological party, although it has assumed a fixed position in the political system and plays what seems to be a preassigned role of tame dissenter. This has caused some dissidence among more militant members. Finally, the language parties are clearly in the nature of organized political movements, seeking to transform the existing political structure of the country by putting electoral pressure on the traditional parties. There would probably be a few extremist members of Parliament, no matter how much satisfaction the language parties gained, but there can be little doubt that these parties exist because of strong public sentiment on the language issue and would lose much strength if public interest were diverted to other problems. To a limited extent, they represent the challenge to the system as it exists, for they seek a fundamental reform of the Belgian state.

The Christian Social party

The Christian Social party (Parti Social Chrétien—PSC; Christelijke Volkspartij—CVP) is Belgium's largest political party. It is the successor of the prewar Catholic party, but in 1945 it was "deconfessionalized"—it gave up its links with the Catholic Church in an attempt to broaden its appeal to voters who wanted a moderate, center party. Nonetheless, it is the only party that many Catholic voters consider acceptable, thus giving it much of its old confessional flavor. In addition, the hierarchy of the Catholic Church continues to act as though the party were linked to the Church, although the party leaders are careful to maintain "correct" relations with it. Thus the party is based on the support of the average Belgian Catholic, which in practice means that it is strongest in the most Catholic part of the country—Flanders.

The PSC/CVP does not require much of a program in order to attract the support of its usual electors; they choose it because of the Catholic tradition or because they prefer the idea of stability to either of the other alternatives offered to them. Indeed, this Catholic tradition does represent more of a sociological attitude than a religious belief. The PSC/CVP has been a consistent supporter of the Belgian farmer, seeking the highest possible prices for him and other guarantees in case of a reduction of farm income. In recent years the party has moved increasingly to attract the support of workers, and its program has begun to resemble that of the Socialists. It places increased emphasis on greater social benefits, including pension and sickness payments, and on efforts to end unemployment. It has pushed for a regional economic policy that would both help the backward areas of the country and provide for economic decentralization, thus giving some satisfaction to the language elements in both parts of the country that are seeking greater autonomy from the central government. It is also active in pushing for urban planning programs. In the field of foreign policy, the PSC/CVP is a strong supporter of NATO and the European integration movement. While it also supports the United Nations, as do other leading Belgian parties, it does not share the fervor felt in the Dutch parties on this issue.

Mass party membership is not characteristic of Belgium, although there are party organizations down to the local level. These groups, made up of party militants, play an important role in selecting candidates for elections. In the PSC/CVP the communal committees are grouped in district organizations corresponding with the nation's electoral districts. The so-called Comités d'Arrondissement can be powerful influences within the national party when they are based in the major metropolitan areas, and this is especially true for Brussels, which is the balancing element between the two linguistic groups. The next level, above the district, is the National Congress, which lays down the general guidelines for party policy at its annual meetings. The actual party leadership is found in the National Committee and its Executive Board, which is responsible for adopting positions on major issues of the day in line with the dictates of the congress. Actions of the National Committee may be reviewed and either approved or rejected by either the General Council of the party (an intermediary body between the committee and the congress) or a regular or extraordinary session of the congress.

As a party with a relatively vague program, the PSC/CVP relies considerably on the appeal of its leaders to attract popular support. These need not be figures well known outside the country, although they are certain to have gained a national reputation for being able to bridge the gaps between the language groups. Such groups are regular, recognized elements of the National Committee and have their own officers. The leading party figures must enjoy the confidence of both of these "wings." A recent example is Paul Vanden Boeynants, a bilingual Brussels politician, who gained a reputation as a dynamic personality and who deemphasized the language split, laying greater stress on the economic development of the country. He proved to be the party's best vote getter in history, although the basis of his strength remained Brussels.

It should be noted that the traditional politicians, particularly those outside the PSC/CVP, have not yet fully accepted the kind of personal appeal that Vanden Boeynants attempts to make to the electorate. They claim that his request for a personal vote of confidence amounts to nothing more than press-agentry. Yet he does appear to be setting a new and modern style in Belgian politics.

The Socialist party

The Belgian Socialist party (Parti Socialiste Belge—PSB; Belgische Socialistische Partij—BSP) is the second largest of the Belgian parties and a direct successor of the Belgian Workers' party, founded in 1885. The only change was in the name, once the term "socialist" had become more acceptable. Begun as a protest again the poor working conditions of the nineteenth century, it has never been an extreme left party and has always sought to work within the national political system. It is, naturally, a nonconfessional party, and as in the Netherlands, it has tended to side with the Liberals in any dispute involving the relations between church and state, although on almost every other issue it differs with the more economically conservative Liberals. The party counts on the support of Belgian workers, particularly those who have moved away from the Catholic Church. In practice, this means that a considerable measure of support has come from Wallonia and makes the PSB/BSP the complement of the other major party, the PSC/CVP. Recently, however, the Socialists have made some inroads into the workers' votes in Flanders, and this in turn has probably been a strong influence on the increasingly Socialist orientation of the PSC/CVP.

The Socialist party favors the strengthening of the national economy through governmental rather than private action, partly because it believes that individual initiative has failed to provide satisfactory solutions to the nation's economic problems. It calls for extensive economic planning in Belgium, a relatively novel concept in this country. Where there are profits from the government's economic expansion program, they should accrue to the state. The Socialists do not, however, favor wholesale nationalizations; they do not oppose free enterprise. They believe that certain key industries, such as coal and steel, should be brought under strict government supervision. The energy sector is of particular interest to the party. The Socialists would like to see limits placed on profit taking. But their major appeal is in their demands that social benefits be increased substantially and that massive help be given to the unemployed, involving perhaps the operation of economically inefficient enterprises. The Socialists are prepared to run a national budget deficit for these purposes. In international relations, the PSB/BSP supports Belgian membership in NATO, although it would like to see the organization transformed into a forum for increased East-West contacts. The Socialists also support Belgian participation in the European Community and stress that the rights of European workers must be protected.

The most striking characteristic of this program is its lack of doctrine. The Socialists are more interested in winning elections than in pursuing doctrinally pure positions. This attitude is also manifest in party organization, where, despite its democratic philosophy, a great deal of power is concentrated in the hands of the leadership. The party structure almost exactly parallels that of the PSC/CVP. There are, however, party congresses at the level of the linguistic regions as well as at the national level. Thus this party reflects the same kind of split as the PSC/CVP. The party leadership does endeavor, however, to take much of the bitterness out of the debate and pushes for some political and considerable economic decentralization of the country. The leadership of the party executive is recognized, and there is good party discipline. This serves to hide the fissures that exist below a patina of party unity. This cannot be sustained indefinitely, however, and some dissidence among Flemish members has been manifest. They argue that the party is too oriented toward Wallonia.

Men rise to party leadership on the basis of faithful service and the ability to bring the two language elements into harmony on the major language issues of the day. The best-known leader of the Socialists has been Paul-Henri Spaak, former prime minister, long-time foreign minister, president of the first UN General Assembly, and former NATO secretary general. Spaak put his finger on the real nature of the party when he said: "There are two kinds of Socialists—Socialists and *real* Socialists. Me? I am a Socialist."

The Liberals

The Party for Liberty and Progress (Parti de la Liberté et du Progrès—PLP; Partij voor Vrijheid en Vooruitgang—PVV), usually known as the Liberals, is the third of the major Belgian political parties. Its historical origins are clearly in the development of the Liberal party in the nineteenth and twentieth centuries. But in 1961 the PLP/PVV sought to break with the traditions of the past. The change in its name was not merely a matter of style; the party hoped to shed its anticlerical image and to become known as a progressive, moderately conservative political group. This change has been effected with amazing success, for the party has increased its electoral standing substantially and has attracted a number of Catholic politicians to its fold.

The party is generally considered to draw its strength from the Belgian business community. It obviously does depend on this sector for its financial support, for it cannot call on large labor unions for aid, as do the other large parties. Yet the PLP/PVV has succeeded in appealing to middle-class voters for their electoral support, if not for their money, and is independent of the control of big business interests.

The PLP/PVV does not altogether scorn the use of the term "businesslike" in describing itself. It seeks to put both its internal operations and its political action on a businesslike or "modern" footing. The party favors greater scope for free enterprise and thus is reluctant to see the role of the state in the economy increase substantially. It recognizes, however, that state aid will be required to launch even the most efficient enterprises in a small country where the savings available for domestic investment are limited. It favors social legislation, not only for the workers but for the small businessman. It attacks the Socialists, however, for wanting to pay out benefits without adequate concern for the national budget and the long-term economic development of the nation. The PLP/PVV believes it can appeal to workers on this basis, because they have become wealthier and thus have a greater vested interest in a moderate and well-balanced social program. In general, the party urges the steady economic development of the country, calling on outside investment and not overtaxing the nation's own capacity over the long run. In foreign policy, there is considerable harmony among the three major parties, and the PLP/PVV gives particular support to the European integration movement.

The renovation of the PLP/PVV injected a new element into the Belgian political scene, although there appear to be limits on the appeal this party can make to supporters of the other two groups. The PLP/PVV, like the Liberals before it, believes its presence is vital to the Belgian political scene to provide a counterbalance to the weight of the labor unions in the other two major parties. Clearly this party does have a built-in appeal to the bourgeois Belgian voter, now that its anticlerical position has been dropped. Its appeal is particularly strong in Brussels and in Wallonia, and it has been striving to draw voter strength in Flanders away from the traditional Catholic party or from the linguistic party.

The internal organization of the PLP/PVV follows the same pattern as the other two national parties, although there are two special characteristics. The first is the absence of two linguistic "wings." The PLP/PVV has succeeded to a considerable extent in relegating the language dispute to a secondary position below the nation's economic concerns. It asks Belgians to be Belgian, and its members follow this principle in their own party actions. Although for the time being this stand will have only a limited appeal, it is obviously the most progressive attitude of any of the three major parties. The second factor is the authority of the party's Executive Committee. The PLP/PVV, at its congresses, has given a high degree of support to this committee, even in advance of its actions, and particularly on language questions. This authority in turn devolves on the party president, Omer Van Audenhove, owner of a successful shoe factory and political activist since 1947. He gets most of the credit for the successful transformation of the party and adheres strictly to the basic principles laid down for its national and non-anticlerical policies. In return he is accorded "full powers" to dictate party policy on his own and has maintained a considerable personal popularity.

Other parties

The Belgian Communist party has been on the scene for several decades and has practically achieved the status of a "traditional" party, although there is no chance that it would be asked to join in a governing coalition. The party advocates much of the traditional Communist program, including state control over key industries and substantial improvement in workers' benefits and rights to determine industry policy. On the language issue, the Communists favor "national self-determination" or, in other words, a federal state. The party has its greatest strength in Wallonia, a reflection of the leftist sentiment in that part of the country. It has been suggested that extremism in Wallonia takes the form of support for the Communists, while in Flanders it is manifest in support for linguistic extremist parties. If this is true, it may explain why the increasing support for language parties in Wallonia has cut into Communist strength. Some elements of the party consider, however, that it has become too moderate, and they have broken away to form a small Peking-oriented party. The Communists do make one gesture to the tradition of party solidarity: all of its members of Parliament contribute their salary to the party coffers and are paid a worker's wages.

The three remaining parties are all linked to the language question. The largest of these is the Flemish United People's party, known as the Volksunie. This group draws all of its support from Flanders and especially from Antwerp. It takes a purely Flemish stand on all aspects of the language question [7] and advocates the creation of a federal state in which Flanders and Wallonia would be the constituent parts. Brussels would form a kind of federal district, although its status has not been made clear. This party has been gaining in strength.

On the other side of the fence are the two French-language parties. In Brussels, there is the French-speaking Democratic Front (Front Démocratique des Francophones—FDF), which has made inroads into the Liberal strength. The FDF wants Brussels left free to enlarge and eventually to establish a link with Wallonia, and it wants the liberty of the father of the family to determine the language for the education of his children. This

[7] See Chap. 2.

would lead to an even greater French-speaking population in the capital. Allied to this party is the Walloon party (Rassemblement Wallon), the latest in the line of French-speaking groups. This party seems to have taken hold in Wallonia and has strong links with the FDF. Although their structures are separate, they may be considered a single party, for they are virtually certain to take identical stands on all issues. The Rassemblement Wallon favors federalism, with links to Brussels and Wallonia. It demands the immediate economic decentralization of the state.

To some extent, these parties are the descendants of the pre-World War II Rexist party. This group, which reached its peak at the end of the thirties, capitalized on the dull and non-controversial political atmosphere that characterized Belgium. The Rexists began as a Catholic revival group but later became Nazi supporters and collaborators with the German occupation. The three present-day language parties are clearly not fascist, but draw on right-wing support and appeal to the same sentiments of people who believe that Belgian politics are too bland and, indeed, corrupt.

These three are essentially one-issue parties, and they do not have a well-developed program. They do not seek a place in the cabinet, for they are unwilling to make any sacrifices in their basic positions. They hope to gain enough votes to force the traditional parties to adopt their views, thus splitting themselves into two parts and hastening the creation of a federal system.

BELGIAN ELECTIONS AND CABINET FORMATION

General elections are held once every four years. They may be held more frequently, and often are, when the king dissolves Parliament as a result of a cabinet crisis. The citizens are asked to vote for members of the Chamber of Representatives, half of the members of the Senate, and the members of the provincial legislatures. The provincial assemblies then choose approximately another quarter of the members of the Senate. The final quarter is selected by cooptation by the members already elected. In theory this is to allow for experts and well-qualified individuals to be chosen, but in fact all phases of the election to the Senate are aimed at electing members of parties in about the same proportion as for the Chamber. Sons of the king or, if he has none, his brothers are also members of the Senate. At present, there is one senator by right—Prince Albert, the King's brother.

Campaigns and voting

The election campaign is short, running forty days or less. Extensive use is made of posters and handbills, which are distributed to every home. In addition, radio and television time is made available to candidates of all parties. Election meetings are also held, but they attract only the party faithful and have little appeal to the average voter. There is little public discussion of the campaign by individuals, but the press, which is highly partisan and widely read, debates all of the major issues.

All Belgians over twenty-one are required to vote. They vote in one of the country's thirty electoral districts, none of which extends outside the limits of any one province. The 212 seats in the Chamber are distributed by district, thus providing about one seat for each 40,000 persons. The largest district, Brussels, has almost one million voters and the smallest about 60,000. A list for each party wishing to submit one (provided a sufficient number of signatures—from 200 to 500—is attached) is run in each district. The names and the order are selected by the party leadership after a "poll" of the party members in the district. The voter may vote by party or cast a preferential vote to a specific candidate. Under Belgium's proportional representation system, this will help assure the election of the candidate wherever he stands on the list. Any excess is distributed in each district according to the votes cast, with a list gaining a seat for each electoral quotient it obtains. The votes not distributed in this way are grouped by province and distributed to previously declared "related" party lists in other districts. The same system is used for the 106 seats in the Senate subject to direct election. In addition, there are 48 provincial senators, one for each 200,000 people in a province and no less than three per province, chosen by provincial assemblies. Finally, there are 24 coopted senators, who are designated by the parties in line with their strength in the Chamber. Because this may not always provide for an exact division, there is often trading off between posts in the provincial assemblies and the Senate.

Table 4–3 shows election results in years from 1946 to 1968. The most striking observation based on these results is the waning position of the Christian Social party. It reached its zenith of political strength after the introduction of the vote for women, who voted in much the same way as their husbands but were somewhat more conservative. The 1954 elections gave a considerable vote of confidence to the Socialists and Liberals, related to a large extent to the school question and indicating a major effort to get out the vote on the part of those opposing the school legislation previously passed by the PSC/CVP. Still another important trend is the elevation of the PLP/PVV from a small "traditional" party into direct competition with the two other parties as a principal power in the country. This was largely due to the ending of its role as an anticlerical party and its successful bid to cast itself in the role of a middle-class group. Here was a case where the party leadership correctly sensed a shift in the political winds and acted to take advantage of it.

Finally, there had been a tendency to believe that the Belgian voter could be counted on to support the same party regularly, but the 1968 elections showed that this hypothesis could be upset by the strength of the language question. The three major parties either did not want or were unable to take a clear stand on a fundamental change in the structure of the Belgian state, although a sizeable number of voters did. The result was a massive shift from the traditional parties to the language groups.

Parties and cabinet

The political parties play a role of immeasurable importance in the Belgian political system. To a great extent they have replaced the Parliament as the legislative branch of government. And they enjoy a freedom of maneuver unknown in the Netherlands, where the parties are rather rigidly tied to an ideology. This flexibility first appears in the formation of a new cabinet after elections. The king is free to ask whomever he chooses to attempt to form a new cabinet. He is likely to call upon a member of the Christian Social party, located at the center of the political spectrum and the largest of the parties. The person designated may then go to either the Socialists or the Liberals in his attempt to form a cabinet. This orientation may result from the mandate of the

Table 4-3 Chamber of Representatives: percentage of votes by party and distribution of seats (in parentheses)

	1946	1949[a]	1950	1954	1958	1961	1965	1968
Christian Social (PSC/CVP)	43 (92)	44 (105)	48 (108)	41 (95)	46 (104)	41 (96)	34 (77)	32 (69)
Socialist (PSB/BSP)	32 (69)	30 (66)	35 (77)	37 (86)	36 (84)	37 (84)	28 (64)	28 (59)
Liberal or PLP/PVV	9 (17)	15 (29)	11 (20)	12 (25)	11 (21)	12 (20)	22 (48)	21 (47)
Communist	13 (23)	7 (12)	5 (7)	4 (4)	2 (2)	3 (5)	5 (6)	3 (5)
Volksunie		2 (0)		2 (1)	2 (1)	4 (5)	7 (12)	10 (20)
French-speaking and Walloon						1 (1)	2 (5)	6 (12)
Other	3 (1)	2 (0)	1 (0)	4 (1)	3 (0)	2 (1)	2 (0)	0

[a] In 1949 the vote for women was introduced.

electors, but it is more likely to reflect the formula that will gain the support of the greatest number of members of the newly elected Parliament. At times, a choice may be made, only to prove to be the wrong one. Then, without elections, the combination of parties in the coalition may be changed. If the king were to invite a member of the Liberal or Socialist parties to attempt to form a cabinet, the person designated would be virtually obliged to enter into discussions with the PSC/CVP—and even then would not be likely to succeed. But the role of the parties does not end once a cabinet has been installed in office.

Many of the most important decisions are made by agreement among the leaders of the two parties in the coalition or even among the three "traditional" parties. These agreements may have to be ratified by the congresses of these parties, but the Parliament as such does nothing more than approve the decision already made. The Parliament itself is organized to allow for the formal existence of political groups, assuring that a spokesman of each party, including the minor ones, has the opportunity to express his party's views on any issue. Individual members of Parliament may be unhappy with this state of affairs, but they have little alternative, because of the strict party discipline. A member straying from this discipline will simply find that he no longer has party support; he will not appear on the next electoral list or will be placed very low on it with no chance of being voted into office again. Thus the individual is beholden to the party and its leaders.

The cabinet must remain in close contact with the leaders of the parties that compose it. There is a give and take between the party representatives in the cabinet and the party leadership. Cabinet members cannot refuse categorically to accept the advice of the party, for the party leaders may threaten to withdraw their support of the coalition. Thus even here there is considerable party discipline. In practice, however, there is little likelihood of a major difference of opinion between the cabinet and the parties composing it.

Table 4–4 lists the party coalitions in cabinets in the years since 1945.

The Belgian bureaucracy is not of sufficiently high caliber to generate many proposals for new legislative action, as in

Table 4–4   Party coalitions in cabinets, 1945–1968

Dates in office	Prime minister	Parties
Aug. 1945–Mar. 1946	Van Acker	Socialist, Liberal, Communist
Mar. 1946–Mar. 1946	Spaak	Socialist
Mar. 1946–Aug. 1946	Van Acker	Socialist, Liberal, Communist
Aug. 1946–Mar. 1947	Huysmans	Socialist, Liberal, Communist
Mar. 1947–Aug. 1949	Spaak	Socialist, Christian Social
Aug. 1949–June 1950	Eyskens	Christian Social, Liberal
June 1950–Aug. 1950	Duvieusart	Christian Social
Aug. 1950–Jan. 1952	Pholien	Christian Social
Jan. 1952–Apr. 1954	Van Houtte	Christian Social
Apr. 1954–June 1958	Van Acker	Socialist, Liberal
June 1958–Nov. 1958	Eyskens	Christian Social
Nov. 1958–Sept. 1960	Eyskens	Christian Social, Liberal
Sept. 1960–Apr. 1961	Eyskens	Christian Social, Liberal
Apr. 1961–July 1965	Lefevre	Christian Social, Socialist
July 1965–Mar. 1966	Harmel	Christian Social, Socialist
Mar. 1966–June 1968	Vanden Boeynants	Christian Social, PLP
June 1969–	Eyskens	Christian Social, Socialist

France. Thus the parties have made themselves the channel between the various interests in the nation and the Parliament. Once a proposal has been given the seal of approval of a party congress, it acquires undeniable political weight.

The subsequent discussion of the decision-making process will shed more light on the role of the parties in Belgium. But it is obvious that relatively little separation of powers exists between cabinet and legislature and that the parties have to a considerable extent superseded the legislature itself. In this pattern, Belgium is not unlike several other European countries including Britain. In Belgium the system works relatively effectively.

FIVE
CONSENSUS
AND CLASH
Groups, interests, and cleavages

The Netherlands and Belgium present strikingly different pictures of interest-group activity, with pressures not directly represented in the political parties being exerted on political decision making. In general, the Dutch society of consensus generates fewer dissident elements that cannot be accommodated within the framework of the formal decision-making apparatus. Once again the Netherlands presents a somewhat unusual case, while Belgium offers the example of a more traditional pressure-group situation, complicated by the numerous splits in the country's social fabric.

RELIGIOUS AND ECONOMIC GROUPS IN THE NETHERLANDS

In the Netherlands, the main patterns of interest concern religion and the socioeconomic structure. With regard to religion, the believer-nonbeliever dichotomy and the Catholic-Protestant division are the most evident. In the socioeconomic sphere, the division between labor and management, or between the lower classes and the upper classes, dominates. The first of these conflicts, concerning questions of belief, is manifest principally in the political parties. As might be expected, they thus assume a less important role in the activities of interest groups. Although the churches do not have direct links with the parties, they can exert considerable influence by way of their common members. Even more important is the fact that the churches and parties find themselves in parallel "pillars" of influence in Dutch society.[1] As a result, the need for direct political pressure is reduced, and many of the desired programs are "built into" the political parties.

The other principal area of interest-group activity, reflecting the second major conflict in Dutch society, is the traditional tug-of-war between labor and employers, in which the state is often called upon to play a role as mediator and to distribute certain benefits that society as a whole has agreed are fair and necessary. Here the Netherlands has developed a virtually unique system of resolving conflict and of channeling demands to the government. A brief word about some of the subsidiary pressures in the Dutch body politic will introduce a closer examination of the system.

Big business

The Netherlands has been characterized as a nation having huge firms, so big in fact that the government is a mere subsidiary of the trusts. This oversimplification represents a misunderstanding of the influence that the major enterprises have on Dutch society. It is undoubtedly true that the government cannot afford to take decisions that run diametrically counter to the interests of firms like Royal Dutch Shell, Philips, or Unilever. But this is not due to the relative weakness of the government when faced with the mammoth industrial enterprises. Instead it reflects the revenues earned for the public coffers by these firms and the considerable number of workers they employ. A visit to Eindhoven indicates the great number of people affected by the major firm, for the city depends virtually entirely upon Philips.

As members of the upper classes of society, the directors of these firms have frequent personal contact with some of

[1] See Chap. 2.

the nation's political leaders. But blatant attempts to lobby members of the Second Chamber or ministers would be doomed to failure, because the public is aware of the potential political force of these firms. Thus a direct pressure approach is ruled out in advance because of the certain negative action. On the other hand, much of the Dutch population sincerely shares the view that the major enterprises should be allowed to thrive.

Rotterdam

Rotterdam is in a position somewhat like that of the great companies. This city, which includes the world's most active seaport, wields considerable influence over the national transportation policy. There is relatively little opportunity for conflict over Rotterdam's demands, although Amsterdam, also a major port, seeks to minimize any competitive disadvantages. Nonetheless, Rotterdam draws considerable strength from its location and seeks to maintain its ascendancy among European ports with the help of the central government. Its municipal services include personnel assigned to "lobby" the government, but not on behalf of private interests. Indeed it is a question of local, but entirely public, interests seeking to have the government adopt domestically and internationally a policy favorable to the continued expansion of the port. Perhaps because of the public nature of this major interest group, it has been almost entirely successful in its efforts, to the dismay of foreign ports that cannot obtain the same kind of backing from their central governments.

Agriculture

Another particularly Dutch interest group is formed by the farmers. Agriculture in the Netherlands faces the same problems of overproduction as in other countries. Because Dutch agriculture is more efficient than in several other Common Market countries, the farmers expect the government to assure them of outlets abroad. The Dutch farmers' unions have the highest percentage of actual as against potential membership of any unions in the Netherlands. With three fourths of the farmers unionized, they are able to bring strong pressure to bear.

Although the farmers represent less than 10 percent of the population, they have succeeded in penetrating almost all political parties and are well represented in the nation's economic advisory organs. They have succeeded, through their pressure within the parties, in forcing the government to offer them direct subsidies of more than $135 million annually plus high guaranteed selling prices. The structural problems caused by too many farmers working too small farms remain, however, and this has been a cause of the revolt against government commodity boards that has had some appeal to a limited number of farmers.

The Labor Foundation

The organization of relations between labor and management and its effect on government is perhaps the most important element in interest-group activity in the Netherlands and is certainly typical of this country alone. It represents institutionalized cooperation that tends to channel pressures into predetermined forums, without stripping them of their force.

The origin of the system lies with the creation of the Labor Foundation in 1945. This body is completely private and was not created by law. Instead, it grew out of the wartime resistance cooperation between workers and management. The Labor Foundation was conceived of as a permanent point of contact between labor and management at local and national levels.

The Labor Foundation is a bipartite body, composed of an equal number of workers' and employers' representatives. Workers are named by one of the country's three major labor union organizations. These are the Socialist Netherlands Federation of Trade Unions (NVV), the Netherlands Catholic Federation of Trade Unions (NKV), and the Protestant National Christian Federation of Trade Unions (CNV), in order of size.[2] There are also three groups of employers, organized along religious lines. Representation in the Labor Foundation of the three major unions has tended to reduce the number of splinter groups. In return for this recognition, the major unions promise to act "constructively" and "responsibly," which means,

[2] There is also an extremely small Liberal labor union.

in practice, that they are willing to forego short-term demands if they believe they can achieve some long-term goal.

The Labor Foundation has important "internal" functions, such as the negotiating of collective bargaining agreements. But it also has been given by law and by the government an additional "external" function as a channel between labor and management and the government. It has become an official advisory body to the cabinet. For example, a decision to shorten the work week originated within the unions of the Labor Foundation and was eventually adopted by the foundation itself. Foundation officials then transmitted the recommendation to both the cabinet and parliament, where it was virtually certain of adoption, for it had already obtained labor and management support. The Labor Foundation has also been given the task of approving virtually all collective bargaining agreements by the cabinet. This allows for a kind of industrial "self-policing" to prevent inflationary accords. Through a process of persuasion, the foundation is able to tone down excessively high wage agreements, which, in a small country like the Netherlands, could have a wide impact in a relatively short period. The powers of the Labor Foundation, having been accepted in advance by all parties, are relatively easy to wield.

The Labor Foundation was one of the primary influences in inducing the government to end its strict controls on wages and prices. By common agreement between workers and employers, the Labor Foundation moved to ask the government to end controls and to allow adoption of a relatively free wage system. A system of "black," or illegal, wage rates was already undermining the government program. Because of the continual pressure on the government, especially the Ministry of Economic Affairs and parliament, this demand was finally granted, marking the major step in the economic evolution of the country in the postwar period.

The Social and Economic Council

In 1950, under the Industrial Organization Act, the Social and Economic Council was created along the lines already established by the Labor Foundation. The council is composed of forty-five members, one third named by the employers, one third by the unions, and one third by the cabinet, as representatives of the general national interest. Unions nominate members in line with their size, while employers' organizations in industry, agriculture, trade, commerce, banking, insurance, and transport—the major elements of national economic life— do the same. The fifteen public members are often university professors. To a certain extent, they can block action by the other two groups if they are able to show that it would not be in the national economic interest. Thus they can, for example, provide information on the effect on hourly wages and unemployment of shortening the work week, which may discourage too rash a move.

The cabinet is required to ask the council for its opinion on all pieces of social and economic legislation it wishes to propose—the bulk of important domestic legislation. The council may, at any time, issue its own unsolicited opinion on economic and social questions. In this way it can provoke cabinet action, and it may make sure that it has rendered an opinion even if the cabinet appeared not to have been ready to ask for it. The cabinet is not bound to accept the advice given, but if the report is adopted by a large majority or unanimously, it is difficult for the minister of economic affairs to refuse to take action. In addition, the council sends copies of all its reports to members of the States General, giving them the opportunity to place pressure on the cabinet if they agree with the council's conclusions. This is likely, for the council represents a sizeable proportion of the national constituency. In one case, the council unanimously adopted a report on the improvement of old-age pensions, and the cabinet and parliament had virtually no other choice but to adopt it. This stands in stark contrast with the prolonged battles in many other countries over increasing pensions. The council has also become interested in the question of profit sharing for workers, an issue that has preoccupied the political parties for some time without having resulted in much legislation. Finally, the council has begun admitting to its subsidiary bodies representatives of the consumer groups. It may do so at its own discretion, thus taking into account changes in Dutch society, for the council is an autonomous body.

The success and efficiency of the Social and Economic Council is all the more striking because it functions in the Netherlands. Traditionally it is the countries of southern Europe, like France and Italy, that have undertaken to provide an institutional framework for labor and management. But nowhere has the system worked as well as in the Netherlands.

The Industrial Organization Act also provides for the creation of general industrial boards for broad industrial groups, industrial boards for specific groups, and commodity boards for specific farm products. There are now two general industrial boards, one for the retail trade and the other for skilled craftsmen. There are forty industrial boards covering such sectors as coal mining, forestry, and shoe manufacture. Finally the fifteen commodity boards cover virtually the entire food industry.

These various groups are composed of labor and management representatives and have broad powers, which, however, are subject to government review. The boards can regulate competition, control the production and sale of goods, and settle social questions, such as wages and other conditions of employment.

The Dutch system for dealing with economic and social pressures is thus highly structured. The interests involved have accepted this system, partly because of the experience of wartime cooperation, which proved effective, and partly because the system provides results. The economic interests are also reflected in the political parties, as noted earlier, but this represents a second stage in the process. Through joint bodies, such as the Labor Foundation and the Social and Economic Council, their desires have a greater chance of being carefully examined and then given the greatest possible political weight even before they arrive at the stage of governmental or legislative action.

Through the political parties and the official and quasi-official socioeconomic organs, the Netherlands has substantially transformed traditional pressure-group activity.

THE NETWORK OF BELGIAN GROUPS

In Belgium, three basic conflicts determine the alignment of the numerous interest groups, most of which attempt to participate in the nation's political system. The first and most traditional is the cleavage between Catholicism and the freethinkers.

Although this issue has largely passed from the political scene as far as the parties are concerned, it is still the underlying motivation for many of the groups. There remains also the traditional split between economic conservatives and progressives. This, too, parallels the divisions among the parties. Finally, the two tendencies most characteristic of the language dispute, centralization versus federalism, are also present in the majority of interest groups. These three cleavages cut across other interest groups, and numerous combinations and permutations of interest-group activity can be found. There are, it should be recalled, three main "families" that transcend both the political parties and the pressure groups. These are the Catholic, Socialist, and Liberal "worlds" or "families." The position of many of the groups can be determined in relation to one of these three constellations.

Varieties of interest groups

In Belgium eight different kinds of groups can be identified. These have a wide range of functions: religious or philosophical, cultural, economic, professional, group service, defense of special interests, regional, and single-issue.[3]

Among the religious or philosophically oriented groups are the churches and, in particular, the Roman Catholic Church. Also in this category are the Masonic organizations and the "free" (that is, not state) universities—the Catholic University of Louvain and the freethinking University of Brussels. The cultural groups are often related either to the nation's political parties or to the language question. Among the most important are the Jeunesse Ouvrière Chrétienne (Christian working-class youth) and the Socialist youth.

The Belgian economy is dominated by a relatively small number of economic "groups," which are formed by direct links, as in the case of cartels, or indirect links, as in the case of holding companies. "The 'group' can be defined as a collection of enterprises among which there is some kind of link, sufficiently strong and durable to permit some degree of common economic

[3] J. Meynaud, *La Décision Politique en Belgique* (Paris: Armand Colin, 1965), pp. 49–58.

policy with regard to prices, investment, wages, etc." [4] This definition leads off a directory of these major "groups," whose existence is thus openly recognized and accepted in Belgium. The world of these "groups" is considered a "subuniverse" without any "visible" relation to political life. But, as in the Netherlands, these groups do have direct access to the minister of economic affairs, and their interests are, to a certain extent, the interests of the country. In addition, they work through professional employers' organizations.

Professional interest groups are "the most powerful, best organized, most active and the most influential on the political level," according to a recent Belgian political study.[5] They exist in six major social areas: employers, middle class, farmers, "liberal" professions (such as medicine and law), civil servants, and workers.

The first among the employers' organizations is the Federation of Belgian Industries (FIB), which is a federation of federations. It groups thirty-five sectorial organizations, many of which are themselves federations. The FIB represents some 35,000 firms of all sizes and serves as a link and arbitrator between them. It also is designated as the official spokesman of management in relations with the government, labor unions, and national economic life. Yet it should not be thought that in relations with workers the FIB represents management; this power still remains with the ownership of the major "groups." Besides the FIB, there is also a Federation of Nonindustrial Enterprises (banks, insurance companies, distribution firms) and a Federation of Catholic Employers, which is more of a cultural organization.

In the sector of the middle classes, organizations may group members according to either their profession or their social status. There is a plethora of groups organized along the lines of social standing, often with a given religious orientation, but these distinctions are gradually fading. The leading professionally oriented groups are composed of independent workers and supervisors. Within the Christian Social party they serve

[4] Meynaud, p. 50.
[5] Meynaud, p. 51.

as a counterbalance for labor groups, but there is also a unit linked to the PLP/PVV. In general these organizations are concerned with protecting the interests of artisans, small- and medium-sized firms, and shopkeepers.

The agricultural organizations are led by the Boerenbond (the Farmers' League), which has much of its strength in the Flemish part of Belgium. The Boerenbond is considered to carry considerable weight, acting on educational, financial, and political levels. The Boerenbond represents much of the middle class of Flanders. Two other farm groups are associated with the Liberals and the Catholics.

The so-called liberal professions have been well organized in Belgium. First, the alumni associations of the various institutions of higher learning play a political role. In addition, "orders" have been created and are legally sanctioned for many of the most important professions, such as medicine, law, pharmacy, and architecture. The struggle among various medical groups to determine which is authorized to speak for the doctors has caused many of the "doctors' strikes" that have swept the country periodically.

Civil servants are organized along both political lines (this may be a factor in determining their appointment) and along language lines (this certainly is a factor in determining their appointment).

Workers (blue collar and white collar) are organized into three major labor unions, each linked with one of the traditional parties. One finds in Belgium the Catholic trade union with the greatest proportionate strength of any western European country. Among the unionized white-collar workers, the Catholic Confédération des Syndicats Chrétiens (CSC) has the support of some 52 percent, while the Socialist Fédération Générale du Travail de Belgique (FGTB) has 41 percent and the Liberal Confédération des Syndicats Libéraux de Belgique (CGSLB) about 7 percent. Among the unionized blue-collar workers, who outnumber the white-collar workers, the FGTB gains the support of 54 percent, the CSC 41 percent, and the CGSLB 5 percent. More than 1.5 million workers, about 60 percent of the labor force, belong to unions.

Some "collective service" groups exist more to provide

services to the public than to promote the interests of a specific group. They are usually organized along confessional or political lines and are vital to the maintenance and strengthening of the fabric that keeps the three major "families" or "worlds" internally united. Among these groups are the "mutualités," both Catholic and Socialist, which dispose of sizeable budgets and operate numerous clinics and health programs throughout the country.

Some groups represent specific interests that are not, however, professional. These include veterans and former prisoners-of-war organizations, the League of Large Families, women's groups, and student associations.

The regional groups embody those who take strong positions on the language question. These may now be losing in importance, as political parties, such as the Volksunie and the FRF-RW, begin to make an appeal for voter support. Previously the most important regional interest groups were the Flemish People's Movement and the Walloon People's Movement.

Finally, there are single-issue groups that do not remain a fixed feature of the Belgian scene. They may find considerable support in existing groups and gain much power for a short period. One example is the Defense Committee for the Borinage, a section of Belgium that was particularly hard hit by coal mine closures.

The "families"

Superimposed on this rather confused mass of interest groups are the various liaison groups that attempt to bring some order out of the chaos. The most important links are those that follow the lines of the traditional three "families"—Catholic, Socialist, and Liberal. There is great parallelism among the three in terms of subgroups and interests represented, and the internal structures of the Catholic and Socialist "umbrella" organizations are almost identical.

On the Catholic side, there is the Agenda Committee, a nonofficial body that groups leaders of the Christian Social party and of the principal Catholic-oriented groups. This committee reportedly plays a determinant role in the development of the general political strategy of the PSC/CVP, even greater than the party's own Council and National Committee. In addition to the Agenda Committee, the Christian Workers' Movement (MOC), grouping all labor, educational, economic, and religious entities linked to the Catholic "world," has considerable power. Similar groups exist in both Flanders and Wallonia, but the Flemings dominate. The MOC is generally viewed as gaining increasing influence over the Christian Social party, possibly moving toward a clear labor orientation.

The Socialists operate the Common Action, which groups all the principal Socialist-oriented interest associations, although it has little real power. But as in the Catholic "world," there is much overlapping of leadership among the various organizations in a single "family" that lends to its internal cohesion and strength.

Interest groups and public policy

How do the groups influence public policy? Not surprisingly, the labor unions and the employers' groups are the most concerned by the evolution of public policy, both because of their roles in the national economy and because their membership dictates a national approach. These groups exercise their influence at three levels: the grass roots of the parties, the party organs, and the cabinet. At the lowest level they in general try to influence opinion without necessarily taking specific positions. They do, however, play a major role, especially in the PSC/CVP, in the "polls" for nominating candidates to be placed on the electoral lists. A struggle may be noticed in the polls between the Christian Workers' Movement and the representatives of the middle and upper classes. Pressure on the party organs can, of course, be exercised through the "polls" and through the overlapping membership of some people in both pressure groups and parties. In the legislature, the groups may seek to influence the party leaders to use their considerable disciplinary powers over individual members or through overlapping membership in the groups and in the Parliament.

The situation is somewhat more complex in relations between the groups and the executive branch. As before, the groups may work through the parties, provided, of course, that a given party with which a group is related is taking part in the cabinet. The minister that a group seeks to influence may be a member himself or may have close contacts with the group. In certain cases the groups have a right to be seen by the minister, when they carry considerable economic weight in the sector for which he is responsible. Finally, the groups can exert "external" pressure on the cabinet through such measures as strikes. But the most usual means of access are through overlapping membership and through the parties. If a minister is not of the same party orientation as the group, the group leaders can reach him through other ministers who are politically "right," for one minister is almost certain to be willing to do a favor for another—the traditional political log-rolling.

Naturally the groups do not seek the same ends, and there are inevitable clashes. Much has to do with the relationship between the group concerned and the parties that support the cabinet. The Socialist trade union, for example, refused to take part in a strike that would have embarrassed a cabinet in which the Socialist party was participating. On the other hand, there are occasions when the interests of all workers, whatever their trade union, transcend confessional differences and they are able to act together effectively.

In general, the groups exercise influence in proportion to their economic strength. A high degree of interaction exists between the groups and the political parties, mainly because of their overlapping memberships and their allegiance to one of the three Belgian "families." The parties have perhaps the upper hand in the relationship, for they are called upon to mediate between the various groups that can make a legitimate call on their support. On the other hand, the party leaders realize that they draw much of their own political power from the support of the parties and thus cannot afford to ignore them.

The cabinet is even more independent of the groups than are the parties. It has a role of integrating the country as a whole, and it has its own sources of expert information. In addition, the cabinet can benefit from the rivalry among groups on a much greater scale than can any of the parties. Yet many of the functions of the cabinet exist simply because of the struggle among the various groups. The cabinet is thus given the role of referee, not necessarily able to impose its own will, but generally accepted as the judge of the relative strength of the various competing groups. This is strengthened by the fact that the administration itself does not generate proposals for government action. Indeed, the basic impulse for government action in Belgium comes out of the sum total of the pressure exerted by the various groups. The parties themselves reflect these pressures. The essence of the operation is to distill a single set of decisions from a wide variety of often conflicting pressures. Nonetheless, the cabinet and the parties can make their own direct appeals to the public will, and do so, thus making the pattern of influence a constantly shifting contest for the allegiance of the voter.

Turning once again to the relationship of interest-group action to the three major questions that split the nation, one finds that the religious controversy as such is losing force. Truly "neutral" organizations exist, like the Federation of Belgian Industries. Where there are conflicts between socialism and Catholicism, they are in fact clashes between economic progressives and conservatives. The economic division of the country has gradually achieved a greater reality than the religious conflict. Finally, the groups do reflect a tendency toward greater decentralization than the cabinet itself has been willing to adopt. There are Flemish and Walloon wings of many organizations, or when the Flemish dominate one of the groups in a given sector, there may be a second "national" group dominated by the Walloons. This is the very kind of division that the parties have been trying to avoid.

Most groups play the political game from inside the same framework as the three traditional parties, and they do not represent a direct challenge to the political system. Even groups divided along linguistic lines do not necessarily advocate a similar division of the country as a whole. Indeed much of the effort to transform that nation has been transferred to the political parties, freeing the groups to devote their efforts more to the traditional clash of interests. Although there is little feeling of common participation in a vast joint undertaking, the Belgian interest groups do tacitly accept the system within which they operate.

SIX
THE SURVIVAL
OF PARLIAMENT
Policy making
in the Netherlands

In a small country such as the Netherlands, the role and function of the national government structure encompasses a large part of the nation's total political activity and reaches each citizen directly and regularly. Although the evolution of the Netherlands since World War II has led to the creation of a national consensus, there remain nonetheless important political issues that must be debated and settled by the national government.

Like many of the world's constitutional monarchies, the Netherlands is one of the most democratic countries. At first glance it seems to follow the traditional continental lines of parliamentary democracy, which, in fact, means considerable power for the cabinet, with the parliament merely called upon to approve or in rare cases to disapprove proposals emanating from the cabinet. But Dutch traditions have led to the development of a major variation on this theme, with considerable functional power in the hands of the States General. As shall be seen, this is the most salient feature of the Dutch political system.

THE EXECUTIVE BRANCH

The theoretical governor of the Netherlands is the prince of Orange, who is the king. Females may succeed to the throne

128

and its present occupant is Queen Juliana, who will be followed by Crown Princess Beatrix. This is a monarchy with all the trappings of divine right rule: the citizens are "subjects," the cabinet acts in the name of the queen, as do the courts, and the queen has the right to accept or reject acts of the States General. But all of this is merely the vestige of an earlier age that came to an end in 1848. Now the queen has few personal powers, although she does have an important role to play in Dutch life.

The queen

Politically, the queen is inviolate and cannot be held responsible for acts of the cabinet in her name; only cabinet ministers can be held responsible. But the queen does serve the purpose of transforming acts of the cabinet into acts of the state. She enjoys the respect of a large part of the population, owing to the services her family has rendered to the country as well as to her own performance. The Dutch are a people with a considerable respect for history, and they recall with some emotion the role of the princes of Orange in their political evolution.

The most important political power of the queen is in the formation of a new cabinet after the general elections or the collapse of a cabinet. The queen consults the head of the Council of State, the presidents of both chambers of the States General and of each of the political parties in an effort to appraise the political climate. Finally, acting completely independently, she names an *informateur* whose job it is to inform her of the best political formula possible for the formation of a cabinet. This informateur is usually a politician himself, and thus his selection indicates something of the way in which the queen is thinking. She may appoint a second informateur if the first fails to come up with workable suggestions, but more usually she will name a *formateur,* the man asked to form a cabinet and in most cases to become prime minister. The formateur has the delicate task of finding a program that covers the basic issues facing the nation and that is acceptable to enough parties to support a cabinet in office. The formateur will, in the first instance, usually be the leader, if there is one, of the party that won the largest number of seats in the new parliament. He may well be the leader of the Catholic party, which is virtually certain to take part in every cabinet. The formateur reports back to the queen on the success of his efforts. If he has failed to come up with an acceptable program and a governing coalition, the queen withdraws his appointment and names a second formateur. There are relatively few such formation periods over a span of time, but in the Netherlands they tend to be extremely lengthy, running from two to four months. During this time the queen is central to the political life of the nation and must be well informed on the political situation, for she is trying to encourage the formation of a cabinet reflecting the nation's political will.

The queen also exercises a political role once a cabinet is installed. Because the cabinet acts in her name, she must be fully informed and consulted on its plans. Differences of opinion between members of the cabinet and the Crown are possible and probably inevitable. However, great care is taken to ensure that the public is not aware of any such disputes. Theoretically, a minister in persistent disagreement would have to resign. Since this does not happen, it is more likely that the cabinet shows some willingness to modify its proposals to take the queen's views into account without changing their basic character.

The Dutch royal family seems secure in the exercise of these powers, although the greatest political crisis involving the sovereign since 1848 is of relatively recent vintage. In 1956 a scandal erupted concerning a certain Greet Hofmans, a faith healer, who was alleged to have powers over the royal family. This modern Rasputin had been reputed to have predicted the Korean War, provided help for the ailing Princess Marijke, and aided one of the consort's horses to win a race in Stockholm. The most important item in her dossier, however, was an address given by Queen Juliana before the United States Congress in 1952, which had been prepared without the advice and consent of the cabinet. The furor that grew out of the alleged role of Greet Hofmans and others in the preparation of that speech endangered the position of the House of Orange. The cabinet stepped in to aid the Queen, although its task was made more difficult by the fact that a new cabinet was being formed at that time. Finally,

Prime Minister Drees succeeded in having the supposed "bad" influences removed from office, and the Queen's position was preserved. This situation represented one of the most serious crises in postwar Dutch history. Other problems of the royal family (Beatrix's marriage to a German and Princess Irene's marriage to a Catholic prince) provided much of the copy for the pulp magazines, but they did not threaten the Queen.

The cabinet

The executive branch is headed by the cabinet, a group of about twenty-five political leaders who assume the posts of minister and state secretary on the basis of a program accepted by their party representatives in the States General. This program is only accepted informally by the parties; the cabinet need not have the formal approval of the States General. This underlines the fact that there is no "vote of confidence" in the Dutch system. Thus the cabinet does not stand or fall on the vote in a given issue, for rejection of the proposal does not mean rejection of the cabinet. There may, however, be a specific question of "no confidence" posed by the cabinet itself. The question of confidence either in the cabinet as a whole or for a single minister, vital in the relations between government and parliament, will be discussed fully later. Without a question of confidence being posed in any way, the cabinet or a single minister can decide that it no longer wishes to assume the powers of the Crown and can resign.

In general, the cabinet as a whole is considered jointly responsible for its policy decisions, which may be adopted by a majority vote. To protect the queen, every act or royal decree must be signed both by the sovereign and by the minister responsible for the legislation and its implementation. Within the cabinet and recently in law, the office of the prime minister has come to be recognized as something more than chief among equals. In addition, deputy prime ministers may be appointed, representing the parties taking part in the coalition other than the group to which the prime minister belongs. As we shall see in examining the legislative process, the minister of finance occupies a key role in the cabinet. This is partly because much of government policy is subjected to parliamentary scrutiny when the budget is submitted. But the minister of finance may veto requests for funds by other ministers when he believes that the proposals exceed the country's ability to pay. He also regulates the expenditure of monies already appropriated. In case of dispute between the minister of finance and another minister, it is the cabinet that must decide.

In most cases, the ministers are in charge of specific government departments. Occasionally ministers without portfolio are named, who are needed for the formation of the cabinet and for their views on the development of government policy, but who only fulfill specific tasks from time to time rather than acting as head of a department. More often, state secretaries are named; they are a kind of junior minister. The state secretary is named by the minister of a given department, subject to the approval of the cabinet. The state secretary acts as a minister for the part of the departmental activities assigned to him, but must act in accordance with instructions from the minister. He is not a member of the cabinet and may attend only in an advisory capacity. When appearing before the States General, the state secretary can be held responsible for his actions. If there is any conflict between his acceptance of orders and his willingness to accept responsibility, he must resign.

The cabinet may meet whenever necessary; it usually meets each Friday. At these meetings the members discuss bills they are preparing to submit to the States General and to the Council of State, the status of relations and negotiations with other countries, and the nomination of officials.

The sum total of the formal powers of the cabinet do not reveal its full role in the governing process. Only in the adoption of legislation—in its relations with parliament—can its full scope be seen.

The Council of State

The Council of State is, together with the States General and the General Auditing Court, part of the High Colleges of State. The Council of State is, in fact, part of the executive apparatus of the Netherlands. Its members, most of whom have previously occupied high political positions, are named by the queen.

At one time this body was attached to the Crown; it now

serves as an adjunct of the cabinet. The queen presides over the Council of State, although only on ceremonial occasions. The vice-president, an appointed official, is the effective head of the body, which has no more than twenty members. The members are divided into sections, each responsible for the activities of one or more government departments. Each section includes three members. There is also an administrative disputes section, which forms part of the national judiciary.

Prior to submission of a proposal to parliament, the cabinet sends it to the Council of State. The council also examines proposed international agreements and proposals to annul a municipal or provincial order by the Crown. Some laws give additional powers to the Council of State—for example, in matters of expropriation. The council may also recommend matters to the Crown that it considers require legislation, and, in general, it may express views on issues of national importance. Finally, under exceptional circumstances, the Council of State may exercise the royal authority until such time as a new sovereign is named.

The role of the Council of State is thus that of elder wise men, able to bring to bear their experience and familiarity with the law in relation to pending legislation, before the law-making process has gone too far. The Council of State has no decisive role in advising the cabinet, but it can, however, act as a check on the government, and the cabinet is responsive to the constructive suggestions emanating from it.

Other executive agencies

The General Auditing Court is a part of the executive structure. Although its members serve as judges, it functions within the various government departments to audit government expenditures. It operates in such a way that the cabinet is forced to ask the States General for authority to spend money when the General Auditing Court refuses its approval, and the court itself is authorized to report to the States General. Thus the legislative organ can be used as a lever of control by the independent auditing institution.

Over the years, cabinets have created a number of permanent advisory councils on specific areas of public policy. These groups, composed of members of high technical competence, cover such subjects as mines, labor, education, and the Zuyder Zee. The reports of these councils are published, unlike the secret reports of the Council of State, and public opinion may thus be aroused on a given cabinet proposal. Although their importance may be diminishing as the various parliamentary committees gain in influence and expertise, they have been given a constitutional status independent of the cabinet.

The administration

The final element of the executive structure is the national administration. This administration provides the chief element of permanence in the executive branch. Only the ministers resign when there is a change of cabinet; the officials are in no way affected. Thus only twenty-five ministers and state secretaries are removed and replaced; even the general secretaries of the departments, the highest civil servants, remain in office. To take one example, in recent years the official in charge of preparing the budget has worked under the supervision of six different ministers, representing three different parties with widely differing views on budget questions—the Socialists, the Anti-Revolutionaries, and the Liberals. The motto clearly is "the ministers come and go; the officials stay."

This, of course, prompts a certain attitude on the part of officials toward their chiefs. In general, they believe that about one year is required before the minister is well acquainted with his job. This means that the top officials exercise considerable influence during this period, not only as departmental heads, but in the training of the new chief. On the other hand, the administrators try to respond to the political orientation of the leadership, even when it changes rather sharply. There is a deep tradition of loyalty by the officials to their political superiors. A story is repeated in the Netherlands of the behavior of three government ministers, all of whom had come from the civil service. They first showed considerable loyalty to their cabinet, which had been placed in serious danger by a revolt of one of the parliamentary parties counted on to support it. When its fall became inevitable, they shifted their support to the leader of the revolt. Then, when a new man was designated to lead the cabinet, they immediately threw their support to him, only to shift course one final time when the new prime minister was designated. All of this is recounted in the Netherlands by way of illustrating the innate loyalty of the civil service to whomever is in charge.

"The Netherlands official is the most anonymous man of all time," says one observer of Dutch politics.[1] This statement reflects the almost surprising position that the civil servant is content to occupy. Although the civil service provides the continuity of government, as in France, it never confuses itself with the cabinet, which is politically responsible.

The administration is, however, called upon to aid the minister in performing his political functions. Ministers must stand on their own on two occasions: under parliamentary questioning and in cabinet meetings. In the first case, almost no minister, however experienced, would appear before the States General without surrounding himself with all the officials he thinks will be necessary to deal with the matters under discussion. Others are held in reserve at the ministry. When the cabinet must prepare an answer or supplementary statement to the Second Chamber, the meeting is interrupted briefly. The responsible minister and his officials huddle in a nearby room and prepare the statement. The officials do not, of course, attend the cabinet session. As a result, a minister may hold a departmental cram session just prior to the cabinet meeting so that his officials can provide him with detailed information.

As advisers to the cabinet and aides responsible for the preparation of proposals, the administrators have a virtually unchallenged monopoly on information. While the interest groups may rival the administration on some points, the parliament and the parties do not. Thus, through assistance to the minister, the civil servants are expected to provide him with a vast supply of facts, to be used to snow under potential objections.

[1] J. van den Berg, *De Anatomie van Nederland,* Vol. 1 (Amsterdam: De Bezige Bij, 1967), p. 105.

There are some 400,000 civil servants, including those who perform service functions in agencies such as the postal administration, the mint, and the harbor administration. The Defense, Education, and Tax departments are the largest employers outside the service units. The civil servants themselves are virtually all university trained at the executive level. Although most are simply regarded as technicians, attention is often paid to the political affiliation of the civil servants when they are named to posts. This is not so much a matter of discrimination as an attempt to obtain the appropriate political balance within each given section of a ministry. Such balance is considered a check on the proposals that emanate from that section; they are politically neutral. Of course, occasions arise when officials are "parachuted" into specific offices for political reasons.

Once in office, an official is allowed to continue and expand his political activities, provided he does not take public positions on issues directly within his professional field. He may be elected to public office, including the States General. In this case, he is paid the difference between his parliamentary salary and his civil servant's stipend, but he is relieved of his official functions. He may reassume them, however, when he leaves his parliamentary post. The best-known example of a civil servant assuming a political position is Foreign Minister Joseph Luns, who went in 1953 from a diplomatic post to the political role of minister. Although he has remained in this post over fifteen years, he would be given an ambassadorial or similar appointment if he left office.

Civil servants are generally held in high regard by the population, and the profession is one considered most worthy of university graduates. The public recognizes the power of the administration and the tradition of attracting well-qualified persons. There is no important opposition to the idea of political "spotting" within the ministries; indeed, it is considered absolutely necessary. In a small country, a higher proportion of the population is involved in public administration, and thus the public is more aware of its existence and role. In the Netherlands, the people are generally satisfied by the competence, role, and objectivity of their civil servants.

THE LEGISLATURE

Dutch constitutional practice indicates that the Crown and the States General are the legislative power of the Netherlands. In a formal sense, this is true, for the cabinet, acting in the name of the Crown, must submit legislative proposals, and the queen must "approve" bills before they become laws. Yet, in the traditional sense, the States General is the legislative branch of the Dutch government.

Composition of the States General

The Dutch parliament had its origin in feudal times and assumed its present form in 1815. At that time an upper chamber was instituted, on the initiative of the Belgian representatives, and was composed of nobles nominated by the king for life. The lower chamber was chosen by the provincial assemblies, themselves elected by the three "estates"—the nobles, the towns, and the country. The Constitution of 1848 wrought great changes in the legislature. The Second, or lower, Chamber was chosen by direct elections, the franchise being limited to certain classes of taxpayers. The First, or upper, Chamber was elected by the provincial councils from among the major taxpayers. By 1922, universal suffrage for men and women on the system of proportional representation came into effect. The First Chamber is still elected by the Provincial Councils, but because these bodies are elected in the same way as the Second Chamber, the composition of the two chambers of the national legislature is virtually the same. The only vestige of an earlier era is the fact that the average age of the members of the First Chamber may be slightly higher than that of the Second.

The regular session of the States General is opened on the third Tuesday in September with the queen delivering the Speech from the Throne, which embodies the cabinet's program. Except for an initial three-month period, ministers and state secretaries cannot remain members of parliament, but must resign their seats in favor of substitute candidates from their list. This is one of the foundation stones of the separation of powers between cabinet and parliament. A number of other posts within government are also incompatible with membership in either house of the parliament. Parliamentary debates are generally open to the public and may even be broadcast and televised, although this happens rarely. Certain provisions of the Constitution require joint sittings of the two chambers. They meet together, under the chairmanship of the president of the First Chamber, when matters are under discussion relating to the regency, guardianship, inauguration, and oath taking of the sovereign, and declaration of war. When there is no successor to the throne, the parliament must choose the new monarch. For this purpose, the size of the States General is doubled; new elections are held to choose what amounts to a duplicate body, responsive to the popular will on this most important issue. The duplicate group serves only for this purpose and then is disbanded.

The members of the two chambers are those party representatives elected by the people and by the provincial assemblies. It will be recalled that the term of office of the members of the Second Chamber is four years, with all being elected at the same time, while that of the First Chamber is six years, with one half elected every three years. Representatives of half the country leave office at the same time, rather than half of the representatives of all parts of the country. The distribution of seats in the 150-member Second Chamber and the 75-member First Chamber is very nearly exactly the same by party.

All members of both chambers are considered to represent the entire Dutch nation; there are no constituency representatives. Members of the Second Chamber receive a salary for their services, but members of the First Chamber receive only a daily allowance. Both of these amounts are determined in part by the distance from The Hague of the place of residence of the member. Within this small country, most members of parliament can return home after each day's session. In neither of the chambers is it expected that the member will give up his regular employment to serve in parliament, although party leaders and a few other officials may have to devote their full attention to their parliamentary jobs. Thus, almost all members continue the professions they held when they entered parliament (see Table 6–1).

Of these members, more than two thirds of the First

**Table 6–1   Professions of members
of the States General, 1965**

	First Chamber	Second Chamber
Business executive	13	5
Middle business executive		7
	4	
Lower business executive		2
Agriculture	—	9
Small independent	—	2
Lawyer	4	13
Journalist	—	11
Other independent professions	4	5
Party official	—	7
Trade union official	8	14
Party/union staff member	—	7
Social organization	—	8
Other political/economic organizations	5	7
Teacher	4	10
Professor	9	2
Other educational	3	5
Civil servant-ministry/national		15
	3	
Other civil servant		12
Burgomaster/alderman	15	7
Other administrator	—	2
Others	3	—
Total	75	150

Source: J. van den Berg, *De Anatomie van Nederland*, Vol. 1 (Amsterdam: De Bezige Bij, 1967), pp. 47–48. By permission of the publisher.

Chamber but only a few more than one half of the Second Chamber have a university education. On the basis of educational background and profession it is possible to conclude that the First Chamber remains a stronghold of privilege, although there is no institutional reason, such as appointment for life as in Britain, for this state of affairs. One possible conclusion is that there remains a conscious desire on the part of the parties and the Provincial Councils to maintain some degree of difference in composition between the two chambers.

The members of parliament are, of course, divided by

party and not by profession. However, within many of the party groups in parliament, members of a given profession exercise a specialized influence and act, to a certain extent at least, as the representatives of the interest groups. Such is obviously the case for farmers and representatives of the labor unions.

Party and parliament

The party group is of primary importance. The parliamentary party, in the case of the five national parties, is quite distinct from the national party organization, although there is, naturally, a great deal of overlapping between membership in the parliamentary party and in the party hierarchy. The chief of the parliamentary group may well rival the party chairman, and he may outweigh even the prime minister of the same party in his influence and importance.

One well-known case will illustrate this. In 1966, a difference of opinion concerning state control of radio, television, and the press arose between Prime Minister Cals, a Roman Catholic, and Norbert Schmelzer, the Catholic leader in the Second Chamber. But the basis of the dispute was Schmelzer's discontentment with the Catholic-Socialist coalition—which indeed had been something of a surprise, after it had been generally accepted that these two parties would be the leaders of two opposing political camps. Schmelzer asked the fifty Catholic members of the Second Chamber to support him in withdrawing his support from the cabinet; forty-six did cooperate with his action. The Catholic-led cabinet thus fell, thanks to a parliamentary move by the Catholic leader in the Second Chamber. This resulted in a protracted period of crisis while a "technocrat" cabinet was constructed and new elections were held. When it came time to find a new Catholic leader to assume the post of prime minister, Schmelzer designated the man who got the job. Thus there could be little doubt about his political power.

A further sequel to this story will indicate the relative lack of party discipline in the Second Chamber. Obviously, Schmelzer himself was not disciplined either by Cals or by the party executive for his maneuvers in bringing the cabinet down. Indeed he emerged stronger from the confrontation, but he in turn did not employ party discipline. Of the four opponents to his move, two voluntarily quit the party more than one year later and two others remained, one of whom became vice chairman of the Catholic party. Schmelzer later had occasion to call upon Cals for party activities, and the two cooperated effectively. A footnote might be added by some political cynics. It is possible that Schmelzer, foreseeing large-scale Catholic defections over the budget proposed by the Cals cabinet, shifted position to get ahead of his troops and thus could count on their support. This would account for the relatively little need for discipline after the event, but would also indicate a high degree of internal democracy, creating a situation in which the leader could not lead.

The legislative process

The principal function of the States General is, of course, to examine and vote on legislation placed before it. Bills may originate either with the cabinet or in the Second Chamber. Parliamentary initiative is extremely rare and usually does not concern major questions of government policy. Most bills are prepared by the civil service under directives of the minister or the cabinet as a whole. During the preparation of the bill, consultations are held with outside experts—either formally, or informally (through special or regular advisory bodies). The political parties and major interest groups are kept informed, normally by the minister in charge of the specific sector. The minister welds into a single proposal the various suggestions he has received, and it is then presented to the cabinet. Within the cabinet there may be additional modifications to take into account the delicate balance of party interests among the coalition parties, although the proposal may be a part of the general coalition program and thus not raise many new controversial questions. In addition, the queen and the Council of State are consulted before the proposed legislation is sent to the Second Chamber of the States General.

When a bill is delivered to the president of the Second Chamber, accompanied by a full explanatory memorandum, the Central Committee, composed of the president and leaders of the five major parties, decides on procedure. In recent years, the normal procedure has been to send the bill to one of the specialized committees (foreign affairs, agriculture, and so on), composed of a limited number of representatives of all major parties and a sprinkling of members of minor groups. Other members of the Second Chamber may take part in the discussion at their own request. The committee holds its debates out of the public view and prepares a preliminary report, which is made public. During the preparation of this report, the committee may ask for written comments or a face-to-face confrontation with the minister responsible and possibly with his civil servants. In general, the result of the committee discussion is a synthesis of various party statements, with majority against minority. The minister may, of course, be influenced to alter the bill if he believes that constructive proposals have been put forward or if the members of the committee are able to swing sufficient strength in the Second Chamber against a part of the bill. Thus the strength of the committee depends to a certain extent on the influence of its individual members.

The heart of the legislative process is the confrontation between the full Second Chamber and the minister responsible for a given bill. A general debate on the subject of the bill is held, followed by a discussion article by article. The committee secretary and officials of the Chamber control the debate, since the minister is not a member of the Chamber. The minister limits his remarks to formal statements on the cabinet's position, although he may find himself drawn into a give-and-take with the members of the Chamber. Any member can speak and many do, particularly if they are unwilling to follow the lead of their party spokesmen. A group of only five members is required to propose amendments to the bill, but even more important is the right of the minister, at any time before the discussion ends, to introduce amendments and, if he feels the bill will be defeated, simply to withdraw it.

The minister, not a member of the Second Chamber, may use a number of tactics to defeat parliamentary efforts to modify or defeat the proposed legislation. Obviously, he will attempt to convince opponents of the value of the bill, but if he runs into opposition from the parliamentary majority, he may have to allow himself to be persuaded by them. He can refuse a proposed amendment as "unacceptable," but it may be voted over his opposition. In this case, the minister and cabinet have a number of options. The minister may withdraw the proposed law, although this might undercut the agreed coalition program. He may threaten to resign as an individual member of the cabinet, or the cabinet as a whole may warn that it will resign if the bill is adopted with the offensive amendment. According to observers, the use of the "unacceptable" procedure has proved effective, serving as a warning to the Chamber without endangering the stability of the cabinet. Actually, individual resignation may be as powerful a weapon as the withdrawal of the cabinet as a whole. If a minister resigns, he may remove an element of delicate balance from the coalition, thus causing the resignation of other ministers. Thus the parliament is handed a cabinet crisis, with no assurance of a better formula being reached.

Because most of these alternatives are rather extreme, ways are found of avoiding them, the most obvious being a compromise between the minister and his opponents. The minister and his civil servants may work feverishly in the antechambers of the Binnenhof, the complex of government buildings where the Second Chamber meets, to come up with a compromise that will save as much of the bill as possible. Finally, with at least half of the members present, the Second Chamber votes. The Chamber then informs the queen if it has rejected the bill or the First Chamber if it has not. The Constitution prescribes the text of the message: "The Second Chamber of States General sends to the First Chamber the enclosed proposal of the queen, and is of the opinion that it should be passed by the States General in its present form."

When the proposal arrives before the First Chamber, it is passed to each of the four general committees, whose membership is determined by lot. Each of these committees examines the same bill simultaneously and prepares its own report. The four rapporteurs then meet and prepare a single report.[2] The minister must also appear for the discussion in the First Cham-

---

[2] A similar procedure was used by the Second Chamber until 1953, when it was superseded by the specialized committee system.

ber. This body cannot amend proposals, but it has an absolute power to reject them. Occasionally, as a condition of accepting a bill, the First Chamber may extract a promise from the minister that he will introduce additional legislation in the Second Chamber. Once again the First Chamber follows a hallowed form once it has acted. If it approves a bill it writes: "To the Queen: the States General express to the Queen their thanks for her zeal in promoting the interests of the State, and agree to that proposal in its present form." Or it may write: "To the Queen: the First Chamber of the States General expresses to the Queen its thanks for her zeal in promoting the interests of the State, and respectfully requests her to reconsider the proposal which has been made." In either case, the Second Chamber is also informed.

In the last step of the legislative process, the bill is sent to the queen for her formal approval. The queen, expressing the will of the cabinet, could theoretically refuse her royal assent if the amendments introduced were unacceptable. But were this the case, the minister would have withdrawn it well before a final vote. The cabinet is able to maintain the role of leader in the dialogue with the parliament, and it can refuse to accept amendments. Its proposals remain before parliament until they are withdrawn, even if there is a new parliament chosen in the meantime. But the parliament has counterbalances: it is master of its own procedure, and ministers are not members.

Legislation in practice

The practical course followed by an important piece of legislation will shed additional light on the legislative procedure in the Netherlands. In July 1962 the cabinet presented a bill to parliament on the creation of a new public authority for the Rhine River estuary. The actual procedure had begun in September 1958, when the minister of the interior appointed a committee to study the administrative problems of the area. The committee report was published in February 1960 and sent to the Provincial States of South Holland and the municipalities concerned. These local authorities suggested some modifications, which were adopted by the committee, and in

July 1960 the Provincial States of South Holland gave its approval of the report. The report and the subsequent legislation called for the creation of a "supramunicipal" public authority for the Rhine estuary, including some twenty-four municipalities ranging from Rotterdam to some extremely small villages. When the bill was introduced into the Second Chamber, debate focused on the organization and powers of the public body, which would, in effect, amount to a new level of government between the municipalities and the province. There was also concern that Rotterdam would dominate the new organization, thus spreading its control over other municipalities. These problems led members of the Second Chamber to propose a considerable number of amendments. This in turn obliged the cabinet to withdraw the proposed law and to submit a complete new draft.

In the new proposal, the municipalities were given the right to appeal to the Provincial States from any directives issued to them by the Council of the Rhine Estuary. If a decision of the Provincial States violates the law or "inadmissibly" infringes upon the interests of a municipality, the Crown retains its traditional right to quash it. An attempt was made, during the discussion in the Second Chamber, to extend the powers of the new authority to include not only coordination but also the promotion of interests that formerly had exclusively belonged to the municipalities. The minister of the interior opposed the suggested amendment, saying that it tended toward annexation of the municipalities. The session was suspended, and the members of the Permanent Committee on the Interior discussed the question, rejecting the proposed amendment unanimously. It was then put to a vote before the Second Chamber, where it was defeated by 102 to 22. Finally on February 25, 1964, the Second Chamber adopted the proposal law, creating a new authority by a vote of 104 to 19. Later that year the First Chamber approved the proposed law, and two days later, on November 5, 1964, the bill was promulgated as an act.

The formal procedure for the adoption of the bill took two years and three months; including the all-important preparatory work, the process lasted over six years. Although not a matter of widespread national controversy, this was a vital constitutional issue, likely to serve as a precedent for later decisions on the organization of local powers in the Netherlands. The interests affected—in this case the municipalities—were consulted, and the parliamentary committee was able to play a decisive role. Indeed, the Second Chamber was able to force the cabinet to remodel its proposal. Thus the actual practice accorded fairly closely with the constitutional guidelines for the legislative procedure.

Representation of local interests

In a country where the members of parliament do not represent local constituencies, one may wonder how the public is able to express its views on pending legislation. First, it should be noted that although members of the Chamber are supposed to and do represent the nation as a whole, they are often voted into office on a list of one of the eighteen electoral districts. Thus they do have a certain tie with a part of the country and will often seek to enhance their standing there. They are open to appeals from residents of that area 'and, indeed, from any other area. In addition, the interest groups transmit the public views, although they do not, of course, necessarily make a public sounding on each issue. Finally, the press serves as a powerful means of communication between the people and their representatives. There is both a national and a provincial press in the Netherlands, and the local papers are often quite influential. They provide a means of expression for residents of a given area. In addition, the press is organized along party lines, giving the faithful an opportunity to express their views to the party leadership both through the media and the party organization. This method of representing local interests does not function to the satisfaction of all Dutchmen. The Democrats '66 party supports the creation of smaller constituencies, mainly to give the voter greater access to his own representative.

Legislative powers of supervision and control

The States General is not limited simply to passing on the cabinet's legislative proposals. It has several other important powers, used mainly as a check on the executive branch. These powers concern control of the administration and financial supervision.

The States General is free to challenge the cabinet on any aspect of the administration that seems opportune, and the members of parliament may be well informed on specific problems through their contact with civil servants. But the parliament is reluctant to overplay its hand, for it probably does not wish to topple the cabinet and create the long period of uncertainty as a new coalition is sought. In addition, the sources of information of the States General are not as good as for the cabinet itself, mainly because of inadequate staff. The civil service must, in the first instance, work for the cabinet, not the parliament.

The parliamentary question is a traditional and frequently used method of checking on the cabinet. Most often, written questions and answers are used, and ministers can rarely find adequate reasons of state to refuse to give an answer. Most questions are on important policy or administrative questions and do not constitute harassment of the cabinet, but rather put pressure on it to develop its policy or to tend to important administrative deficiencies.

A more formal and thus stronger weapon is the interpellation. An individual member asks permission of his Chamber to discuss a specific issue with a minister. The Chamber generally grants its permission, and the minister attends a meeting and replies to the questions of the member or others. At the conclusion of the questioning, the Chamber may adopt a vote of thanks to the minister, a motion expressing its views on the subject, which the cabinet is free to accept or reject, or a motion of no confidence in the cabinet based on its replies to the questions put during the interpellation. Indeed, the purpose of an interpellator may be to try to provoke the fall of the cabinet.

Special debates, usually proposed by the cabinet, can cover a major area of government policy without there being a specific piece of legislation before the Chamber. The cabinet may seek to test its major hypotheses before the Chamber prior to drawing up draft laws. The Chamber may also ask the cabinet to present a basic document covering its orientation in a given sector. Budget debates also allow for a general policy examination as well as discussion of minor grievances. The budget debate remains the most important confrontation of parliament and cabinet each year.

A final weapon in the arsenal of the States General is the parliamentary inquiry, usually dealing with a specific problem. Committees of inquiry can call witnesses and experts, who are obliged to provide information, subject to arrest and prosecution if they refuse. Cabinet representatives may refuse to give information, although they are generally cooperative. Often the cabinet itself will carry out the inquiry, and members of the Chambers will be invited to serve on the committee. But major parliamentary inquiries can mark turning points in the nation's history. Two of the most important concerned the situation of the working class (in the nineteenth century) and the conduct of the government-in-exile between 1940 and 1945.

In addition to the States General's various instruments of control over administration and public policy, it also exercises financial control of the executive branch. The budget consists of a series of bills covering each department and explained in a memorandum called the *millioenen nota*. The specialized committees of the Second Chamber discuss parts of the budget with the ministers concerned. The debates do not concern financial administration and there are few amendments concerning specific expenditures. Instead, the Chamber questions the government policy. The minister of finance plays a key role at this time, for all proposals to authorize expenditures must be discussed with him by the minister concerned. However, the cabinet is responsible for the budget as a whole, thus presenting the Chamber with the need to accept it in its entirety. Yet individual debates tend to concentrate on single issues, and there are the usual demands to increase or cut the budget in line with the pet peeves of a given member. If the States General votes to increase the budget of a given minister, he is not obliged to spend the money. Thus he cannot be directly controlled in this way. On the other hand, ministers must remain sensitive to the comments expressed in the budget debate, for they indicate the general orientation sought by the parliament in the conduct of government affairs.

A further power of the States General is the amendment

of the Dutch Constitution. A law may be proposed, almost always by the cabinet, stating that a constitutional amendment is necessary. Once this law is adopted, the parliament is automatically dissolved and new elections are held. Actually, when parliament is about to be dissolved in any case, such a law may be passed. The new parliament is considered a "constituent" assembly and it may adopt the amendment by a two-thirds vote of both chambers. Thus the election serves something of the purpose of a referendum on the proposed amendment, but with the other issues normally present in a campaign, the amendment may be a subsidiary matter.

THE SEPARATION OF POWERS

This review of the legislative process in the Netherlands and the instruments of control at the disposal of the States General underlines the most significant characteristic of the Dutch system of government—the separation of powers between the executive and the legislative. This will not seem surprising to an American student of political science, but it is quite unusual in most other countries. In the United States, the Congress wields a power virtually unheard of in any other nation of the world. It is not subject to the executive branch, and the executive cannot count on its automatic support. Instead the President must court the Congress to pass the legislation he wants, and he must be prepared to modify his proposals in order to obtain their passage. The Netherlands provides a rare example, perhaps the only other one in the modern world, of a legislature that is not only legally but in fact independent of the executive and thus plays a key role in the governmental process.

Independence of the States General

The reasons for the special position of the States General in the Dutch political system are numerous.

In legal theory, the cabinet is formed at the queen's command, and indeed the queen does exercise some personal discretion in choosing the prime minister designate. Once the ministers are appointed and resign from the States General, as is usually necessary, they alter their political style. They have assumed the responsibility of the nation's government and have left more partisan stands to the parliamentary parties. It should also be recalled that some "expert" members of the cabinet have never served in parliament and are relatively far removed from the political wars.

The civil service, which stands behind the cabinet and together with it constitutes the functioning executive branch of the government, has retained something of the aura of a governing class. Obviously the civil service is operated demo-cratically and is not closed to any class of society. But at the highest level, civil servants seem still to believe "that government should be for the people and from the people, but by civil servants." [3] The parliament, as the popular representative, is thus held at arm's length by the civil service.

The confessional parties are alleged to have an impact on the separation of powers between cabinet and States General. They each have a general philosophy of government that is fundamental to their very existence. Political parties are merely instruments of this philosophy, which dictates that government exists to serve the fundamental faith. This does not mean that the confessional parties are reluctant to assume power. But they distinguish between the authorities placed over the people by God, on the one hand, and the people and its representatives, on the other. This implies that the parties are not to intervene in the inner workings of government but to sit back and wait for its proposals. In addition, it raises political debate to the level of theology, which, in itself, allows for less discussion about authority. This explanation should, of course, be kept in perspective. In essence, it means that Dutch political life is subconsciously affected by these considerations of hierarchy.

The party system itself is a powerful influence on the separation between cabinet and parliament in the Netherlands. With the distinctions among parties and their inability and lack of desire to create larger political groups by compromise,

[3] Hans Daalder, "The Relation between Cabinet and Parliament in the Netherlands" (Paper presented to the International Political Science Association, 1958), p. 12.

no party or group of parties sharing a basically similar philosophy is able to find a clear majority for governing. A purely confessional coalition is unlikely because of mistrust among these parties and their generally centrist and weak program orientation. A coalition among nonconfessional parties would probably not achieve a majority. Thus the remaining solution is a combination of confessional and nonconfessional parties. But this inevitability does not make the formation of a coalition any easier, because each potential partner has good reasons for not compromising its basic position in order to come to an agreement. In the last analysis, the party's unique position is what it uses to attract voters from other parties, especially those with which it is likely to join in a coalition. For the centrist confessional parties, there remains the problem of which major option offered by the nonconfessional parties is the best choice. Overenthusiasm for any option may encourage voters to shift their own support to another party. Thus the parties must be equally ready for an alliance with one side or the other.

This situation results in a tendency on the part of the parties and their parliamentary delegations to stick as closely as possible to distinctly party principles and to compromise as little as possible. They accept the need for the party to make some compromises in order to form a coalition, but they are reluctant to give away more than is necessary. Thus the agreed cabinet program is the result of much hard editing and is subject to continual scrutiny to see that the permissible compromises are not being stretched too far. And proposals outside the program are not likely to find easy going in the States General. Thus there is a tug-of-war between the parties in parliament seeking to maintain philosophical purity and the party representatives in the cabinet, who find themselves facing the challenge of governing a nation. This leads to a distinctly different approach between cabinet and parliament.

The position of two parties, the Christian Historicals and the Catholics, merits special attention. As indicated earlier, the CHU is somewhat more loosely organized than the other major political parties, and its members have less of a coherent philosophy to unite them. Yet the party is in the middle of the political spectrum and often takes part in governing coalitions. It is difficult to know, however, what the party, either in the cabinet or in parliament, is likely to demand because of its fluid political position. The Catholics, on the other hand, play a clear role in cabinet formation: they want to be part of the coalition and have been in every regular cabinet since World War I. If they refused to participate, the nation could only be governed by a "technocrat" cabinet. But the Catholics, fighting the belief that the Dutch nation is basically Protestant, do not always push their political strength to the utmost. Others in coalitions tend to take Catholic support for granted and make few concessions to the KVP. The main Catholic leaders have thus preferred to remain at the head of the parliamentary Catholic party and outside the cabinet. This helps strengthen the parliament in its balance with the cabinet.

Still another factor in the independence of cabinet and parliament stems from the lack of party discipline on the British model. Although members of the party do depend on support from the national leadership in order to be placed on the electoral list, they are not in the same position of absolute dependence as in Britain or other continental nations. This is due in part to the Dutch mentality, which includes a considerable streak of independence and respect for the individual. Thus it is simply harder to impose an intellectual discipline, and others are likely to admit that any position may have some merit to it and deserve more than rejection out of hand.

If the party went so far as to impose discipline, it would run another risk in any case. A dissident party member could simply refuse to accept his expulsion and decide to run his own ticket in the elections. Defections of certain elements from major parties are not unheard of, and small parties are continually being formed. If the dissident represented any opinion that had attracted some support, he might well draw voters away from the main party. Hence it may be desirable to keep the dissident element within the party, maintain the voting strength of the party, and seek to work out differences within the family. The independence of the individual member of parliament contributes to the independence of the institution, for the cabinet cannot always be sure of the votes it can count on with regard to a given proposal.

Relations between cabinet and States General

What, then, is the state of relations between the cabinet and the States General? In simple terms, there is clear separation between the two, but, at the same time, they are inextricably linked in the governing process.

The parties themselves are tied to their own programs, which may prevent them from being adequate vehicles of public opinion. Elections in general do not result in major swings from one party to another, but the growth of the Democrats '66 movement and the Boerenpartij may represent something of a change in this trend.

Cabinets are difficult to build and difficult to destroy. The process of seeking informateurs and formateurs and their search for an acceptable cabinet formula is difficult, which in itself discourages frequent efforts to topple the cabinet. The carefully balanced program is likely to be respected by all parties. The members of the cabinet are themselves chosen by the parties to ensure that none will be too overtly opposed to their interests.

The job of the cabinet is to have the agreed program passed by the States General. The method of operation is up to the cabinet itself, as are decisions on dealing with new problems not included in the program. The cabinet may, of course, be subject to party pressures. The parties publish their views, and the politically oriented press prints the differing views within the party on issues before the cabinet. Indeed, ministers may seek to provoke a party clamor in order to strengthen their own position. Yet the cabinet remains a distinct body and it must take a decision in common. Indeed, personal differences within the cabinet may play a greater role than party influences.

Parties act differently in the cabinet and in the parliament. This results from the previously mentioned difference in roles—the cabinet is to govern the nation; the States General is to represent the collective interests of the nation.

Despite the considerable independence and power of the parliament, there is little doubt that, as in all modern democratic states, the executive branch has come to weigh more heavily in the governmental balance. This is part of the cause for demands to strengthen the States General, particularly in terms of increased candidate contacts with the people.

One of the major reasons for the shift toward the executive is the need to be able to make decisions quickly and without having divulged all of the cabinet's intentions well in advance through public debate. Thus the parliament is induced to lay down general policy guidelines and delegate some of its legislative powers to the cabinet.

The complexity of governing in a modern society also helps build up the influence of the cabinet, which can call on civil servants and experts with far greater ease than the parliament. The parties have tried to lessen this advantage somewhat by including on their electoral lists experts, who have not necessarily taken an extremely active part in party activities, but who can be counted on to support it and to provide it with needed information.

The cabinet must often consult major groups—Calvinist, Catholic, and neutral (Liberal or Socialist)—in the preparation of a bill. The Social and Economic Council may have rendered an opinion that led the cabinet to propose legislation. In either case the cabinet is extremely reluctant to tamper with an existing compromise, even to please the parties. Thus the parliament may well have to acquiesce in compromises made outside the Chamber. This situation is not, however, as usual in other continental countries, such as Belgium, where the Parliament may become little more than a rubber stamp.

Finally, the extensive participation of the Netherlands in international organizations, particularly the European Community, removes many matters from the direct purview of the States General. The cabinet is responsible for carrying on the negotiations, and it cannot always keep in close contact with the parliament. When an agreement is reached with a number of other nations, the parliament is most unlikely to overturn it by vetoing the action of the Dutch representative. The fact that the Netherlands is a small country further discourages the States General from upsetting the international apple cart. Once again the cabinet gains powers in the process.

This, then, is the system by which laws are passed and public policy created in the Netherlands. It is a virtually unique system, which, for all its weaknesses in representing the popular will, provides for an effective system of checks and balances, a rarity in modern government.

SEVEN
THE ECLIPSE
OF PARLIAMENT
Policy making
in Belgium

The national government in Belgium is the principal instrument for resolving the crises that periodically threaten the nation's fabric. In each case, the government has found a workable compromise, sufficiently displeasing to all parties to make it acceptable.

THE EXECUTIVE BRANCH

An initial observation on government in Belgium is that the executive branch exercises many of the powers that should normally be in the domain of the Parliament. Yet even this is a formalist explanation of the way in which the political system works. The national debate on any major issue extends far beyond the formal political structure, thus requiring a solution to be sought among the various major groups in the population. For this task, the cabinet is obviously better qualified and equipped than the Parliament, and it profits from its role as mediator to strengthen its own position in the political system.

The king

Like the Netherlands, Belgium has a constitutional monarchy and a democratic form of government. There are, however, major differences of style between the Belgian and the Dutch monarchy. One of the reasons that prompted Belgium to opt for independence from the Netherlands was the imperious style of the Dutch king William. The Belgians were determined to give their king a more democratic aspect and create what one member of the national Constituent Assembly called "a constitutional monarchy, resting on the most liberal, the most democratic and the most republican principles." [1] The result was a monarch designated as king of the Belgians—a leader of the people—but not king of Belgium—not the sovereign of the nation.

The king's role has been twofold. He is the natural symbol of national unity, the figure around whom all elements and representatives of all parties can rally as a sign of their support for the Belgian nation. This role can be accomplished relatively passively, although most of the Belgian kings have been very active in promoting the well-being of their country and have attracted the warm support of the people. Indeed, the existence of the monarchy seems to fill a need in Belgium for some subject of popular enthusiasm, and there is no republican movement at all in the country. In this respect, the Belgian royal family seems one of the most secure remaining in the world. The second part of the king's role has been a manifestation of the personalities of the various occupants of the throne. With the probable exception of the present king, Baudouin, each of the others has had a personal policy, discernibly independent of the government and having a direct impact on the nation.

The so-called royal question, discussed earlier, marked a turning point in the relation of the king to government and probably ended much of his independent role. The interpretation that the Constitution gave some powers directly to the king, particularly the post of commander of the army, probably originated with King Albert, who acquired the reputation as savior of his country for his military opposition to the German invasion in World War I. In addition, the position of Leopold III was strengthened during the 1930s by the chaos of the

[1] André Mast, *Les Pays du Benelux* (Paris: Pichon et Durand-Auzias, 1960), p. 84.

parties and the weak cabinets. Thus he was able to play a leading role in shaping Belgian foreign policy, and he chose to take personal leadership of the army during the eighteen-day Belgian battle in World War II. In this situation, the distinction between the constitutional myth that the king has some powers and the reality that indicates that they are not personal powers, but are exercised by the cabinet, became obscured, and the cabinet was in part at fault. Traditionally, the king is inviolable, and the cabinet is supposed to take the responsibility for actions in his name. The situation developed that the king in fact was taking the responsibility for the cabinet, and after the policy of neutrality proved a failure, the king was not able to remain in office.

The affair led eventually to a reexamination of the royal prerogatives, but this resulted in no major changes in the constitutional rules or political practices governing the king. Nonetheless, the relative discretion exercised by King Baudouin reflects a change in style as a result of the "royal question." A report on the royal prerogatives, issued in 1949, stressed that king and cabinet might differ, but, in the last analysis, the king would have to bow before the will of the people as expressed through the parliamentary majority supporting the cabinet. The report added that the king sheds his inviolability when he acts without prior approval by the cabinet. Finally, the report said that if the king takes personal command of the army, he is no longer able to act as chief of state.

At present the actual powers of the king are limited to those exercised at the time of the dissolution of Parliament and during the formation of a new cabinet. The king does not, of course, decide on his own volition that the Parliament should be dissolved. In a situation where the cabinet has fallen because it has lost the support of a majority in Parliament, the outgoing prime minister calls on the king and requests him to dissolve the legislature. The king is not bound to accept this advice if he believes that a new cabinet can be formed without elections. In any case, the king may judge when it is opportune to dissolve the Parliament, although the political situation often does not leave him any real choice.

The king begins his consultations in meetings with the presidents of the two houses of Parliament, the outgoing prime minister, and the presidents of the three "traditional" parties. The king does not call on leaders of the other parties, whatever their role has been in the fall of the cabinet or their strength following elections. Finally he designates an *informateur,* who is to examine the possibility of finding a program that will be backed by a parliamentary majority in the shortest possible time. Often the informateur will become the *formateur*—the prime minister designate of the new cabinet, if he succeeds in finding a satisfactory compromise among two of the three major parties. If he does not, the king may designate some other political leader to try to form a cabinet. Even in this process the king may play a role, using his personal prestige to persuade politicians to take part in a cabinet or not to oppose its formation. He may help in the actual formation of the cabinet by urging some personalities to join it. Thus at this stage the king plays an entirely independent role, although he must not lose sight of the political realities of the moment.

The cabinet

The cabinet that is named by the king must present its program to Parliament, where the majority is certain to support it. The cabinet that will carry out the program is an amalgam of the country's political and social forces. The cabinet will probably be known by two names, that of the prime minister, who is a member of the senior party of the coalition, and that of the vice prime minister, a member of the junior party. Actually, the Constitution makes no provision for such posts, but they have grown up over time. Obviously the prime minister becomes identified in the public mind as the head of the cabinet, and he is its unchallenged leader. He takes great care that the vice prime minister is associated with him, so that the public is made continually aware that both parties to the coalition agree on government policy. The remainder of the members of the cabinet are in charge of government departments, as is the vice prime minister. The cabinet will usually include several officials bearing the title "minister-state secretary," not foreseen by the Constitution, but indicating a junior minister. It should be noted that the cabinet is divided exactly equally according to the first language spoken by its members. Occasionally, a minister from

Brussels is counted as bilingual. The regular use of French at cabinet meetings, held each Friday morning at the Parliament building, has given way to simultaneous interpretation of both French and Dutch.

Members of the cabinet are usually members of one of the two houses of the Parliament, and they are not obliged to give up their seats when appointed to the cabinet. It is possible for experts to be appointed to serve in the cabinet who have not been elected to Parliament. The cabinet as a whole is politically responsible for the acts of each of its members.

The cabinet contains several smaller bodies that are of considerable importance in the formulation of government policy. The "Restricted Cabinet" is an executive committee, the successor of earlier organs known as the Inner Cabinet and the Political Coordination Committee. This body examines in advance questions that will come before the full cabinet, seeking any potential problem that may arise in the plenary meeting. The Restricted Cabinet is especially important when the budget is prepared, as it formulates proposals for the cabinet on each department's budget.

An institution that rivals the cabinet itself in importance is the Ministerial Committee on Economic and Social Coordination. With the prime minister as chairman, as in the case of the Restricted Cabinet, this committee is composed of about half the members of the cabinet. Its task is to prepare the guidelines for the cabinet's policy in the economic, social, and financial sectors. This is the heart of government policy in Belgium, and each cabinet is certain to be called upon to prepare an overall orientation on these matters at least once in its term. The public watches with great interest the work of this committee as it prepares guidelines that the cabinet and Parliament are almost certain to accept.

A third group is the Ministerial Committee on Budget Management and the Civil Service, also under the chairmanship of the prime minister and comprising more than one quarter of the cabinet. This body controls the budget and administration and ensures that public investment schemes, adopted by the Committee on Economic and Social Coordination, are carried out.

Finally, the Ministerial Committee on Scientific Policy, also headed by the prime minister, examines draft legislation concerning science and technology and is in charge of suggesting the broad policy outlines in these sectors. These matters are of greatest importance in Belgium, which has fallen somewhat behind other western European countries in this area. Thus the prime minister also in effect serves as minister of science, although no such formal post exists. The result is the relatively unusual situation of a prime minister also occupying himself with a specific portfolio.

The cabinet governs in place of the king between his death and the oath taking of his successor.

Other executive organs

Other organs, created by law or the Constitution, play a role as part of the executive branch of government. In 1946 a Council of State was created with primarily judicial functions. It does, however, have a legislative section that is to examine most pieces of proposed legislation and royal decrees and to render an opinion to the cabinet. It is also consulted by the president of either house of Parliament concerning proposed laws. This body, composed of experienced politicians, is able to inform the cabinet and Parliament whether a proposed law or decree will be constitutional and whether all of its provisions are legally acceptable or must be redrafted. In a position to give technical advice, the Council of State is removed from the hurly-burly of daily politics. It should not be confused with ministers of state, the nation's elder statesmen, who occasionally advise the king on the nation's political situation.

The complexity of the problems facing the cabinet and the need to consult a wide variety of interests in the formulation of policy led to the establishment of a considerable number of national consultative committees. These committees are constituted by the cabinet and provide it with technical information. Members of the committees, representatives of various interest groups, are made to believe that the cabinet is listening to them. At the same time, a problem may be buried, temporarily at least, by reference to one of these committees.

Two of the most important of these committees are the

Central Economic Council and the National Labor Council. In composition, the first, representing industry, labor, and artisans, and the second, representing employers and workers, parallel the Dutch Social and Economic Council and the Labor Foundation. But the Belgian groups wield much less power, partly because they need not obligatorily be consulted by the cabinet or Parliament. The National Labor Council can regulate wages and conditions in a single industry, but it cannot deal with the economy as a whole. At that level, the cabinet itself steps in. Both organs were able to play an unofficial role when, in 1955, the workers demanded the reduction of the legal work week. But it was the cabinet that acted to introduce progressively the shorter work week, with the consultative organs left far in the background.

The relative failure of the consultative committees in Belgium reveals something of the method of operation of both the cabinet and Parliament. The cabinet prefers to rely on its own experts for technical advice and on the union and management leadership directly for soundings on their possible attitude toward proposed action. Thus the cabinet finds little need for an additional body of wise men. In addition, the cabinet can turn to the Council of State for technical and political advice. The Parliament, on the other hand, considers itself the representative of the nation and consequently believes it is not required to consult other groups to determine public sentiment. The Parliament also does not have the taste for a battle of experts, pitting those of the advisory committees against those of the cabinet. At the same time, the Parliament, or the majority at least, is required to show some confidence in the cabinet. As a result the social and economic forces of the nation cannot be channeled into an institutionalized pattern of cooperation with the cabinet, which makes for a far less coherent and manageable system than in the Netherlands, but spares any group from being accused of having "sold out" to the system.

The administration

The administration, a part of the executive branch, is a continual subject of public scrutiny and debate. This stems as much from the public image of the national administration as from any other factor. Most Belgians appear to believe that the national administration is too large, that it is not staffed by the most competent people available, and that it is organized inefficiently. The general public attitude is thus not favorable to the public administration, and this is reinforced by the feeling of frustration a Belgian experiences in his dealings with his government.

This public view is probably somewhat more negative than is warranted, but nonetheless contains a large element of truth. The Belgian administration is more than an accurate portrayal of the divided society in which it exists. It also suffers from its struggle with the individual Belgian, who is determined to obtain full vindication of his "rights" in his relations with administration. The administration must allow for a linguistic balance, which makes for excessive size and slowness. Duplication is the rule because officials of both language groups perform the same function. The obvious solution would be bilingualism, which does exist in some departments, but this tends to favor the Flemings (who often know French) and to disadvantage the French-speaking Belgians (who often do not know Dutch). A Walloon official can favor his part of the country, because he feels that he will be replaced sooner or later by a Fleming who will then favor Flanders. This results in a kind of pendulum effect in some ministries. It also hampers coordination among ministries, which may be headed by civil servants of different language groups.

Appointments to administrative positions are often determined more by political allegiance than by ability. Thus even a university degree and professional experience may be outweighed by party loyalty. The result is to drive the cream of university graduates into business rather than public service and to lower the public's opinion of politics in general. The public has become inured to a kind of spoils system that gives the vacant posts to the party in power. It may be argued that this results in a distribution of posts among all major parties, as each has its chance periodically to serve in the cabinet, but this does not assure that the views of all political elements in the administration will be taken into account, for the governing parties tend to rely on their "own" officials. It is interesting that in terms of recruitment the Ministry of Finance adheres best to objective criteria; this ministry has the reputation of being the most efficient in the country.

The actual size of the national administration, estimated at some 213,000 in 1965, is not as great as many Belgians believe. It has nonetheless increased rapidly—for two reasons. First is the proliferation of tasks the central authority has been called upon to assume in modern society. In Belgium a number of quasi-official authorities have been created, staffed by civil servants. Second, expansion has become a way of solving many of the nation's political problems. When faced with a conflict, the cabinet will often expand government services to each of the conflicting groups. This inflates the national budget and creates additional posts in the civil service.

Officials at the highest level of administration tend to shed some of their links to their party or linguistic group and appear to adopt a more national attitude. This may be a reflection of their regular contact with ministers, also imbued with something of a national perspective, and of the increasing sense of professionalism that results from years in the civil service. These become the regular advisers of the cabinet and play much the same role as the civil servants in the Netherlands. But this class is small. It does extend into the Ministry of Foreign Affairs, which in some ways is distinct from the remainder of the national administration. The concept of bilingualism, for example, is an accepted rule for members of the diplomatic service.

This sketch of the mechanisms and institutions of the executive branch only hints at the considerable powers of this element of the governing system in Belgium. It must be viewed in comparison with the legislative branch before a complete idea of its actual powers is possible.

THE LEGISLATURE

Legislative power in Belgium is exercised in law by the king, the Senate, and the Chamber of Representatives, and in fact by the latter two, which together constitute the Belgian Parliament. The cabinet, acting in the name of the king, sits within Parliament, with the full right to participate in debates and to vote, and its presence helps shape the legislature's character.

From the outset, the Chamber was considered to be the direct representative of the nation; thus, in theory at least, it stands at the summit of the Belgian political institutions. The Senate was, in the early years of the kingdom, open only to the most wealthy citizens and served as a brake on the more "popular" Chamber. The Senate, beginning to decline in importance in the first part of the twentieth century, was accorded the power to initiate financial legislation, just as the cabinet and the Chamber. This marked an improvement in its fortunes, and it has become more of a partner of the Chamber than in the past. But it clearly has remained a subsidiary house, and its atmosphere is considerably more calm than that of the Chamber. Major bills are still introduced in the Chamber before they are presented to the Senate.

Both bodies had to be chosen more democratically as suffrage was extended. During much of the nineteenth century, the Chamber was chosen by only 2 percent of the population and the Senate by even less. Since the introduction of full suffrage (women's voting rights since 1948), both houses have been elected, directly or indirectly, on the basis of the greatest democracy possible.

When the parliamentary session opens, generally in November, there is none of the pomp of a speech from the throne by the king. The cabinet does not, in fact, publish a program for the year, covering major aspects of its policy. And in case the cabinet should wish to make a general policy statement to the Parliament, its spokesmen are members of Parliament with the right to speak at any time. Although this kind of overlapping of functions is permitted, members of Parliament cannot ordinarily hold other posts where the state pays the salary. Parliamentary debates are open to the public, although discussions within the committees may be closed. The two houses do not meet in joint session for any purposes laid down by the Constitution.

Composition of Parliament

The 212 members of the Chamber of Representatives are chosen by direct election every four years, or more freqently if the Parliament has been dissolved by the king. The Senate members are designated in four different ways. A number equivalent to half the members of the Chamber—106—are elected directly to the Senate at the same time as the Chamber. The Provincial Councils name one senator for each 200,000 inhabitants, with a minimum of three for a province and a senator for any number more than 125,000 after the final 200,000 slice. These senators are designated by the Provincial Councils, chosen at the same general elections as the Chamber. A number of "coopted" senators equal to half the "provincial senators" is then chosen by the duly elected members of the Senate. Finally, male members of the royal family in line to succeed to the throne are members of the Senate with the right to vote, although they do not exercise it.

The Senate is thus chosen according to a considerably different process than the Chamber and, in addition, according to widely differing criteria. All citizens over twenty-five are eligible to become members of the Chamber. The Constitution lays down no fewer than eighteen categories, in any one of which a person must qualify in order to be elected to the Senate, and he must be forty years of age. The original intention in creating these categories was to allow in the Senate only the most responsible representatives of society. Among the groups are former high-ranking officers in the army and navy, heads of industrial enterprises with more than 100 workers or a farm with more than 123.5 acres, and taxpayers who pay at least 3000 francs ($60) in direct taxes annually. These classifications may have had some meaning in the past; they have little practical importance now. Almost any person over forty who might conceivably want to enter the Senate could easily fulfill one of these criteria.

The Senate is virtually the mirror image, on a reduced scale, of the Chamber, but there are a few slight differences. Voters show a 2 to 3 percent variation in the voting for members of the two houses, probably attributable to the factor of personality of the candidates. In addition, the less-populated areas are better represented in the Senate than in the Chamber, which is chosen on a strict basis of population. A few constitutional powers, such as the right to impeach ministers (Chamber) or the right to nominate judges of the highest court (Senate), are reserved to a single house.

The need for the bicameral system in Belgium may appear doubtful, with both houses of a virtually identical composition. The traditional answer, as in other bicameral systems, is that the upper house can correct the mistakes found in the legislation passed, perhaps too hastily, by the lower house. The Senate does fulfill this function, but the record indicates that it sends bills back to the Chamber in less than 10 percent of the cases. But the bicameral system does permit for a more extended public debate of the issues. The discussion in the Senate is virtually certain to take place at a different time and in a different atmosphere than in the Chamber and is widely reported in the press. Thus the people get a second chance to hear the arguments, some perhaps new, and to react.

Most members of Parliament continue with their professions (see Table 7–1) while in public office, but they must sub-

Table 7–1   Professions of the members of Parliament (Chamber and Senate), 1964

	Number	Percent
Lawyers, judges	96	24.8
Doctors, pharmacists, veterinarians	9	2.3
Engineers, architects	17	4.4
Businessmen, bankers	27	7.0
Professors	13	3.4
Journalists, writers	20	5.2
Small businessmen, independents	19	4.9
Farmers	9	2.3
Secondary teachers	17	4.4
Primary teachers	8	2.1
White-collar workers	53	13.7
Social workers and officers of social and workers' organizations	46	11.9
Labor union secretaries	31	8.0
Workers	4	1.0
Pensions and no other job	18	4.6
Total	387	100.0

Source: F. Debuyst, *La Fonction Parlementaire en Belgique* (Brussels: CRISP, 1967), p. 95.

stantially reduce their activities—probably more than in the Netherlands. Almost all members of Parliament commute from their homes to Brussels, which enables them to keep in touch with their job and constituents.

The apparent underrepresentation of workers is not as acute as it might appear, for many of the members began their careers as workers. Participation in political life tends to have an influence on the development of the individual's career. The strong position occupied by journalists and teachers indicates a broad public acceptance of these two professions. The journalists have often been writers for newspapers with a party orientation before coming to the Parliament. The high representation of the legal profession goes far to explain the style of the Chamber, which is often a raucous debating society, with a relatively high premium being placed on speaking style. With so many trained orators and legalists, however, it is often difficult to maintain order. The Belgian Chamber reflects the rough-and-tumble of the more Latin style, in sharp contrast with the more orderly "Northern" style in the Netherlands. As for education, almost 60 percent of the members of the Chamber have a university education, which compares favorably with most western European standards, although it is well below the 84 percent level of the United States Senate.[2]

Loyalty to party and constituency

Members of Parliament can be expected to show allegiance to their party and to their constituency. The party has chosen them to appear on its electoral list, and the central party organization has the right to expect their loyalty. In addition, members of parties represented in the cabinet may feel that it is desirable to keep their party in office as long as possible in order to improve the chances of passage of the legislation they consider important. On the other hand, whatever the merits of a given proposal, the minority can be counted upon to oppose with great discipline, this being the only way of bringing about the fall of the cabinet and thus creating an opportunity to enter the coalition. Defections do take place, but they are relatively rare. In recent years, they have resulted from the

[2] Debuyst, pp. 109–110.

reorientation of the Liberal party, which attracted a certain number of conservative Catholic politicians and those dissatisfied with the PSC/CVP structure, who were no longer barred from Liberal party membership on confessional grounds. The language question has also drawn members away from the "traditional" parties to the extremist groups. But these defections rarely take place during a session. It is much more usual for realignments to take place when the election campaign is in progress.

Party discipline was at the heart of the cabinet crisis of 1968. The PSC/CVP parliamentary delegation split along linguistic lines on the stand the party in the cabinet should take on maintaining the French-speaking section at the Catholic University of Louvain, in Flemish territory. The PSC/CVP ministers were unwilling to demand the expulsion of the French-speaking section immediately, and the Flemish parliamentarians then demanded that the Flemish PSC/CVP ministers quit the cabinet. When they did, it fell. The fundamental question of language acquired in this case a far higher priority than party discipline, and it was the party as a whole and the cabinet that had to pay the price.

Loyalty to the constituency is a natural outgrowth of the individual electoral lists for each district; there is no national list in Belgium. Thus candidates are chosen and make their appeal partially on the basis of local interests. This is particularly true for the language question, where candidates will try to sense the temper of their voters and respond to it. In 1968, for example, the Socialist party in Brussels placed two Flemish candidates far down on their list. These candidates then chose to run on their own Socialist list and were elected handily. This in turn led to the creation of a Flemish-Socialist organization in Brussels, thus indicating a greater Socialist response to the demands of the Flemish population of the city than had been true in the past.

The legislative process

The chief function of the Parliament is to pass laws, according to the legislative procedure laid down by law and practice. Formally, virtually all proposals originate with the cabinet. In preparing its proposals the cabinet inevitably consults the major interest groups concerned, often through the intermediary of the parties that compose the coalition. Then follows a series of parallel negotiations between the party representatives and the party leadership. The dual roles of the members of the cabinet indicate a fundamental difference between cabinet and party activities. The debate within the cabinet may be relatively relaxed, for the ministers gradually come to have a similar view of the national interest on many major questions. The parties, on the other hand, have a better-defined program on certain basic questions. They also reflect their related interest groups, which are even less willing than the parties to make concessions of principle. Thus the alternative for the parties may well be either to support a cabinet proposal, perhaps with some modifications, or to run the risk of toppling the coalition because it was willing to stray too far from its base of support. As the case studies that follow illustrate, this is the heart of the legislative process. If the cabinet, majority parties, and interest groups can come to terms, there is little doubt that the proposed legislation will pass Parliament.

Unless an urgent matter is under consideration, the cabinet consults the Council of State before submitting a bill to Parliament. Bills go to either house, although most often to the Chamber, where they are referred to the competent committees. There is generally a committee in each house for each of the government departments. The responsible minister and his assistants appear before the committees in both the Chamber and the Senate and are called upon to defend the proposal. The debate, however, usually holds few surprises, as does the report of the committee. Majority and minority views are pitted against each other. The report is sent to the full house where a similar debate, once again with ministerial participation, takes place. Once it is adopted, possibly with a few minor amendments acceptable to the government, it is sent on to the other house, where the same procedure is repeated. The bill as adopted is sent to the king for his signature. There is, of course, no doubt of either his personal approval or that of the cabinet that has guided the bill through its legislative course.

One of the major complaints against this procedure is the length of time required for the consideration of most legislation. Some administrative measures have been adopted to speed up the process. In the Chamber, permanent sections have been created that can act in the name of the Parliament as a whole. Any member is free to attend if the section is considering a matter of interest to him, and the plenary session retains the right to decide on all issues. In addition, on proposals of great importance and urgency, the Parliament has shown itself able to act with considerable speed.

An examination of several major cases of decision making in recent years will indicate more about the nature of the process and the relatively subsidiary role of the Parliament.[3]

Decision making: the schools question

A particularly good example of decision making in Belgium was the "Schools Pact" of 1958. It grew out of the conflict between church-related and secular groups and concerned the secondary schools, just as the first "Schools War" in the nineteenth century had concerned the primary schools. In 1950 the PSC/CVP was returned to Parliament with an absolute majority; thus it was able to govern without forming a coalition and could enact much of its program concerning the schools. This program provided for extensive subsidies to all schools, but in such a way as to favor the growth of private education and the continuation of the public or lay schools in a subsidiary position in the nation as a whole. Mixed commissions were created to render opinions on the programs both of the new official schools and of Church-related schools seeking official approval. It should be recalled that the PSC/CVP was no longer a religious party at this time. But in its basic program, as an obvious bid to maintain its traditional electorate, the party had favored this schools program, aimed at strengthening the private (mainly Catholic) schools.

The Socialists and the Liberals in the opposition attacked these laws, because of the high subsidies provided for private schools. In addition, they regarded the creation of mixed commissions as a wedge opening the way for Church control of

---

[3] Case studies drawn from J. Meynaud, *La Décision Politique en Belgique* (Paris: Armand Colin, 1965).

public as well as private education. These parties ran on a program of opposition to the schools laws and the teacher-appointment procedures of the PSC/CVP cabinet. They did not oppose aid to Church schools, but complained of the inferior position of public schools and the fact that they did not exist in sufficient numbers at all levels. The 1964 elections ended the PSC/CVP majority and brought into office a Socialist-Liberal coalition.

In the four ensuing years, the pendulum moved in the opposite direction. The cabinet announced it would cut subsidies to private schools. The PSC/CVP and the Catholic Church united in remostrating against the proposed "anticlerical" measures, and violence threatened to break out in the streets of Brussels. The cabinet nonetheless pushed through its major schools bill, which cut subsidies. The cabinet accepted a number of amendments in Parliament, including one giving the state the right to decide if there were a need for new (mainly public) schools. In the 1958 elections, both sides demanded freedom of choice for parents in the selection of schools, each feeling it would gain strength by choice unconstrained by Church or law. The PSC/CVP, in a shift of position, did announce in favor of free education for all until age eighteen. The elections resulted in an absolute majority for the PSC/CVP in the Senate, but not in the Chamber.

Some elements in the PSC/CVP wanted new elections immediately, in hopes of strengthening their position in Parliament, but these political conservatives did not prevail. The party chiefs recognized that they could not continue the war of schools legislation and thought it best to try "surprise by moderation." Unable to form a coalition, the PSC/CVP agreed to govern as a minority. At the same time, the Socialists began to feel that the battlefield was not well chosen and decided to avoid new elections, fearing they might lose in Flanders. A movement within the Socialist party began for dialogue with the Catholics. The claim was generally rejected that Socialist influence could be spread in Flanders through the public schools. Thus within the two largest parties there was a growing disenchantment with the issue, mainly because it blocked any progress toward economic development. The Liberals, anxious to get back into the cabinet, seemed ready for peace as well. The problem for all three was how to find a procedural way to settle the schools question.

The PSC/CVP minister of public instruction proposed the creation of a national committee to discuss the problem, and the Socialists agreed, insisting that it be composed of members of Parliament. This procedure was adopted. Why did Parliament agree to this extraparliamentary body? First, a desire existed to create a pact, a kind of national agreement, rather than merely to pass a traditional law. In addition, the settlement had to have some degree of permanence, requiring the support of all three parties, no matter what the current coalition might be. This was to be a political, not a legal settlement, and hence the negotiations were to be on a political text, not one susceptible of passage as a law. Outside Parliament, committee members might be more willing to retreat from their public positions, and it was hoped that the committee would work outside the glare of publicity. Then, too, if agreement were reached, the parties could be asked to ratify it, forcing the members of Parliament to approve the accord without further debate. Finally, the questions to be discussed were highly technical, beyond the grasp of many parliamentarians.

Thus, two months after the national elections, a tripartite national committee of eleven members of Parliament was constituted. A draft was placed before it by the minister of public instruction, and a second committee, composed of technical experts, was appointed to supply additional information. With Parliament in summer recess, the cabinet was spared intensive questioning by members who might have opposed the national committee. The political parties left the negotiations in the hands of their representatives on the committee, although the PSC/CVP members were in regular consultation with high-ranking officials of the Roman Catholic Church. Finally, in November 1958, the Schools Pact was initialed by the members of the national committee, which had completed its work in three months.

The agreement gave satisfaction to the demands of both sides, largely through massive spending for the educational system. The accord, signed on November 6, 1958, was ratified by the three parties ten days later. The PSC/CVP extraordinary

Congress supported it unanimously, the Socialists voted in its favor 659 against 231 with 18 abstentions, and the Liberals' Permanent Committee gave it a 117-to-6 victory with 4 abstentions. The Schools Pact was formally signed in the prime minister's office four days after ratification. An additional four months were required before the Chamber received a bill prepared by the Permanent Committee for the execution of the Schools Pact. In May it was adopted with only the Communists opposing in both the Chamber and the Senate. The pact, once signed by the king, opened a twelve-year period of "truce" between the two sides that was virtually certain to last indefinitely and to settle a major national problem.

The most outstanding feature of the process of adoption of the Schools Pact was, of course, the exclusion of the Parliament from the legislative process. The actual vote by the Parliament had no real importance and came well after the flames of controversy had died out. Thus the "representative of the nation" was shunted aside in order to allow extraconstitutional institutions to arrive at a solution to the national education problem. Some of the reasons for recourse to a national committee have already been mentioned. The most important of these was the desire to obtain the accord of the three major parties, virtually impossible in the Parliament where the rules of the game provide for a continual struggle between majority and opposition. Parliamentarians could not be counted on to abstain from behaving in a "demagogic" or "partisan" manner. Even after the text was agreed upon, the party leaders did not turn to the parliamentary delegations to determine whether they would approve it. Instead they consulted the parties themselves, leaving the members of Parliament no room for maneuver. The party leaders undoubtedly believed that they were acting in a more democratic fashion by turning to the party meetings, for they were composed of a greater number of people, directly representing a wide variety of interests. In effect, the "representative of the nation"—the Parliament—enjoyed this title more in theory than in practice.

The Schools Pact itself illustrated one of the legislative practices of Belgium: the use of a "truce." This is acceptable to all major parties when they wish to focus their attention on other problems and to place a divisive national issue on ice. The hope is that "it is only the temporary that lasts," and the truce will stretch on indefinitely. Although the parties have tied their hands for several years in the future, they leave themselves the option of returning to partisan politics once the truce has expired. For example, a two-year language "truce" operated satisfactorily, but when it ended in 1968, the parties chose to readopt full freedom of action.

Decision making: economic expansion

Another major national question that illustrates aspects of the decision-making system was the so-called Single Law on Economic Expansion, Social Progress, and Financial Improvement. This law grew out of a prolonged period of deficit in the national budget and a sizeable increase in the national debt. The cabinet of Gaston Eyskens, a PSC/CVP-Liberal coalition, was already under heavy fire in 1960, when the problem of the Single Law arose. A wide gap existed between the labor-union element of the PSC/CVP and the conservatives of the Liberal party. The Catholic labor union was unhappy about being so closely linked with this cabinet, while the Socialist labor union remained entirely free to make the demands it saw fit. The Catholic union experienced a high degree of militancy, despite the PSC/CVP coalition with the Liberals. Eventually the Catholic union was led to cooperate with the Socialist union.

The cabinet's problems were increased in July 1960 with the crisis over Congolese independence, and Eyskens considered reshaping his cabinet, while the king thought its outright resignation would be desirable. But Eyskens remained and obtained the support of the Parliament, partly because of the Congo troubles, for an austerity program. The cabinet was reshuffled in the fall, a vote of confidence was obtained, and Eyskens published in November the proposed Single Law. He announced to the PSC/CVP parliamentary group that, the project having been approved by the cabinet after consultation with the Catholic labor union leadership and industry, they would have to take it or leave it. The compromise made both sides unhappy; the Liberals did not like the tax increases, and the union elements of the PSC/CVP did not approve wholeheartedly the cut in spending.

Opposition both in the ranks of the Catholic union and the Socialist union mounted. From the end of November, the Socialist union initiated a series of strikes that began to assume the proportions of a general strike. The Catholic union finally decided not to follow the strike movement, partly because the cabinet had made a gesture to it by delaying the scheduled linguistic census of 1960. The Flemish PSC/CVP labor leaders opposed this census, which might show a greater French-speaking strength in Brussels than they were willing to admit. The general strike itself drew public attention away from the voting of the Single Law, which took place in January 1961.

The cabinet itself was to be the victim of the crisis over the Single Law, mainly because the Liberals thought they would benefit from new elections by capitalizing on public disapproval of the general strike. When the PSC/CVP leadership refused to accept an electoral reform that might have helped the Liberals gain a few seats in Parliament, the Liberals resigned from the cabinet. Liberal ministers immediately ceased participating in the cabinet, thus attempting to block the adoption by the cabinet of royal decrees needed to implement the Single Law. The king refused their resignations and dissolved the Parliament. Although the cabinet was only responsible for current business, it adopted the necessary decrees, despite the opposition of the Liberals. Thus the PSC/CVP and the king were able to prevent the last-minute defection by the Liberals from blocking the application of the Single Law. The PSC/CVP-Liberal coalition gave way after the elections to a PSC/CVP-Socialist Cabinet, which in the next four years managed to modify and weaken the Single Law.

The passage of the Single Law indicated that a cabinet could withstand serious pressure from the nation's major interest groups, but the cost was high. Not only did the cabinet itself fall because of the dispute, but the position of the unions was strengthened. The PSC/CVP-Socialist coalition was more to the liking of the left-wing elements of the PSC/CVP and represented a vindication of the Socialist opposition to the Single

Law. In later years, it would be impossible for the major parties to take such a strong stand against the manifest interests of the unions, which constitute Belgium's major pressure groups. The crisis indicated that the cabinet could no longer adopt any policy it wished, even if it could argue that it was in the national interest, when the interest groups were opposed. It should be noted that in this case the cabinet was in the pivotal position. The unions tried to influence it, not the members of Parliament, who followed the party directives fairly faithfully. Finally, the language question played a role in the resolution of the issue, proving once again that it is rarely absent from most of the major policy decisions in Belgium and may influence parties and interest groups to forsake other of their demands, if they can gain some satisfaction on matters of language.

Decision making: the language question

The attempt to settle the language question by parliamentary action indicates that in this most important area the Parliament retains much of its legislative powers. The language question in Belgium is complex and has its roots deep in the nation's history, but it has achieved an overwhelming political importance in the 1960s. The creation of a linguistic border between the French-speaking and the Dutch-speaking parts of the country, to be used for administrative and educational purposes, illustrates the nature of the political debate.

A growing sentiment for increased cultural autonomy has been felt in both parts of Belgium. The Flemings are particularly concerned with stemming the inroads of the French-speaking population and the French language in their sections of the country. On the French-speaking side, a federalist-separatist element seeks to create a bastion for itself in Belgium. This element has been gaining strength in Wallonia to the detriment of the more moderate French-speaking population, which favors the maintenance of a unified Belgium both for patriotic reasons and because it would allow gradual expansion of the French-speaking influence in the country. In 1961 the cabinet decided to prepare legislation establishing a linguistic border in Belgium. A proposed line was suggested to the Parliament, with the only major problem arising over the fate of six communes, known as the Fourons. They were considered mainly Dutch-speaking, despite a vote in favor of a French-speaking status by the population as early as 1947. Many judged this expression as a plebiscite rather than a declaration of fact as to the actual language situation there. These six communes, it was proposed, should be transferred from the French-speaking province of Liège to the Dutch-speaking province of Limburg. The Chamber adopted a bill proposing this transfer without strong Walloon objections. Some of them felt the time had come to make peace with the Flemings; others, more federalist-minded, favored the drawing of an immutable border at almost any cost.

But the 4200 inhabitants of these villages vigorously protested the Chamber's action, thus arousing a wave of public opinion in favor of the right of the individual to choose his own language. When the Senate received the bill in July 1962, it voted by 73 to 71 with 2 abstentions against the transfer from one province to another of these six communes and by 72 to 70 with 2 abstentions against their being left within the province of Liège. The communes were nowhere, for the moment at least. Yet three months later the Senate voted 91 to 68 with 4 abstentions in favor of the transfer. The cabinet had put great pressure on its supporters, indicating that it would fall if some satisfaction were not given to the Flemings. The final vote was Fleming against Walloon, and the latter were victims of their numerical inferiority in the country as a whole. The issue came before the Chamber once again, because of several new amendments, and the transfer was confirmed by a vote of 122 to 72 with 3 abstentions. Only one Fleming, who voted against the transfer, broke the linguistic voting pattern.

The fact that voting had taken place so clearly along linguistic lines on major legislation concerning the use of languages led to a growing desire to amend the Belgian Constitution to take into account both the existence of language regions and the minority rights for language groups. This was, in some respects, a counterpart for the adoption of the language frontier and the transfer of the Fourons to Limburg.[4] The procedure

---

[4] It should be noted that certain areas contiguous to Flanders have been shifted to the control of a noncontiguous Walloon province with much less disturbance.

was initiated in April 1962, when a political working party, composed of ministers and members of Parliament, was created to examine ways of amending the Constitution. This was the beginning of a procedure similar to the one used for the Schools Pact. But the Liberals refused to take part in this group, claiming that the cabinet as such should not participate in this working party.

The group examined ways of changing the composition of the Senate in order to allow for fair representation of the two language groups. This possibility was, however, rejected, for it was feared that it might prove impossible to form a new cabinet with two different parliamentary majorities. Yet it was recognized that some form of a special majority vote in Parliament would have to be used in a number of cases: municipal and provincial legislation, education, cultural matters, organization of the judiciary, social legislation, and regional economic legislation. The working party report was eventually sent to a national commission in January 1964. This commission contained representatives of the three parties, but final agreement had to be worked out among the three party chairmen themselves.

Then, in January 1965, the Liberals announced that they could not accept, without further study by the national commission, any agreement leading to the constitutional creation of the language border, which would make it virtually inalterable. The Liberal attitude stemmed in part from opposition to the final transfer of the Fourons and from a patriotic sentiment that opposed dividing the nation permanently. The national commission issued its report without Liberal support, and it was approved by the PSC/CVP and Socialist party congresses by overwhelming majorities. Thus Belgium still has pending a constitutional amendment, designed to alter voting in the Parliament. However, the two parties that support it would have to hold more than two thirds of the seats in both houses to pass the amendment, and until 1969 they had failed to achieve sufficient strength to assure passage.

According to the proposed amendment, laws on administrative, legal, military, educational, local, cultural, and certain business matters would be subject to a special vote. Even if the proposed laws gained the needed majority vote, this majority would have to include a majority of both language groups or the law would not be passed. In addition, three quarters of the members of either language group could declare through a "motion of exception" that any other bill passed by a parliamentary committee was likely to cause "serious prejudice to the relationship between the two national communities and to be liable for submission to special procedure." This procedure would require two readings for any bill that was opposed by two thirds of the members of either group. If this vote were repeated a second time, the rejection would not be considered final, but the bill would be referred back to the cabinet. The entire procedure could then be repeated. The cabinet is to "draw the political conclusions from any repetition of such procedure involving the same bill." Thus, in case of repeated rejection of a particular bill, the crisis would, in fact, be reopened.

This affair illustrates the importance of the Parliament on the language question. There can be no recourse to pressure group tactics, nor can the parties themselves resolve the matter. The Parliament, in this case, represents the Belgian people, a people deeply divided over the language issue. The use of the extraparliamentary procedure of the national commission cannot bring a solution unless there is advance agreement that some solution is better than none at all. The Liberals probably realized that the solution proposed would not be satisfactory to the entire nation, representing a political rather than a more fundamental socioeconomic settlement of the language question. The growth of linguistic extremist parties since the conclusion of the work of the national commission indicates that this appraisal was probably correct. Yet the three traditional parties are committed to some solution that would end the gradual drift toward federalism. They recognize that any vote that would directly pit one part of the nation against the other could only accelerate this process. Thus, on this issue, the Parliament does stand as the representative of the people, and only when it can come to an agreement will the problem be settled. And this agreement must involve some change in voting in the Parliament itself to prevent the Flemings from having the untrammeled right to outvote the Walloons.

The decision-making procedure illustrated by these case studies reveals that a remarkable amount of procedural ingenuity is needed to extract a compromise from Belgium's parties and interests. The cabinet may well be insufficiently strong to channel conflicting interests into an agreement. This leaves only the need to maintain the state itself as a sanction, and even the Belgian nation's very existence has been challenged by the struggle over the language question. Our survey has shown three levels of decision making: the major economic questions that can be settled by cabinet and the interest groups, the major issues of society for which a solution can be found only if the other alternative is prolonged chaos (for example, the schools question), and finally the language question, which has resisted any form of decision making.

Other parliamentary powers

In addition to legislative powers, Parliament may, as in the Netherlands, ask questions and hold more formal interpellations of the cabinet. Questions are used with great frequency, and as a result they concern minor or special-interest matters. A single member may ask hundreds of questions in a single year, mostly on local matters. In this way, he can demonstrate to his constituents that he is attempting to protect their interests. But the impact of any one question is diminished by their great number. Interpellations do help the cabinet to formulate policy on major issues by indicating Parliament's concerns. The responsible minister may use an interpellation to explain new developments in cabinet policy, with little risk that he will then be faced with a vote of censure that cannot easily be beaten down by a vote of the majority against the opposition. For this reason, the language question is often carefully avoided as a subject for interpellation, and when it arises it may lead, even unintentionally, to the fall of the cabinet.[5]

THE LACK OF SEPARATION OF POWERS

In Belgium there is no real separation of powers between the executive and the legislature. The ministers are members of

[5] An interpellation by a Flemish PSC/CVP member brought on the fall of the cabinet in 1968.

Parliament, and the Parliament and cabinet are linked by political parties that impose a strong discipline. The parties themselves act as a liaison between the interest groups and the powers of the cabinet. Thus neither cabinet nor Parliament can afford to affront the parties, for, in so doing, they would be opposing the very people who are their traditional electoral supporters.

The cabinet predominates over the Parliament partly because it is a more manageable body and contacts can be maintained easily between it and the parties. The cabinet represents the forum where compromises on the principles of the parties can frequently be worked out or at least where agreement can be reached on a procedure for dealing with major issues acceptable to all parties. In addition, the cabinet has access to both the parties and the administration, the best available sources of information on the legislative needs of the nation. Only occasionally do members of Parliament find themselves personally in a position to sense a ground swell of support for needed measures and thus introduce legislation without cabinet initiative. About ten times more Belgian laws are initiated by the cabinet than by Parliament.

The Parliament is often called upon to delegate some of its legislative powers to the cabinet. This is often done in the name of speedy action, and there is no doubt that the cabinet can act more quickly than the Parliament in discussing and agreeing upon legislation. The "laws on special powers" that the Parliament accords to the cabinet do not cover administrative matters alone but extend to policy making on major economic issues. The Parliament has little choice in relinquishing its powers; it does so as a faithful reflection and support of the cabinet, which in turn relies on a solid parliamentary majority. This majority is merely recognizing openly what is already an established fact: the parties, as joined together in a governing coalition, have the real power to make laws—and indeed to make parliamentarians.

For this same complex of reasons, the notion of ministerial responsibility has lost its traditional meaning. Formerly, ministers were said to be representing the king and the "governmental concept," while the Parliament represented the people. There would be an innate conflict between the two, it was thought.

The record indicates that the cabinet and the Parliament are dominated by the same parties at any given time and that the relationship between the parliamentary majority and the cabinet is direct and absolute. Thus the ministers, subject as they are to the parties, do not represent some undemocratic and essentially different political force than the Parliament.

What then is the role of Parliament in Belgium? It plays a double role. First, it is the scene of general debates, often upon the presentation of a proposed law or on the occasion of an interpellation. This permits the cabinet to be informed of the public view on important issues. The cabinet is not tied by what it hears in the halls of Parliament, but it cannot afford to flaunt a clearly expressed opinion that appears to represent the views of a large part of the population. Thus the Parliament assumes the role of one of the most important consultative organs available to the cabinet. The Parliament has, as its second function, the right to have the "last word" in the decision-making process. As one Belgian observer says: "Keeping for itself the last word, it lets the executive say all the rest." [6] The problem is whether this last word has any real meaning. It would if the cabinet were ever unsure of the outcome. Occasionally, it is, as in the case of the language dispute. If, however, the Belgian Parliament accedes to the role of being merely a rubber stamp, its powers may become as symbolic as those of the king.

[6] Mast, *Les Pays du Benelux,* p. 194.

EIGHT
GOVERNMENT
AND JUDICIARY
Law and the
judicial process

The administration of justice in both the Netherlands and Belgium is distinct from the decision-making process, and the law is regarded as a function of the state quite separate from the hurly-burly of everyday politics. This approach engenders a considerable public respect for a legal system viewed as an impartial arbiter between individuals and the state. However, it removes from the governing mechanism an element of control and review that other nations, such as the United States, have found a vital part of their decision-making apparatus.

DUTCH LAW

The Dutch Constitution lays down the guidelines for both the law and the judicial system of the nation. A vestige of the divine right theory, it says that justice is rendered in the name of the king. Civil, commercial, military, and criminal law are all to be regulated by codes, according to the Constitution. The Dutch legal system was originally based on Roman law, the foundation of much Germanic law. This system was built on notions of authority and the need to right individual wrongs. But the French occupation at the beginning of the nineteenth century set the tone of the Dutch legal system in succeeding years. Indeed, the code governing tort law, the attempt to vindicate one individual's right against another with the state acting as referee, is only now undergoing its first revision since it was adopted early in the last century.

The civil law system, as it is applied in the Netherlands, prescribes that the law shall be found in the codes that are adopted by the States General. The idea of a codified law enacted solely by the legislature rules out the possibility for the courts to "make" law through decisions on a number of cases. Under the common law system, such decisions may be taken by other courts to indicate what the law means. In the Netherlands, the judge is to have recourse to the code in order to determine what the law is. This also implies that the rule of *stare decisis,* under which earlier court decisions may serve as a precedent and may be referred to as an authority, does not exist in the Netherlands. It should be noted, however, that the lines of demarcation between the common and civil law systems are blurred and that instances can be found where precedent does play an important, if subsidiary, role in Dutch justice.

Although the Dutch Constitution does not include a formal bill of rights, many of its provisions are aimed at assuring the individual certain rights. Rules governing expropriation of property are included, and Dutchmen are guaranteed that conflicts concerning property rights must be settled only by the courts. The Constitution also pledges that no person shall be transferred from the jurisdiction of one judge to another without his consent. Arrest is made subject to the issuance of a judicial order, as is the right to enter a dwelling for purposes of search. Privacy of the mails is guaranteed, and no person can be forced to forfeit his goods as a penalty for a crime. Trials and decisions of courts are to be public. The Constitution assures equal rights for all citizens and guarantees freedom of expression, petition, association, and assembly. In addition the Netherlands has fully accepted the European Convention on Human Rights, which allows individuals to bring cases against their own state in instances where human rights violations are alleged.

Both the police power and the judicial power were under

the authority of the municipality or province during the Dutch Republic. But the Napoleonic occupation led to the creation of a centralized, national legal system with a single body of law for the entire nation. Of course, under the unitary system, the individual has been guaranteed a number of rights, including those mentioned specifically in the Constitution, with the entire state apparatus prepared to enforce them.

As might be imagined, the Dutchman is much attached to the notion of individual liberties, and the Netherlands has long been known as a tolerant state where all segments of the population could expect fair treatment at the hands of the administration, the law, and the people. Although this situation remains true today, there has been an inevitable shift away from emphasis on individual rights toward social rights. A Dutch observer has noted that this analysis by the Swedish economist Gunnar Myrdal seems to apply well to the Netherlands:

> The sanctity of private property rights to do what one pleases with a piece of land; or the right to keep all, except a nominal tax charge, of one's income and wealth for private consumption or investment; the freedom to enter upon any profession one wants at one's own risk; the right of the employer to negotiate individually with his workers, to pay the smallest salary he can for the job, and to hire and fire whom he wants, when he wants; the right of the worker to leave the shop, as and when he desires; indeed, the free choice to own, acquire and dispose, to work or to rest, to invest, to trade, to move—all these time-honored individual liberties are gradually eaten away by the controls of organized society.[1]

DUTCH LEGAL INSTITUTIONS

The court system in the Netherlands is organized along strictly hierarchical lines. At the lowest level are the sixty-two Cantonal Courts (Kantongerecht), having jurisdiction over all civil cases involving less than 500 guilders,[2] tenancy claims and disputes

---

[1] Myrdal quoted in Johan Goudsblom, *Dutch Society* (New York: Random House, 1967), pp. 79–80.

[2] One guilder equals 27 U.S. cents.

concerning rents, contracts of employment, and time payments. These courts also hear criminal cases involving certain misdemeanors such as tax offenses and violations of economic legislation. Small Cantonal Courts may have only one judge, although those in larger cities may have as many as nine. These Cantonal Courts are the main courts of the first instance in the Netherlands.

The nineteen District Courts (Arrondissementsrechtsbank) are courts of appeal for the Cantonal Courts and have certain functions as courts of first instance. Divorce and bankruptcy cases and criminal cases involving almost all felonies and the misdemeanors not dealt with by the Cantonal Courts come before the District Courts. There are from six to thirty-eight judges on such courts, and they work in specific divisions: juvenile, criminal, and indictable economic offenses. The president of a District Court has powers relating to judicial procedure, and he may issue judgments enjoining or forcing action.

Many of the economic matters that might ordinarily come before either Cantonal or District Courts never enter the formal legal system. Arbitration on points of civil law is frequently used, and arbitral bodies have been established by many professional groups. It is, however, often possible to appeal to the national courts from arbitral decisions.

Just as a certain number of Cantonal Courts must direct appeals to a single District Court, the District Courts fall within the appellate jurisdiction of one of the five Courts of Appeal (Gerechtshof). These courts, organized in divisions and with from nine to twenty-five judges, act solely on appeal from the District Courts. The appeal structure includes one Tenancy Division, which receives appeals from Cantonal Courts throughout the Netherlands.

At the summit of the judicial structure is the Supreme Court (Hoge Raad der Nederlanden), composed of twenty justices working in four divisions of equal size. The powers of this court are outlined in the Constitution. The Supreme Court supervises the administration of justice by all courts in the land. In addition, it is the trial court for leading officials—including members of the States General, king's commissioners in the provinces, and heads of ministerial departments—for indictable acts performed in connection with their official duties. Naturally the Supreme Court is the highest court of appeal for decisions by lower tribunals, but it judges solely on the basis of the law, not on the facts of the case, which are to have been determined by the lower courts. In this respect it is similar to the United States Supreme Court. If the Dutch Supreme Court considers a lower court decision erroneous, it will send the case back down for a new hearing. It is also allowed to let a decision stand, while declaring that in the future the decision shall be considered to have been reversed. This procedure is quite unlike the American practice, which requires that decisions must involve specific cases under adjudication and not merely represent a declaration for the future.

For matters involving the treaties and rules of the European Community, the Dutch courts have jurisdiction. But any court may choose to transfer the case to the Court of the European Community in Luxembourg, and if the case should reach the Dutch Supreme Court, it is bound to make such a transfer of jurisdiction. This ensures uniformity among all six member countries of the European Community in the interpretation of these rules.

Administrative law is in the domain of special courts covering such areas as social insurance, civil service, and other economic and social matters. Judges may render decisions in cases where the state itself is sued for tort, but they cannot question government policy. Appeals of administrative orders can be carried to the Council of State, which since 1964 has been given power to hear complaints against the Crown in its Administrative Disputes Section. Once an affair has been heard by the Council of State, it submits a recommended decision to the cabinet—and, in fact, to the minister of justice. In most cases he will accept the advice of the Council of State. If he does not, the cabinet publishes its own decision, a statement of its reasons for deviating from the advice and the text of the suggested decision by the Council of State. This practice differs from that in other countries, where the decisions of the Council of State on administrative matters are final and the cabinet must adhere to them. In the Netherlands, the cabinet is given the right to refuse to amend its allegedly offending actions.

It will be recalled that the Council of State also advises the cabinet on the annulling of provincial or municipal regulations when they are in conflict with the national interest or law.

Parallel to the court structure is the Department of Public Prosecutions, which has the exclusive right to bring criminal cases, although individuals may appeal to the Courts of Appeal if the public prosecutor fails to act. The department is organized on a hierarchical basis in line with the court structure, with an attorney general (Procureur-Generaal) at the Supreme Court. Only he can institute an appeal to the Supreme Court, and he is asked for his opinion by the Court before it renders its own decision. The Department of Public Prosecutions, which he heads, has great independence in the Dutch system. It follows the rule of opportuneness (prosecuting cases that it believes should be brought to law) rather than the rule of legality (the prosecution of all violations of the law). But the Court of Appeal, the minister of justice, and the attorney general at the Court of Appeal can order a prosecution.

The police in the Netherlands consist of a national force and municipal forces. The National Police Force is directly under the control of the minister of justice and operates in all parts of the country. In 122 municipalities, most of which have more than 20,000 inhabitants, there are local police forces. They, too, are subject to the national government through the burgomaster, himself appointed by the cabinet in The Hague. The municipalities pay part of the cost of their own police forces. Finally, the Royal Military Police has the civil function of guarding the frontier.

DEMOCRACY AND LAW IN THE NETHERLANDS

The Dutch judicial system is oriented toward "authority" rather than "democracy." Thus there is no jury system whatsoever in the Netherlands; the last jury existed in 1840. The Dutch believe in the professional administration of justice by judges who have no political links. The national government appoints judges for life (they serve in fact until age seventy), and there is little chance for popular influence. In some respects, the judiciary is part of the civil service, for judges may begin in the lower courts at a relatively early age and work their way to higher courts. But no judge may be forced to accept a transfer if he prefers to work in a given jurisdiction. This system generates considerable public respect for the judges and the legal system.

The lack of democracy in the Dutch legal system is counterbalanced by the guarantees of individual rights in the Constitution and laws—and by two other features. First, the courts have absolutely no power to declare acts of parliament or royal decrees (legislative acts of the cabinet) unconstitutional. There is remarkably little concern that the States General will enact legislation that violates fundamental guarantees of individual rights. The public shows great confidence that the parliament and cabinet will maintain fair legal standards. This almost amazing confidence in the parliament is also an indication of the important role it plays in national political life.[3]

Although no national laws can be declared unconstitutional, nor indeed can international treaties to which the Netherlands has subscribed, provincial and local rules are subject to reversals by the cabinet. When a court is, in fact, faced with what seems to be a conflict between a law and the constitution, it must interpret the law as if the legislature had meant it to conform to the Constitution. If, however, the States General believe that the courts have gone too far, they may pass another law specifically denying the court's interpretation. Thus, judicial review as known in the United States does not exist.

A second democratic element of Dutch justice is the lack of binding decision by the Council of State on administrative matters. Here the cabinet, indirectly chosen by the people, has the last word.

The average citizen comes into contact with the law in the great majority of cases when he receives a ticket for parking or for a traffic violation and in the case of marriage and divorce. In the Netherlands, an individual who receives a parking ticket may pay his fine to the police officer at once, thus liquidating the matter with no formality and without question of its appearing on his judicial record. As for marriage and divorce, the law

[3] See Chap. 6.

requires no special advance agreement on the ownership of property, and the court decides on the distribution of goods and the custody of children in case of divorce. This will not seem exceptional to the student familiar with the Anglo-American legal system; it indicates the extent to which the Dutch system represents something of a bridge between the Continent and the common law. It also explains why the Dutchman does not have a negative impression of a judicial system that creates relatively few complications and is impartial. Yet the contrast with Belgium with regard to these two examples will show how widely Dutch practice differs from that of its neighbor and other continental nations.

BELGIAN LAW

The Belgian judicial system in essence resembles closely the legal structure and philosophy in the Netherlands. However, it represents a purer version of the civil law system, with the Germanic legal tradition playing a smaller role. In a nation where each individual customarily insists on the full exercise of his rights, the Belgian legal system has come to reflect this situation.

The origin of the Belgian legal philosophy can be found in the reaction to the tutelage of King William at the time of the Belgian move for independence. The framers of the Constitution sought to protect the individual against the arbitrary actions of a central administration with excessive powers. They thought that "the government that governs best, governs least," and they established the judicial system to protect the individual.

The Belgian Constitution enumerates at considerable length the individual rights of the Belgians. They are guaranteed equal treatment by the state, and individual liberty is assured. No person can be taken from the jurisdiction of a judge, nor can a penalty not prescribed by law be imposed. Among the penalties that may not be meted out are confiscation of property and the civilian death penalty. Due compensation must be paid for expropriation of land, and the home itself is inviolable unless a proper warrant is obtained. There is complete freedom of worship; none can be obliged to attend a religious service. The state is pledged not to intervene in the appointment of ministers of religion, although it does provide for their salaries. The freedom of education, the press, assembly, association, and petition are guaranteed, as is the secrecy of the mails. Also, indicating the Belgians' right to challenge a harsh administration, there is the right to bring suit against a civil servant without having to obtain prior permission.

In theory, at least, the Belgian Constitution allows for a judicial review of administrative acts to determine if they are in line with the law. This is clearly not a matter of constitutionality, although it resembles it in some ways and has been the source of much discussion among lawyers in Belgium. Article 107 says: "The courts and tribunals shall not apply any general, provincial, or local decrees and regulations save insofar as they are in accordance with the law." Thus, the courts are not given the power to judge acts of Parliament, but rather administrative decisions made by executive authority and decisions of local and provincial institutions. This article merely buttresses another article barring the cabinet from adopting decrees in violation of existing law. The courts are, in fact, seldom led to render a decision under Article 107, in part because of the discretion of the executive and in part because the judiciary does not want to plunge into the "political thicket." This lack of any real form of judicial review in terms of constitutionality is similar to Dutch practice. The ultimate expression of the will of the people is the Parliament, and thus its acts should not be subject to review by the courts. This presupposes general satisfaction with the Parliament as an institution and a belief that if the legislature strays too far from the Constitution it will be checked at the next general elections.

This state of affairs removes from Belgian (and Dutch) political life one of the conflicts familiar to Americans. Whereas—as in the United States—the courts must decide if laws are in accordance with the Constitution, they may be criticized for "making" law by modifying from time to time their interpretation of the Constitution. In the Belgian system, the Constitution is kept up to date by Parliament itself, which may adopt amendments by a simple vote. Thus the judiciary retains its independence from the political wars and its status as arbiter. The Belgian system does, of course, remove any check on a legislature swept up by the temporary tides of opinion on a given issue.

Belgian constitutional law has not yet determined the exact relationship of international agreements to the Constitution. In the United States and, as has been seen, in the Netherlands, international accords assume a position equal to the Constitution.

Article 107 treats general, provincial, and local regulations on the same footing, but elsewhere in the Constitution provincial and communal legislation is given a subsidiary position to the national laws. It is not the courts, but rather the king and Parliament that determine the compatibility of the provincial and local rules with the "general interest."

BELGIAN LEGAL INSTITUTIONS

The Constitution creates a formal separation of powers and indicates that all judicial power is to be exercised by the courts and tribunals. The Constitution also draws a line between the judicial and administrative authority, noting that all questions of civil rights are in the jurisdiction of the courts, but that matters involving political rights may be removed from such jurisdiction by law. This last statement has the effect of including the major part of administrative disputes under a special judicial system, and this has been strengthened by the creation of administrative courts. Among the so-called political rights are the right to vote, to assume public office, to be taxed fairly, and not to be forced illegally to do military service.

The lowest judicial instance is the Justice of the Peace, of which there are 230 in Belgium. Their courts are empowered only to deal with minor criminal offenses and civil suits involving relatively small sums. Next on the judicial ladder are the twenty-six Tribunals of First Instance. Each of these is composed of three judges, who sit in almost all civil cases and in criminal cases where the maximum possible penalty is five years. More serious cases may be heard in the first instance by

Superior or Circuit Courts (Cour d'Assise), which meet once every three months in each of the nine provincial capitals of the country. These courts are composed of three judges, one from the Court of Appeals and two from Tribunals of First Instance. A jury is impaneled to decide on the merits of a case by a majority vote. When the court does not agree with the majority, it may adopt the minority position, thus acquitting the person on trial. If, on the other hand, the court concurs in the jury's decision, it listens to the jury's opinion on the sentence to be meted out.

Thus Belgium, unlike the Netherlands, uses the jury system. The Constitution prescribes that it shall be employed in all criminal cases and "for political and press misdemeanors." The fact that popular appreciation of the law is called upon in certain cases does not mean that the judicial system overall is any more democratic than in the Netherlands, but rather that in certain categories of cases the legislature considers that it cannot foresee all possible political aspects of a case and that the people must therefore be given a means of expression.

Appellate jurisdiction is exercised by three Courts of Appeal—Brussels (bilingual), Ghent (Dutch language), and Liège (French language). Two additional Courts of Appeal are being created, one for each language group. Five judges constitute the panel of these courts, which hear appeals from lower jurisdictions only on points of law, the questions of fact having been settled below. They also act as courts of first instance for cases involving top-ranking government officials. Appeals from these courts go to the nation's single Court of Cassation.

The Court of Cassation, at the summit of the Belgian judiciary, is composed of a civil and a criminal section, each of seven judges. This court, too, decides only on questions of law. Where it rejects a lower court decision, the matter is referred to another jurisdiction on the same level as the court initiating the appeal procedure. If the lower courts again fail to follow the reasoning of the Court of Cassations (literally *cassation* means "breaking" a decision), the highest court may issue a binding judgment.

The Court of Cassation is also responsible for deciding in cases of conflict of jurisdiction, especially between civil and administrative courts. Its functions in the European Community legal system parallel those of the Dutch Supreme Court.[4]

A number of jurisdictions exist outside the framework of the civil courts. The tribunals of commerce, whose members are chosen by the business community, act as arbiters of commercial agreements. The Counseils de Prud'hommes are concerned with questions of labor law. Appeal from both of these to the civil court system is possible. A plethora of special commissions also exists for military, unemployment, disability insurance, war damages, and similar matters. Among the purely administrative tribunals are the Provincial Executive Councils and the Council of State.

The original function of the Council of State in France was to allow some measure of judicial control over acts of the parliament, following the revolutionary period in which the parliament had reigned supreme. This was not at first deemed necessary in Belgium, but in 1946 it became evident that special courts were needed to deal with conflicts involving the state itself, particularly as society became more complex and the state intervened more frequently. At that time, the administrative section of the Belgian Council of State was modeled on the French.

The Council of State can judge whether administrative authority has exceeded the powers accorded to it by law. At the same time, it acts as a court of cassation for the lower administrative instances, including the special commissions, although military appeals still go to the Court of Cassation itself. Traditionally only the civil courts have been allowed to order payment of damages, and this authority was thus withheld from the Council of State. It is thus left to the administration itself to decide whether damages will be paid. The Council of State also has assumed some powers formerly attributed to the king concerning the communal electoral laws.

All judicial hearings and judgments are open to the public, and the decisions must include the reasoning of the court.

[4] Belgium also takes part in the European Convention on Human Rights. Belgian appeals to the European courts follow the same course as described for the Netherlands earlier in the chapter.

The status of judges in Belgium is similar to that in the Netherlands, although the selection procedure removes some of the power from the government. Justices of the Peace and members of the Tribunals of First Instance are directly chosen by the cabinet, but Counsellors (judges) of the Courts of Appeal and the president and vice-presidents of the Tribunals of First Instance are chosen on the basis of two lists, one submitted by the courts concerned and the other by the Provincial Councils. As for counsellors of the Court of Cassation, they are chosen from two lists, one submitted by the court itself and the other by the Senate. This prevents the cabinet from making political appointments, gives the courts themselves a say in their composition, and includes a democratic element in terms of the participation of the Provincial Councils and Senate. Judges are appointed for life, cannot be transferred without their consent, and cannot accept other governmental appointments unless they do so on an unsalaried basis.

The judge is thus an essentially nonpolitical figure, who acquires the standing in the public view of an impartial arbitrator. Trained lawyers can make their careers within the judiciary just as in the Netherlands. The legal profession is composed of both solicitors (who advise their clients on the law) and barristers (who appear in court). In general, the lawyer is well respected, and the individual himself takes a great interest in the law. It is not uncommon to find soft-cover editions of the Civil Code on sale in bookshops throughout Belgium.

The Department of the Public Prosecutor is much the same in Belgium as in the Netherlands, with a hierarchy paralleling that of the courts. This department is entirely free from political pressures and represents a possible career area for young lawyers. In one respect—criminal procedure—the Belgian system is patterned on the French. A *juge d'instruction* is assigned by the Tribunal of First Instance to investigate a case and determine if there is enough *prima facie* evidence to warrant a trial. If so, the accused must be indicted before appearing in court.

The police are organized on both a national and a communal basis, the latter under the authority of the communal government. The national police operate on major highways and at the frontiers, but they are also permitted to exercise jurisdiction within the communes.

THE INDIVIDUAL AND THE LAW

The Belgian judicial system follows the traditions of the Continent and of the civil law tradition; it is heavily influenced not only by the Napoleonic code but by French history. It represents an attempt to combine some of the elements of the authoritarian Dutch judicial system with democratic elements. The law in Belgium is of prime importance to the life of the nation, for the Belgian expects the law to vindicate his rights. If we look at the same cases of law in daily life as we examined for the Netherlands, we shall see that this combination of factors produces a far greater complexity in Belgium.

If an individual receives a parking ticket, he cannot pay it immediately. He will receive from the police of the commune a statement of the violation, indicating the nature of the offense. Later he will be called to his own communal police station to give his version of the event. Still later a local police official will call at his home with a document from the Department of Public Prosecution, stating that he has been found guilty of the violation in question. The document is called a "transaction," for it permits the individual to pay a fine in order to "induce" the public prosecutor not to place a record of the traffic violation in his criminal dossier. The existence of this dossier and the elaborate efforts to avoid any "bad marks" in it are characteristic of the continental civil law system. By contrast with the Netherlands, if a Belgian chose to challenge the parking ticket and lost, he would have the matter placed in his record and would have to pay court costs. Both of these measures are also a far cry from the common law system used in the United States and Britain.

On the question of marriage and divorce, the other frequent occasions on which individuals come in contact with the law, a formal contract must be prepared between both parties indicating the exact disposition of their property once married. The wife retains an independent standing in Belgian law, even being called by her maiden name throughout life. Thus she has certain rights even in marriage, which in some ways simplifies property settlements upon divorce. The notion of an agreement between two parties, rather than a fusion of their belongings, is also characteristic of the civil law system.

The law represents both a source of comfort and an element of complication in the life of Belgians. Its peculiar character shows how a generally used system can be shaped to suit the needs of even a small nation.

NINE
POLITICS
IN LUXEMBOURG
Survival of a viable "ministate"

The mid-twentieth century has seen the appearance of a multitude of ministates, and the question is legitimately asked what role they may play in international affairs. Europe is the home of a number of minuscule semistates and one true ministate, endowed with all the attributes of a full-scale nation. This is Luxembourg, the third partner in Benelux.

Luxembourg has faced severe tests that swept many larger entities off the map entirely. Although its territory was repeatedly reduced, the nation managed to survive; in its essential policy—continued national existence—Luxembourg has achieved success. Whatever their divisions on political questions, all Luxembourgers cling tenaciously to the notion of their state as a separate and sovereign entity. The national motto: "We want to stay what we are."

Luxembourg lies between Belgium, France, and Germany, and all three have strongly influenced its development, yet the country has retained its own character. Three languages are commonly used, creating amazingly few problems. All citizens speak the local dialect, Luxembourgeois, which is a version of German. They are educated in German and to a lesser extent in French. Newspapers are often published with all three languages on a single page, although the official publications of the state are in French. This complete mixing of languages has helped prevent the growth of any settled language groups as there are in Belgium.

THE LUXEMBOURG ECONOMY

Just as Belgium and the Netherlands find economic issues in the front rank of national policy, Luxembourg must give prime attention to its economic well-being. As perhaps the most successful of the very small states, Luxembourg owes most of its strength to its unique economic position and the character of its people. Traditionally, the nation has depended on its massive steel industry to provide jobs and national income and has acquired a key position on the international money market. But both the steel industry and the financial center have been challenged in recent years. Steel has suffered because of a worldwide increase of supply, outstripping demand. At the same time, the existence of the European Community has threatened the privileged position of the money market.

Yet these have not been unmitigated disasters for Luxembourg. There is still a market for a major part of its steel production, and the government has pushed a diversification program that has brought in a number of foreign firms outside the steel sector. This, too, may have had an effect on the nation's foreign policy, although it is difficult to measure. The major Luxembourg steel concerns had traditionally been partly owned by French firms, and this link may have discouraged the government from taking an overly independent stand from France in international affairs.[1] Increased diversification may have freed Luxembourg from some of these restraints on its policy. As for the money market, Luxembourg has thus far succeeded in protecting its privileged position.[2] But even if its privileges are

[1] The major Luxembourg steel firm, Arbed, is largely owned by Schneider, the French producer.

[2] The principal pressure for an end to Luxembourg's privileged position has come from France, but economic difficulties there in May and June of 1968 would appear to further delay any chance of a major modification of the European money-market structure.

modified, Luxembourg will have drawn much compensating benefit from the European Community. Not the least of this profit has been drawn from the European Coal and Steel Community, which has had its headquarters in Luxembourg since 1952; Luxembourg remains one of the "temporary" capitals of Europe. Merely being one of "the Six" has enhanced Luxembourg's international prestige in a way unprecedented in the nation's history.

Luxembourg believes it must make its way on a footing of equality with other nations, big and small. It is not a developing country, not an island, not a great tourist center, not strategically located. Thus the internal organization of the state must be one of the sources of its strength. As a result, the Luxembourg political system is characterized by both a sense of reality and economy.

GOVERNMENT INSTITUTIONS

Luxembourg is a constitutional "monarchy," the throne being occupied by the grand duke, a member of the same family as the Dutch royal house. The traditional ties of the two nations are illustrated by their flags, which are virtually the same. But in terms of constitutional organization Luxembourg follows closely the pattern laid down by Belgium, and indeed many articles of the two constitutions are identical.

The grand duke is the symbol of the existence of the state and enjoys considerable popularity with the Luxembourgers. He has few political powers of his own, beyond the nomination of the prime minister designate. As in most constitutional monarchies, the cabinet, theoretically named by the grand duke, constitutes the executive power and acts in his name.

The chief of state does, however, play a role in government. He is consulted by the prime minister concerning legislation that will be submitted in his name and that he will eventually sign. In accordance with his appointive functions, his views are asked before he sanctions the nomination of officials. Thus, the grand duke has the right to be consulted, a traditional right of the sovereign in constitutional monarchies, and he apparently takes great interest in performing his duties.

The cabinet is always formed by a coalition, since no party has had a sufficiently large majority in the parliament to support a cabinet in office by itself. Since World War II every prime minister (known formally as the president of the government and minister of state) has been a member of the Social Christian party, the largest in the nation. The grand duke is thus virtually certain to call upon a member of this party to form a cabinet, who in turn will attempt to do so by establishing a coalition with either the right or the left. The options are therefore quite limited, and governmental crises are not usually lengthy. In addition, there is a remarkable continuity in the office of prime minister; since the war there have been four. With minor reshuffling, a cabinet can expect to remain in office for the entire five-year period between general elections.

The organization of ministries is in the hands of the cabinet. The prime minister himself is in charge of the Ministry of State, which coordinates all activities of the nineteen other ministries. The national administration is amazingly small; each minister holds several portfolios. A cabinet reshuffle may merely indicate an exchange of portfolios among them. Recently the grand-ducal government has adopted the institution of state secretary, a kind of junior minister. In the cabinet formed after the 1964 elections, eight ministers and two state secretaries shared the nineteen ministries.

In addition to the cabinet, the Council of State has been established to advise the grand duke on matters of policy and to act as a high administrative court. The Luxembourg Council of State is based, as in Belgium, on the French example. But Luxembourg, with a unicameral legislature, permits the Council of State to play part of the role of a senate.

The Council of State is composed of twenty-one members, eleven of whom deal with administrative disputes. Its members are named by the grand duke, acting in turn upon the advice of the cabinet, the Chamber, and the Council of State itself. Thus, the council is able to maintain some degree of independence from the current political scene. All members of the Council of State compose its General Meeting, which takes part in the legislative procedure. The council may be consulted by the cabinet on all decrees and administrative decisions. The council must be consulted by the cabinet before a bill is submitted to the Chamber. In urgent cases, it may submit a bill to both simultaneously, but the legislature cannot act without having received the opinion of the Council of State. This opinion is, however, in no way binding.

The council does have one direct power in the legislative process. To make up for the fact that Luxembourg has a unicameral legislature, the Constitution prescribes that every law shall be adopted twice by the Chamber with a three-month delay between the two votes. But the Council of State may waive the delay if it sees fit. If no waiver is granted, the Council of State is thus able to exercise a temporary veto, assuring that the public will have sufficient time to be made aware of the legislature's intentions. Finally, in its judicial role, the council can decide in cases of dispute between the cabinet and the state financial control authority, the Auditing Court. Thus an appointive body, largely free from cabinet control, can still play an important role in the governing process.

The election of the Chamber of Deputies, the nation's legislature, represents the high point of Luxembourg political life. The voter's choice is usually made from among three principal parties, although small parties also take part in the campaign. The citizen, required by law to vote, may have kept himself well informed of the political activities of the Chamber, for he is regularly provided free of charge with a summary of the debates.

POLITICAL PARTIES

The Social Christian party, the biggest vote getter among the political groups, has long been dominant in Luxembourg politics. It represents the bourgeois values of the predominantly Catholic population. Internally, the party supports a middle-of-the-road program, which in national terms allows for support for the extensive social welfare program. In addition, the Social Christian party has pushed protective legislation for farmers and small businessmen.

The close relationship between the party and the Roman Catholic Church is natural, although it shows signs of undergoing a significant modification. This may be due partly to the example of the Belgian party of the same name and partly to the gradual disappearance of church-state issues from political life. The school problem does, however, remain a potential threat, and both Church and party favor a maintenance of the existing close relationship of the state and private schools. But there are those within the Social Christian party anxious for an end of the party's confessional character and who would be prepared to accept a revision of the current legislation.

Still another stand peculiar to the party is its opposition to giving workers a say in the management of firms where they work, a policy supported by the Socialist party. Finally, the Social Christian party must bend its efforts toward renewal, for it is thought to be losing its dynamism.

The Socialist party was founded at the turn of the century as the protector of the working class and the opponent of clericalism. By the period immediately preceding World War II it had entered the governing coalitions. The party draws much of its support from the labor union movement, with considerable overlapping in the leadership of party and unions. This party has been the chief force behind much of the nation's progressive labor legislation and the increase in social benefits, including pensions for retired workers and extensive worker's compensation and social insurance.

The Socialists in Luxembourg, as in many other western European nations, are concerned about projecting a more youthful image and dealing with the problems of a society much more sophisticated than fifty years ago. The Socialists in Luxembourg appear to be meeting these problems with some success, and it is possible that they may gain the political leadership of the nation, marking a radical change from its traditions.

The third major party is the Democratic party, an outgrowth of the liberal movement. As such, it has traditionally adopted an anticlerical attitude and remains opposed to links between church and state. Although it supports the extension of labor legislation, the Democratic party relies on the nation's middle class for its support; hence it is more restrained in its social welfare demands than are the other major parties. The nation appears to be moving toward a two-party system, with the liberals of the Democratic party becoming a minor party. It would, however, be conceivable for the Democrats to gain strength if elements of the Social Christian party grew increasingly discontented with the confessional character of that party.

The Luxembourg Communist party draws most of its support from the industrial areas of the country. The party's recent gain in parliamentary strength was part of a protest against the traditional political framework, rather than a slide to the left. The party follows an expectable Moscow-style Communist line but could hardly be considered revolutionary. It does manage, however, to maintain its own newspaper, its chief means of influence. The Communists remain outside the councils of government, and there appears to be no reason why their parliamentary strength would allow them to force their way into any coalition. They can be counted on to provide regular opposition to all cabinets, even when their opposition "partner" is the Democratic party.

The final party represented in the Chamber following the 1964 elections is the Independent Popular Movement. This is essentially a party of protest, following in some respects the path laid down by the Poujadist episode in France. The party offers little in the way of a constructive program, limiting itself to an essentially negative attack on the government. Of its two original members in the Chamber, one defected to the Social Christian party. This party did not have a long life.

VOTING IN LUXEMBOURG

The Luxembourg electoral procedure is unique, reflecting the situation of a small country in which there are some 190,000 voters. The nation is divided into four electoral districts. Formerly elections were held in two of these at a time, resulting in a partial renewal of the Chamber of Deputies. The cabinet would be reconstituted after each election. Now the parliamentary elections take place in all four districts simultaneously. The number of seats per district is apportioned in terms of population; there is one deputy for each 5500 people and for any fraction above 4000. Thus the largest district, which includes the industrial area, has twenty-three deputies and the smallest has seven.

Each voter is given the same number of votes as there are candidates to be elected in his district. For example, in the smallest district he has seven votes. If he likes, he may vote for one of the lists on the ballot, and his seven votes will be distributed among the candidates on the list. He is also authorized to cast two votes for a single candidate and to vote for candidates on different lists. A survey of the electoral lists reveals that many voters do not vote a straight party list. The seven seats are distributed on the basis of proportional representation among the lists. Votes cast for an individual do not usually help him personally to be elected, and the division of seats takes place by cumulating the total votes for each list. If the division of seats does not come out evenly, a second distribution is made to determine what party would have the highest number of votes per seat if it were given the fractional remainder, and that party gets the additional seat. Although there is to be one member of parliament for each 5500 people, the smaller parties often seat candidates with fewer votes. This system of according to each voter an often considerable number of votes is only possible in a small country. It permits the elector, who may well know the candidates personally, to distribute his votes exactly in line with his preferences.

The results of the national elections (Table 9–1) show a

Table 9–1 Distribution of seats in parliament following national elections

	1951[a]	1954	1959	1964[b]	1968
Social Christian	21[c]	26[c]	21[c]	22[c]	21[c]
Socialist	19[c]	17[c]	17	21[c]	18
Democratic	8	6	11[c]	6	11[c]
Communist	4	3	3	5	6
Popular Independent Movement				2	
Total	52	52	52	56	56

[a] Elections in two of the four districts.

[b] Number of seats in Chamber of Deputies increased to reflect population increase.

[c] Participated in cabinet.

remarkable stability in voting preferences. Not only has the Social Christian party led every cabinet, but the Socialists have almost invariably been its coalition partner. This will help explain the extensive social legislation adopted in Luxembourg, for both parties have bid sufficiently high to attract a considerable number of voters and have paid off on their promises once in office. The period when the Democrats were in office reflected a decline in the fortunes of the Social Christian party (PCS) to the advantage of the more conservative Democrats. The recent increase in protest voting appears to pose no threat to the two major parties.

In addition to voting for members of the Chamber of Deputies, Luxembourgers may be asked to vote in national referendums, although these are quite rare. The Chamber determines when a referendum is to be held, not as in France, where the executive decides and may thus circumvent the legislature. In 1919 the people were asked whether they favored the continuation of the monarchy and whether they desired an economic union with France. On the first question, they voted by a four-fifths majority in favor of maintaining the Grand Duchess in office. By holding a referendum on this question, the cabinet itself was spared direct involvement in the issue, raised by her alleged collaboration with the Germans in World War I. The nation also voted three to one in favor of economic union with France, but this was later rejected by the French. The Luxembourgers were not subsequently consulted about the economic union with Belgium, created in 1922. In 1937 a referendum was held on a proposed law that would have brought the dissolution of "the Communist party and groups and associations which, by violence or threats, aim to change the Constitution and laws of the country." This open attempt to outlaw the Communists were very narrowly defeated and brought a cabinet change in its wake.

LEGISLATION

The members of the Chamber chosen at the national elections are allowed to continue with their professional activities, although they may not occupy certain administrative posts at the same time they are deputies. In addition, deputies who are named ministers in the cabinet are obliged to resign their elective office. This attempt to separate the executive from the legislative is further strengthened by rules banning members of the cabinet from serving on the Council of State. The ministers can, however, be asked to attend sessions of either the Council of State or the Chamber of Deputies, and they regularly defend proposed legislation there.

Most legislation originates with the cabinet, arising from the program it published upon entering office as well as the international commitments of the country. Individual members of the Chamber may submit bills, but this serves mainly to stimulate cabinet action, rather than to lead to the passage of the proposed legislation. The cabinet consults the Council of State on proposed laws; the council, through hearings and debates, examines each proposal thoroughly and often modifies it. The cabinet then submits the proposed law to the grand duke and, after receiving his approval, sends it to the Chamber.

The Chamber of Deputies is composed of a number of permanent committees covering the various sectors of government activity. In addition, there are permanent committees for financial control and for petitions. The Executive Committee of the Chamber may send a bill to one or more of the permanent committees or else may decide to create a special committee to examine the text. Each committee receives the bill and a complete cabinet statement on it as well as the proposed text of the Council of State if it differs from the cabinet proposal. Following committee consideration, the full Chamber discusses and adopts the law. Unless it receives the assent of the Council of State, the Chamber must wait three months before recommencing the entire legislative procedure. The version of the bill finally adopted is usually the text proposed by the Council of State.

In fact, passage of most legislation is a foregone conclusion. The cabinet consults both the parties and the principal interest groups, most importantly the labor unions, in advance, and a basic agreement is usually reached among them. The cabinet is also required to consult one or more of the professional "chambers"—agriculture, trades, commerce, private employees, and labor—on any bill affecting them. The parliamentary majority usually ratifies the cabinet's proposal and makes it law.

The Chamber of Deputies has certain nonlegislative functions. As noted earlier, it nominates some of the candidates for membership in the Council of State. It receives petitions, and it may conduct investigations, ask questions, or interpellate the cabinet. On questions of general policy the Chamber may adopt motions, and it may withdraw its confidence from the cabinet either by a special vote or by a negative vote on a question that the cabinet has designated as a matter of confidence in its stewardship.

LOCAL GOVERNMENT

Owing to its size, Luxembourg is subdivided into communes without any intermediary unit between the local authorities and the national government. The system of local government is in many ways similar to that of the Netherlands. The communes have considerable internal autonomy, although strictly limited to local matters. The Communal Council is elected every six years, independently of the national elections. It acts as the legislature of the locality and is presided over by the burgomaster.

The executive, with the responsibility of daily administration, is the College of Burgomaster and Aldermen, a group of three persons in all communes except the city of Luxembourg, where there are seven. The burgomaster, as in the Netherlands, is named by the chief of state, and he need not be a member of the council. Thus he has a direct link with the national administration and a degree of independence from local pressures. He is in charge of the investigatory police attached to the courts and may be called upon to act as public prosecutor.

The commune has taxing power, subject to approval of the national government. The cabinet can control the communes and prevent them from acting contrary to the national interest through district commissioners, appointed by the central authority and responsible to it. The cabinet is empowered to annul many decisions within the realm of communal authority if it sees fit.

In the organization of justice Luxembourg resembles Belgium. However, because of the country's size, the Higher Court of Justice acts as both a court of appeals and a court of cassation. International agreements occupy a place beside the Constitution, and laws are subordinate to them. There is no jury system.

SOCIETY AND SOCIAL WELFARE

The position of labor in Luxembourg merits special attention, for the nation is highly industrialized. One aspect of industrialization has been the substantial influx of foreign workers, dating from before World War II. These workers, now mainly Italian, Spanish, and Portuguese, retain their nationality and do not participate in the nation's political life. Yet they have caused concern about the maintenance of the national identity because they amount to about one seventh of the total population. In general, however, they have been well received, for most Luxembourgers recognize the need for outside labor. In recent years, there has been sufficient turnover in the foreign population to preclude prolonged concern about their becoming rooted in Luxembourg. They may, of course, become naturalized if they are willing to fulfill the legal requirements.

Other aspects of the industrial strength of the nation are its high standard of living and its extensive social benefits. These national assets are the direct result of the postwar period, when the Luxembourg steel industry was working at full capacity to meet demand. Although these social gains are not likely to be repealed as national growth slows, they are not expected to be improved as radically in the future as they were in the past.

In terms of standard of living, Luxembourg leads the six Common Market countries and compares favorably with the United States, as Table 9–2 indicates. Luxembourgers also have a higher per capita consumption of energy—almost twice that in the United States—and are better housed in terms of living space and supply of running water than people in other Common Market countries.

The social welfare legislation covers health and accident insurance, disability and old-age benefits, unemployment com-

Table 9–2   Comparison of standards of living

	Autos	Radios	TV	Tele-phones	Doc-tors	Hospital beds
		(per 1000 population)			(per 100,000 population)	
Luxembourg	187[a]	365[a]	93[b]	224[a]	98[b]	1230[a]
United States	385	1244	408	462	204	930
USSR	4	320	68	29	149	900

[a] First in Common Market.
[b] Last in Common Market.

pensation, family allowances, and public assistance. Virtually the entire population is covered. Public aid is an example of the extent of the social welfare program. It provides that, in addition to regular welfare payments distributed through the communes, any person, whether Luxembourger or not, may receive temporary assistance from any commune where he may be. Beyond the regular welfare program, a National Solidarity Fund ensures that older persons and persons unable to work receive payments to prevent them from falling into poverty. Thus the situation where insufficient pensions lead to poverty, occasionally found in Europe, is absent in Luxembourg, where it can be said that serious indigence does not exist.

The study of the political system of Luxembourg illustrates that institutions may be adapted to a particular status, such as that of the ministate. Luxembourg fulfills all the characteristics of the modern state but has developed a political system in line with its traditions and its size. With a recognition that national survival is in the interest of all, the Luxembourg people have shown a remarkable aptitude for collective action based on private enterprise. And the nation has realized that it must be willing to cooperate closely with its neighbors in international affairs.

TEN
THE "INTERNATIONAL" NATIONS
The Benelux nations in world affairs

Foreign policy and domestic policy are often intermingled and indistinguishable in the Benelux nations. Everyday life there virtually entails not only a desire but an obligation to play an active role in world affairs. The Benelux nations cannot afford to be isolationist.

INTERNATIONAL INVOLVEMENT

The predominant cause for international involvement is the dependence of the Benelux economies on outside factors. These nations derive a higher percentage of their gross naitonal product from foreign trade than do almost any other nations of the world. Their foreign policies must, therefore, be devoted to opening avenues of commerce and preventing political controversy from closing them. The chief foreign policy objective of these countries must be to maintain conditions of commercial growth and stability while avoiding unnecessary political involvements.

Coupled with this essentially economic approach is a desire, born of the experience of two world wars, to promote international conditions that will make the recurrence of war unlikely if not impossible. These two strands of foreign policy can be woven together harmoniously through the Benelux organization itself and more importantly through the European integration movement.

As a result of their membership in a wide range of international organizations, relatively few areas of national policy remain outside the scope of the Benelux nations' international commitments. All are members of the United Nations, the Organization for Economic Cooperation and Development, NATO, the Council of Europe, and the European Community. They are bound to consultation and cooperation on maintenance of international peace and security, aid to developing countries, and economic policy. But they have undertaken internationally binding commitments in the field of human rights (through the European Convention on Human Rights), military affairs (through the assignment of almost all of their military forces to NATO), and trade and economic affairs (through the European Community).

These obligations have been undertaken with more than a sense of duty and after relatively little domestic political debate. As small nations, the Benelux countries have made international cooperation the keystone of their foreign policies. Because of Europe's wars, they are in general agreement that nationalism is an outmoded policy and insufficient for solving their own problems. Indeed, by comparison with the larger nations, a relatively higher degree of idealism is present in their foreign policies. Perhaps the most extreme example has been the Dutch decision to distribute the greatest part of its foreign aid through multilateral organizations, the reverse of normal national practice.

The international "vocation" of these nations is the result of a number of factors: location, language, history, and economic strength.

The Benelux nations occupy a pivotal position in Europe. Lines of communication and transport linking parts of northern and southern Europe and Britain and the Continent pass through their territory. They possess the greatest port complex in the world. Their peoples have a generally friendly attitude toward foreigners.

In the three countries, four languages—Dutch, French, German, and English—are widely spoken. The language education of Dutch and Luxembourg schoolchildren has become virtually proverbial. This emphasis on language stems from a recognition of the need to function effectively in a larger world.

Because of their pivotal position, the Benelux nations have experienced countless invasions and occupations. These incursions, while demonstrating the faults of nationalism, have also hindered the development of overweening national identity, particularly in Belgium. In the Netherlands and Luxembourg, a sense that nationalism has outworn its usefulness is widespread. The combined effect of these trends has been to favor an open and pragmatic mentality in foreign affairs.

Finally, these three countries have flourished economically. Despite their size, they have become major economic powers. If the Common Market were excluded from consideration as a single unit, Benelux would be the world's fourth largest trading entity. In addition, Benelux holdings of international reserves open the way to the highest circles of international finance. As the world has come increasingly to face its economic problems and to accord them a high priority, the Benelux countries have been thrust into roles of central importance.

Four areas of Benelux foreign policy merit special attention. Belgium and the Netherlands have gradually disengaged themselves from their foreign colonies, which had imposed special burdens. At the same time they have pushed ahead with both Benelux cooperation and European integration. Finally, they have chosen to play leadership roles in the Atlantic Alliance.

COLONIAL POLICY

The colonial policy of the Netherlands and Belgium is an unhappy page in their political history. Their tribulations with dependent areas reveal that these small countries, like the greater powers, were unable to cope with the transformation of their colonies into independent states. Their failure to avoid bloodshed and a loss of international prestige resulted partly from the untoward haste of the colonies to seize the attributes of sovereignty for themselves without full regard for the need for adequate political structures and procedures. But the Netherlands and Belgium appeared reluctant, both because of an honest concern for the stable development of the colonies and because of their strong colonial attachments, to part with those sovereign prerogatives when the time came.

Netherlands and Indonesia

The Netherlands was once one of the world's great powers, and its greatness rested on its colonial empire. The jewel of that empire was the East Indies, later to become Indonesia. In 1619, the Dutch East Indies Company founded Batavia (later Djakarta) on the island of Java and from this base spread its control over most of the Indonesian archipelago. The East Indies Company through a worldwide trade sought to capitalize on the wealth of the Indies. Although it did not actually govern Indonesia, the company was able to intervene in the politics of the local maharajahs through the use of Dutch troops. This ensured that Indonesia remained a relatively docile colony.

When the East Indies Company was disbanded in 1798, the Dutch government succeeded it as the highest authority in Indonesia. Thoughout the nineteenth century the government ruled directly, and it attempted to exclude other nations from the development of the Indonesian economy. In 1860 slavery was ended. By the beginning of the twentieth century a more open economy had been allowed to develop, and a semblance of self-government was introduced. Although the Dutch kept ultimate political control in their own hands, this first gesture toward allowing Indonesians to be consulted through formal organs of government opened the way to greater demands for self-government.

The Dutch administration tended to draw a demarcation line between Indonesians and Europeans. Indonesian students were allowed to study at European universities, but were then relegated to the Indonesian civil service, which was kept distinct from the Dutch administration and subordinate to it. In the interwar period, a growing disaffection of the natives from their colonial rulers developed, and Japanese commercial influence grew.

World War II brought satisfaction for many of the Indonesians' unmet demands for self-government. The Japanese, as allies of the Nazi government that already occupied the Netherlands, moved into Indonesia in February 1942. They acted as liberators, giving Indonesians a considerable measure of authority, although they were naturally directed to support the Japanese cause. The Indonesians were given a hold on self-government they would later be unwilling to loosen.

In 1942 the Dutch government promised that after the war a partnership would be established between the Netherlands and Indonesia, with each completely independent for internal matters. But the Indonesians seized independence for themselves in August 1945, immediately after the Japanese surrender. The Dutch, dependent on British arms to maintain their influence in the area, were compelled to accept this de facto state of affairs. In talks between the Netherlands and Indonesia, it was agreed that a United States of Indonesia would be created, representing a federation of the islands of the East Indies, and that this entity would in turn enter into a union with the Netherlands. This union meant, to the Dutch at least, a strengthened version of the British Commonwealth. But the agreement was short-lived, because the Dutch believed they should maintain control in Indonesia until the formal union of the two was created. In July 1947 the Dutch embarked on the "First Police Action," aimed at asserting Dutch control. This move brought the United Nations into action, and eventually, in January 1948, a truce was arranged. By virtue of United Nations intervention, the Netherlands lost its argument that the affair was a purely internal matter.

The Dutch elections of 1948 revealed that a majority felt the cabinet should deal sternly with Indonesia. In December of that year the "Second Police Action" was initiated, and the Dutch succeeded in displacing the chief Indonesian leaders, although they did not gain complete control of the country. Once again the United Nations took the matter under consideration, prompting a cease-fire and a round-table conference in August

1949. Three months later it was agreed that by December 30 a federal Republic of the United States of Indonesia would be created as well as a union between the Republic and the Netherlands. But later events were to show that this agreement could not last. Indonesia's Sukarno insisted on a centralized state rather than on a federation, and the union was never operational because of Indonesian fears that it would be used as an instrument of continued Dutch domination.

By the mid-1950s the Indonesians had adopted an overwhelmingly hostile attitude toward the Dutch, and many Dutch nationals and business firms were forced to leave the country. This was a blow to the Netherlands, but far more psychologically than financially. Many Dutch had long and deep attachments to the East Indies. In addition, there was real concern about the fate of peoples on outlying islands under the centralized rule of Sukarno. The dispute was not allowed to die down, because of the continued Dutch presence in West New Guinea, known to the Indonesians as West Irian. The Dutch claimed that the people of this area were racially distinct from Indonesia, but Sukarno maintained that his nation was, in any case, a mixture of races and that the Dutch had agreed to turn the area over to Indonesia. Finally, in 1962, an American mediator brought a solution to the problem that provided a face-saving device for the Dutch and an ultimate victory for the Indonesians. The area was first transferred to the United Nations and after seven months was placed under Indonesian rule.[1]

Dutch relations with Indonesia have reflected the general improvement in relations between the West and the sprawling island nation since Sukarno was replaced by a military coup and Communist influence was ruthlessly reduced. With Indonesians showing a willingness to repay their debts, which Sukarno had repudiated, the Dutch have taken the lead in providing renewed economic assistance to the country.

The transition for the Netherlands was indeed painful and was made no easier by the often unreasonable attitude of

[1] According to the formal arrangement, a plebiscite was scheduled to determine the people's wishes, but it was considered a foregone conclusion that they will join Indonesia in law as well as in fact.

Sukarno. In the immediate postwar period the Dutch proposed a series of measures that would have more than met the Indonesian prewar demands. As in many instances of decolonization, the moves by the mother country were too little and too late.

According to one analyst, the Indonesian problem "produced serious strains in Dutch domestic politics, similar in nature but to an even greater extent than the internal political tensions in the United States over the Vietnam issue." [2] Cabinets managed to govern in the Netherlands despite underlying disagreement about colonial policy. Many in the Netherlands, particularly the Conservatives, believed that the Dutch should not give up control in Indonesia because of the danger to national economic interests and the lack of adequate preparation for independence. But there was also a strong element of idealism, urging that colonies such as Indonesia should be accorded self-government. The ultimate decision was not, however, in the hands of the Dutch parties or even of the Dutch government, and it was necessary to adjust to the inevitable. Perhaps the greatest blow was to find the Dutch in opposition to the bulk of opinion expressed in the United Nations, an organization enjoying wide respect in the Netherlands.

Other Dutch colonies

The West Indies gave the Netherlands an opportunity to show it had learned the lesson of Indonesia. Both Surinam, on the South American continent, and the Netherlands Antilles have been made full parts of the Kingdom of the Netherlands and have been accorded self-government. These arrangements were established in 1954, and since that time there has been no appreciable unrest in these areas.

In general, the Dutch have a keen sense of obligation to aid the developing nations. Political parties debate the extent of increases in foreign aid, not how to cut it. Indeed, the Dutch attitude is almost idealistic. Most aid is naturally reserved for former dependent areas of the Netherlands, but a high per-

[2] Arend Lijphart, *The Politics of Accommodation* (Berkeley and Los Angeles: University of California Press, 1968), p. 101.

centage is channeled through such organizations as the United Nations and the European Community.

Belgium and the Congo

In 1960, with the breakdown of public order in the Congo, Belgium found itself branded as an old-fashioned colonial power, having failed to equip a territory under its control for over eighty years with the elementary ability to govern itself or to merit international respect.

Although in fact the events of July 1960 took place after the Congo had been granted its independence, international opinion was first awakened at that time to the uncomfortable relationship between the former mother country and the former colony. Yet the Congo had played an important role in the nation's political life for decades.

The Congo was, at the outset, the personal fiefdom of King Leopold II. Acting as a private person, Leopold began acquiring unoccupied tracts in central Africa in the hinterland of the Congo River. The famous explorer H. M. Stanley acted on behalf of the King in exploring and claiming the territory. At the Berlin Conference of the major European powers in 1885, the Congo Free State was recognized with Leopold as its king.

In Belgium, the spread of Leopold's influence throughout the territory and his attempt to develop its natural resources for commercial purposes were regarded with a benign eye. Leopold was regarded as an international promoter, who was doing much to advance the Belgian economy and who might do the same in the Congo. Many felt that the Congo should remain the personal property of King Leopold, completely separated from his European base.

Two factors militated against the maintenance of King Leopold's personal rule in the Congo. The first was his lack of sufficient capital to develop the Congo. The second was his use of outright slavery to force Congolese to labor on his enterprises. Indeed the two were related, because the King attempted to channel all economic activity under state control to extract maximum profit from the area. Both in Belgium and elsewhere in Europe, opposition to the King's methods mounted, and finally he felt compelled to turn his private domain over to the

Belgian state. In November 1907 the Parliament, not without some hesitation, made the Congo a Belgian colony.

The Congo, eighty times the size of Belgium and with a larger population, presented a considerable challenge to a country that had no experience as a colonial power. The government set as its goal the ultimate creation of a modern nation, governed by Africans. Yet the Belgian government did not want to see the Congo become a drain for Belgian resources, and in one of its earliest acts declared that the colony was open to foreign investment and trade and would not be tied economically to the mother country's apron strings.

An effort was made to provide an economic infrastructure, mainly through the construction of railroads, and to improve the standard of living for the mass of the people rather than for an elite that would then take charge. Thus, in practical terms, an attempt was made to provide a primary education for all, but none was made to provide a university education for any Congolese. This policy was to cause the new country grave difficulties after independence.

Despite Belgium's direct involvement in the Congo, individual Belgians at first felt a sense of detachment. But gradually, after World War I, Belgians began moving to the Congo to take charge of the colony's commerce or to manage its mines. For those Belgians who went to the Congo—and at times they numbered more than 100,000—the colony represented something like what California meant to the "Okies" of the 1930s. It was a sunny land, with unlimited economic opportunity, in sharp contrast with the dour Belgian climate and the stratified society at home that precluded the life of luxury they could live in the colony.

World War II stimulated the economic development of the Congo, as the Belgian government-in-exile called upon its resources on behalf of the Allied war effort. At the same time, more Congolese were attracted to the towns and to education, and they became increasingly aware politically. The second wave that swept the Congo toward independence was the freedom movement in Africa—and in particular the creation of the French Community after General de Gaulle returned to power in 1958. Political parties were founded in the Congo in that year; some Congolese leaders were fortuitously thrown into contact at the Brussels World's Fair; and finally the Accra Pan-African Conference revealed the Congolese Patrice Lumumba as a first-rank fighter for African liberation. Belgium began to feel the stirrings of discontent with its rule and the growth of a demand for independence. The new cabinet of Gaston Eyskens announced that it would decide on the future of the Congo in the light of these pressures.

Clearly the Belgians still believed that the Congo would long remain a colony because its people were not "ready" for self-government. In general, Belgians felt that they had done much to prepare the Congolese for independence, but that progress was bound to be slow. The Congolese and especially the leaders of the budding political parties felt a far greater sense of urgency. On January 4, 1959, rioting, focusing on the theme of independence, broke out in Leopoldville, and forty-nine people were killed. These riots profoundly shook Belgium. Nine days later a cabinet declaration stated: "Belgium plans to organize in the Congo a democracy able to exercise sovereign powers and to decide on its independence." The mere mention of the word "independence" was a fundamental transformation of Belgian policy. It was made possible by the open support of the Catholic Church for the independence movement, passive acquiescence by the business interests in the Congo,[3] and the faltering opposition of the colonial administration.

The only question remaining was when the Congo would be granted its independence. But the only way of delaying an immediate grant of independence was by sending military forces into the Congo. Both the Catholic Church and the Socialists opposed such a move, and the cabinet's plan to do so had to be dropped. Once again Belgian business interests with a large stake in the Congo stood by passively. This was probably due to the intermixing of their Belgian and Congolese interests. Had their interests been solely in the colony, they might have demanded

---

[3] Some observers believe that Belgian firms had already written off the Congo, expecting the violent turn its history would take. But Belgian political observers discount this reasoning. See J. Meynaud, *La Décision Politique en Belgique* (Paris: Armand Colin, 1965), pp. 345–361.

the use of force. But with their other bases in Belgium, they knew they would have to pay at the other end for any military action in the Congo.

In January 1960 a round-table conference was held in Brussels to set the date for independence. Early agreement was reached on the date of June 30, 1960, but the Belgians sought to maintain some role in the government of the Congo after that date. The Congolese refused categorically. Thus the Belgians were forced to accept full independence on that date, although no responsible leader believed that the Congolese would be ready for self-government. The Belgian decision was widely called "the Congolese bet."

In just a matter of days after the Congo had attained its independence, the "bet" was lost. The Congolese National Army revolted against its Belgian officers, and Belgian troops were employed without the consent of the Congolese government to assure the safety of Belgian nationals in the former colony. Thus began a prolonged period of Belgian involvement in Congolese affairs in an effort to protect Belgian lives and to a lesser extent Belgian business interests. Although much of the international community chose to hold Belgium responsible for the chaos of the ensuing years, the Congo actually became a classic battlefield of great power politics, with the United Nations called upon to restore order. It may be true that during the disturbed period of the following seven years, Belgians became more intimately involved in Congolese affairs than ever before. But Belgium did not enjoy the role of international villain thrust upon it nor the periodic killing of Belgian nationals in the Congo. Gradually Belgians abandoned their support for such leaders as Moise Tshombe, the leader of the Katanga secession. At the same time, the Congolese government achieved a semblance of control over the entire country and could reasonably claim to speak for it. By 1967, the Belgian government could say that it would treat the Congo as any foreign country. It banned Belgians from serving as mercenaries there. The Congo would remain the principal recipient of Belgian foreign aid, and Belgian business would continue to have interests there, but the Belgians felt able to reduce that aid if necessary and to withdraw guarantees of protection made to business interests. In addition, they acceded to Congolese nationalization measures, although they continued to operate major industrial plants.

The Congo maintains a "special relationship" with Belgium, but the disengagement of the two countries required as many years as Belgian colonialists had predicted. The fact that the disengagement came after independence undoubtedly contributed to the Congo's importance in world affairs. It appears correct to say that neither Belgium nor the Congo was "ready" for Congolese independence in 1960.

Other Belgian colonies

In addition to the Congo colony, the territory of Ruanda-Urundi, formerly a German possession, came under Belgian control by virtue of a League of Nations mandate in 1924. The territory, less attractive to business interests than the Congo, is located on the eastern border of the former Belgian colony. In 1962, Rwanda and Burundi, two separate states, were given their independence by the ending of the United Nations Trusteeship Agreement that had replaced the mandate. Relations between Belgium and these states have been cordial, causing no serious problems, mainly because of their limited size, rudimentary economic development, and the overshadowing presence of the Congo.

Belgium's colonial experience demonstrates the virtually insurmountable tasks facing a small country entrusted with a major colony relatively late in the colonial epoch. The Belgians acted in the belief that their policy was enlightened and constructive. It was, however, lacking in a sufficient comprehension of the scale of the problems they faced. Like other colonial powers, Belgium was unable to channel or control the onrushing demands for independence that developed in Africa in the late 1950s. At the same time, the Belgians in the Congo and consequently the Belgian government clung, perhaps too long, to a colonial mentality—even after Congolese independence. A further complicating factor, not present to the same extent in Indonesia or other former colonies, was the direct interest of the United States and the Soviet Union in the fortunes of the Congo.

The Congo experience did much to sour Belgians on the

question of aid to developing countries and to solidify "colonialist" attitudes among much of the Belgian population. Nonetheless, Belgium is active in providing technical assistance and still maintains a major aid program in the Congo.

THE BENELUX ORGANIZATION

That Belgium, the Netherlands, and Luxembourg have decided to create a single economic union of the three nations comes as no surprise to the student of their common history. Geographical and economic considerations virtually dictated some form of cooperation—and with the political recognition that small states could not go it alone, the conclusion of a formal agreement was relatively easy. Benelux was created on September 5, 1944.

Evolution of Benelux

The precursor of Benelux was the Belgium-Luxembourg Economic Union (BLEU) of 1922. Although this accord did not provide for a perfect union—agricultural trade was only partially covered—it did represent a pooling of tariff-negotiating authority and the creation of a single customs area. The BLEU has remained as a permanent element of the broader agreement, which in fact is an accord between the Netherlands and it.

The idea of close cooperation among the small states of Europe gained some acceptance as early as 1930 with the Convention of Oslo, in which seven nations pledged to limit their freedom of action in increasing tariffs. Two years later the Benelux nations agreed to reduce some trade protection and not to increase any existing protection. These moves were opposed by the larger states of Europe, who claimed that they represented discrimination against them. In effect, the major powers were saying the best way to keep the small states down was to keep them weak, independent economic units.

World War II swept such objections aside. While the Benelux governments were still in exile in London they agreed to create a customs union of the three countries, abolishing tariffs for trade among themselves and creating a single external tariff for trade with others. Such a move was relatively easy to accept, for each of the three had a tradition of trade liberalism and had not depended on high protectionism. Yet the agreement did not come into effect until January 1948 because of the striking difference in the postwar recovery of Belgium and the Netherlands. The Belgian economy had been spared much of the damage of the war, and both production and wages rose more quickly than in the Netherlands. But by 1948 the Dutch felt it possible to abolish at a single stroke all tariffs in trade with the BLEU.

Benelux did not, however, stop with the customs union. Periodic meetings of representatives of the three countries extended cooperation further into the realm of economic policy. On February 3, 1958, the treaty instituting the Benelux Economic Union was signed at The Hague. This accord, containing exactly one hundred articles, represented a distillation of previous agreements reached by the three countries. Like the Rome Treaty creating the European Common Market, the Benelux agreement represents a series of goals that the states agree to achieve, rather than a plan for immediate action.

Why create an economic union of the Benelux nations just when the Common Market, in which all three were members, was just getting under way? The answer was never made clear by the leaders of the three countries. In part, the economic union was a natural outgrowth of the customs union. In addition, it was felt during the 1950s that if European integration became bogged down, the Benelux countries might still be able to push their own cooperation. But relatively few appear to have envisaged a Benelux Economic Union as a force within the framework of the Common Market itself. Indeed the Common Market so overshadowed the Benelux move that neither public opinion nor political leadership demonstrated any appreciable interest in the new treaty.

The Economic Union agreement came into effect in November 1960, but for the next seven years efforts were concentrated on the completion of the customs union rather than on the coordination of economic, financial, and social policies. This lack of emphasis on rapid progress toward economic unification was due mainly to the early and rather spectacular successes of the Common Market itself. Trade restrictions among the six-nation

Community were quickly reduced, and free movement of labor among them became almost an accomplished fact. Enlargement of the European Community also seemed to be a real possibility, which pushed Benelux efforts further into the background.

Renewed interest in Benelux

Work on economic and legal cooperation began to accelerate after the first French rejection of the British application for membership in the European Community in January 1963. Yet Benelux officials were the first to admit that Benelux itself yielded no "spectacular" results. They attributed this state of affairs to the slow and painstaking work required to weave often differing legislative patterns into a coherent whole. But much of the relative lack of color must be attributed to the underlying agreement of the Benelux countries about their ultimate goals. There were simply no major political clashes among them, and the technical work proceeded at a rather leisurely pace.

The second French veto of the British application for Common Market membership in 1967 and the growing realization that France was determined to block any "supranational" pooling of decision making within the Common Market stimulated a far more dramatic response from the Benelux nations than in 1963. They announced that they would proceed at full speed toward the completion of the economic union, perhaps as early as 1968, and they would extend their cooperation to political areas outside the scope of the Benelux treaty.

Events in the Common Market were the principal impetus for this decision, announced in January 1968. But political relations among the three nations had also matured to a point where such a move became possible.

Luxembourg became increasingly willing to enter into close political relations with the Netherlands and Belgium. This change was due, at least in part, to the realization that France opposed the special position of the Luxembourg money market and to the decreasing dependence of the Luxembourg economy on France. Another element, difficult to evaluate fully, was the attitude of Prime Minister Pierre Werner, who sought an increased voice for his country in Europe's councils.

Closer cooperation between Belgium and the Netherlands received support from Belgian Minister of European Affairs Renaat Van Elslande. He turned to Benelux as a field of action, after most avenues to rapid progress in the Common Market were blocked by French intransigence. As a Fleming, he felt at home with the Dutch. In addition, a strong working relationship developed between the Dutch Foreign Minister Joseph Luns and Pierre Harmel, who succeeded Paul-Henri Spaak at the Belgian Foreign Ministry in 1966. Harmel was willing to cooperate with the Dutch in adopting a hard line in relations with France, in contrast with the conciliatory attitude of his predecessor. All this added up to a renewed cordiality in Benelux relations. Although some in Belgium and the Netherlands saw this as a kind of escapism from the problems facing Europe, many others felt that Benelux had at last had some life breathed into it.

The Benelux Economic Union requires free movement of goods, persons, capital, and services among the three members. Economic, social, and financial policies are to be coordinated, and any changes in the exchange rates of the three national currencies are to be agreed upon in common. The three nations have decided to adopt and pursue a common policy in their economic relations with other countries.

The Benelux accord is an intergovernmental agreement; there are no elements of supranational decision making in it. Majority voting and an independent executive, integral parts of the Common Market, are excluded. The reasons for this approach are self-evident. First, there is a wide area of agreement among the three partners and little likelihood of a major policy dispute among them. In addition, a qualified voting scheme among just three countries would be extremely difficult to envisage. Indeed, the Netherlands, with a majority of the Benelux population and an economy larger than those of its two partners combined, would have to have the preponderance of voting power and an absolute veto.

Benelux institutions

Yet Benelux has been endowed with a complex institutional structure. Virtually all decision-making power is in the hands of the Committee of Ministers, composed of three members of the cabinets of each of the Benelux nations. Each state has one vote, and all decisions must be taken unanimously, although an abstention does not constitute a negative vote. The Committee of Ministers sets up working parties, composed of high-ranking civil servants, and delegates many of its responsibilities to them. A Council of the Economic Union, also composed of civil servants, is given the task of supervising the implementation of ministerial decisions and coordinating the activities of the committees and special committees, discussed below.

Under the customs union agreement, an Interparliamentary Consultative Council was created. All proposed Benelux agreements are sent by the Committee of Ministers to this body, composed of members of national parliaments. Amendments are proposed frequently, and they are almost invariably accepted by the ministers, thus assuring subsequent parliamentary approval when the agreements are presented for ratification before the national parliaments. This influence of parliamentarians on Benelux decisions is far more effective than parliamentary control by the European Parliament in the framework of the Common Market. An Economic and Social Advisory Council also renders opinions on proposed decisions and may, on its own initiative, submit resolutions to the Committee of Ministers. It exercises little effective influence.

The agreement also provides for a number of committees and special committees, assigned the task of ensuring the ministerial decisions are carried out by national administrations. On the basis of their experience with the implementation of decisions, they may submit proposals to the Committee of Ministers. These committees represent a unique substitute for direct execution of Benelux decisions by an independent Secretariat. They provide the link between the Benelux decision makers and those who will carry out policy on the national level. But members of the various committees regard themselves as national delegates, as is considered appropriate to an essentially intergovernmental organization. In practice, however, this means committees are not a dynamic element in Benelux unless the ministers provide a strong political impetus for action.

A General Secretariat has been established, but its functions are almost purely administrative, and its officials, about sixty in number, are not considered to be independent of national administrations. In recognition of its geographical location, Brussels is the administrative center of Benelux. In recognition of Dutch economic and demographic strength, a Dutchman is always secretary general.

An Arbitral Tribunal is available to settle disputes arising from the application of the Benelux agreement. A final administrative body, mentioned in the accord, is the Joint Service, but none has ever been created. Presumably, such an organ would group services of the three members and would be a direct administrative agency of the Benelux organization.

The Benelux structure offers little out of the ordinary among intergovernmental organizations, and its accomplishments are far from dramatic. In only one respect does it appear to go beyond a simple forum for cooperative action. In foreign economic and financial relations, the three often choose to act as a unit. A single negotiator represents them in talks with other countries, which may result in so-called Benelux commercial agreements. This common bargaining position strengthens the hand of a negotiator, indeed making an accord with Benelux more attractive to other countries than two separate agreements (with the Netherlands and with the BLEU) would be.

Both the evolution of the Benelux organization and its institutions indicate the extent to which political agreement and will to act among the three members is a prerequisite for almost any kind of action. In the absence of such a political will in the early years of the economic union, Benelux was subject to a stifling lassitude. Only when outside events reawoke interest in its potential did Benelux begin to make real progress toward its announced goals.

Fields of activity

There are no real obstacles to an effective economic union among the three Benelux nations. But even if it is achieved, the union will function on the basis of coordinated action rather than through pooled decision making and administration. This makes virtually certain the need for repeated nudges by the nations' political leaders to the officials and experts who staff the organization's institutions. In addition, certain areas cannot be effectively treated by Benelux. Agriculture, the source of considerable controversy within the Common Market, cannot benefit from an adequate policy in the restricted territory of these three small countries, especially when many believe that the Europe of the Six is too small for a common farm policy to function properly. On the other hand, the customs union can be completed easily, and greater attention can be given to regional development in an area free of the conflicting nationalisms characteristic of the Common Market.

Harmonization of law is being extended in Benelux. Legal experts have been able to make progress in aligning legal dispositions, for example, in the field of police control.

Cultural cooperation presents serious obstacles, largely because of the language question. French-speaking Belgians tend to regard Benelux as an essentially Dutch-speaking community, in some ways opposed both to France and the French language. This sentiment is enhanced by cooperative work carried on by Dutch and Flemish scholars to make language rules common to both areas. While the need for scientific cooperation is recognized, joint action in education appears excluded by the underlying distrust of the two language groups.

In the political domain lies the most fertile field for making Benelux a meaningful organization. Government leaders in all three countries appear to recognize that by speaking with a single voice, or at least by taking the same approach, the Benelux nations will carry more weight in the Common Market. They are reluctant to see any further institutionalization of their political cooperation, however, because they fear they would actually lose voting strength in the European Community. As separate states, the Benelux nations have five votes in the European Community's Council of Ministers, while a single state such as West Germany has only four. But, thanks to the precedent set by the Franco-German cooperation agreement of 1963, they are increasingly willing to meet as a Benelux group in advance of Common Market sessions to develop a common position. This process is still at its earliest stage of evolution and promises more than it actually provides.

Yet Benelux seems destined to remain a secondary organization. It has not caught the imagination of the peoples of the three countries to the same extent as the Common Market itself. Although the three small Benelux countries recognize the imperative necessity of pooling their strength in a larger framework if their economic potential is to have any real meaning, they prefer an enlarged European Community, with an outward-looking approach, to a "little Europe" of the Six or a "micro-Europe" of Benelux. As small states with full voting rights in the European Community they believe they can exercise some real influence there. Although their powers are greater in Benelux, the power of Benelux is small.

THE BENELUX NATIONS AND EUROPEAN INTEGRATION

Allow me to refrain from comparing the diplomatic positions of Belgium and the Netherlands. They are in conformity with traditions which are not identical. Each of these diplomacies springs separately from its respective government and parliament.

That the small States of the (European) Community try to agree to unify if possible their points of view seems to me a good practice, and we have been pleased each time we were able to achieve concrete results. But none of us has abdicated the smallest part of our sovereignty in these matters.[4]

This statement by Belgian Foreign Minister Pierre Harmel, made early in 1968, is perhaps the best distillation of the Benelux approach to the problems of European integration. The statement was, in fact, made at a time when cooperation among the three countries on matters concerning the European Community was at an all-time high.

Two considerations are meant to be understood in the Harmel statement. First, it is a Belgian declaration of independence from the Dutch approach, because the Netherlands has almost always represented one of the extremes in the discussion of the political unification of Europe. The second consideration is that Luxembourg is not mentioned and cannot be ex-

[4] From interview of Foreign Minister Pierre Harmel of Belgium in *Le Soir* (Brussels), February 6, 1968, p. 2.

pected to influence Benelux cooperation, although it has in recent years drawn closer to Belgium and the Netherlands. Only on one matter, the transfer of some European institutions away from Luxembourg, did the Grand Duchy show itself ready to take a political initiative in European Community debates.

European integration takes place on two planes: the economic and the political. In both cases, it may appear that France plays a dominant role in the Community. French intransigence, when it comes to creating any Community procedures that would shift part of traditional national decision-making power to Community institutions, has undoubtedly been a principal cause of the gradual slowdown of integration. And without a feeling of continued momentum, all members of the Community tend to defend their individual economic interests with even greater tenacity, resulting in even more foot-dragging. This in turn influences prospects for common political action, where there is no perceptible movement at all.

Thus French policy has been instrumental in slowing down the process of European economic integration and in preventing any real progress toward European political integration. This may appear to be an essentially negative approach, although the French would have wished otherwise. Indeed, General de Gaulle made a series of proposals, aimed not only at preventing the development of a supranational Europe, but at creating a "Europe of the Fatherlands." But repeated French initiatives (as opposed to French vetos) have been blocked, and at least a spark of the original idealism that animated the founders of the European integration movement has been kept alive. This has been principally a result of the policies of the Benelux nations.

The six member nations of the European Community can be arranged in something of a spectrum. At one end would be France, opposed to any pooling of political power, opposed to enlargement of the Community for the foreseeable future, and opposed to cooperation with the United States. At the other end would be the Netherlands, in favor of supranationalism, enlargement of the Community, and Atlantic cooperation. For most of the period since 1958, when the Common Market was founded and de Gaulle returned to power, the other four members—

Belgium, Luxembourg, Italy, and West Germany—have sought to be pragmatists, finding a middle ground between these two extremes and thus allowing the enterprise to advance, however slowly. Perhaps the only change in this alignment during the entire period has been the gradual drawing together of the Benelux group.

The European Community has faced four major political crises: the Fouchet negotiations of 1961–1962, the first French veto of British membership in 1963, the French walkout of 1965–1966, and the second French veto in 1967. The Dutch reaction, and to an increasing extent the reaction of its two Benelux partners, can be characterized as one of steadfast opposition to the French stand.

The Fouchet negotiations

As early as 1960, General de Gaulle began discussing with other political leaders in the Six the possibility of creating institutions for political cooperation among them. As the French proposals evolved, they came to include regular consultations by chiefs of government and foreign ministers on such matters as foreign policy, defense, economic policy, and cultural affairs. Agreement was to be sought on the basis of unanimity, and without benefit of proposals from an independent agency such as the Commission of the European Economic Community. Hence the French proposals called for traditional intergovernmental cooperation as a means of extending European integration, the very concept that had been rejected as unworkable prior to the proposal for the European Coal and Steel Community some ten years earlier.

In 1961 France met with opposition from several of its partners on the inclusion of economic affairs in the realm of intergovernmental cooperation, since they were already covered by the European Community, and because of France's apparent desire to separate European defense policy from NATO. By November of that year Christian Fouchet, a French official, had submitted a proposal that deleted these disputed points but kept the basic elements of intergovernmental cooperation. During talks late in 1961 other countries asked for institutional means of strengthening cooperation, mainly through the creation of an independent secretariat. Then, to the surprise of France's five partners, a new Fouchet draft was submitted in January 1962 that retreated from the earlier proposal and included economic affairs once more as a fit subject for cooperation.

Throughout the talks to this point, the Dutch had been reticent to proceed with the Fouchet plan. They insisted that Britain, which by this time had applied for membership, should be allowed to take part in the talks. And they demonstrated a rather open mistrust of French intentions. The result of the second Fouchet proposal was to push the other four toward the Dutch camp. Working without France, the Five prepared their own version of a treaty for political cooperation that dropped mention of economic cooperation, called for an independent Secretary General, and required less than complete unanimity for decisions. Yet differences remained among the Five, with the Dutch continuing to take the most uncompromising attitude toward France. In any case, the talks gradually ground to a halt later that year, and the Fouchet plan was dead.

On the surface it would appear that all five opposed the French position, and this was the reason that France did not gain satisfaction. Yet some of the Five were ready to compromise with the French (although the French did not seem interested), and it was mainly the Dutch and the Belgians who forced the hard line that the French would not accept. Those who believe the Fouchet plan would have been better than nothing blame the Dutch and Belgians for its failure.

Foreign Minister Paul-Henri Spaak of Belgium, along with the Dutch, insisted that the drafts under consideration in early 1962 could not lead to an agreement without British participation. Some observers believe that Spaak's *no* to more talks was a tactic aimed at extracting further concessions from the French rather than at actually getting Britain to the negotiating table. Spaak undoubtedly would, however, have been happier with more supranational decision-making provisions in the treaty for political cooperation. Before the Belgian public, Spaak was careful to say that he did not believe his actions had led to the end of the Fouchet talks, although in fact they had been a direct cause.

While the Belgians appeared to believe that with sufficient

supranationalism, the small states would be adequately protected under the new treaty and could proceed without Britain, the Dutch were more wary. They steadfastly opposed the various proposals made in the course of the Fouchet talks, leading at least one observer to the conclusion that the Dutch were even opposed to supranationalism, despite all their talk in favor of European unification.[5] There can be little doubt that the Dutch, by virtue of their history as world traders, were more attached to the idea of an open Community and in particular to the introduction of British democratic procedures. In addition, they did not wish to see the Atlantic alliance placed in jeopardy.

This cautious Dutch attitude might suggest that the Netherlands talked much in favor of full integration, but did not support the policy when an occasion arose to take a step forward. However, such a conclusion fails to take into account the fundamental Dutch distrust of French policy within the European Community. Foreign Minister Joseph Luns was concerned that the wishes of a small country such as the Netherlands would be ignored in a tight supranational entity of the Six in which the French could swing the compromisers to its side, leaving the Dutch virtually isolated. For this reason he pinned his hopes on British membership, which would offer the prospect of a counterbalance to French domination. As for intergovernmental cooperation, the Dutch saw no reason to subject their clearly defined national policy—including an open Community and good Atlantic relations—to discussion among the Six when they knew in advance that there was no possibility of agreement between France and the Netherlands. Indeed, the Dutch could later point to the Franco-German agreement of 1963, a kind of bilateral Fouchet plan, as a failure by de Gaulle's own admission, because of the lack of fundamental agreement between the two parties and an overt French attempt to dominate.

If there is such fundamental political antipathy on European political questions between the Netherlands and France, one may question why both find themselves in the European Community. Undoubtedly the Dutch felt a strong commitment to European integration, both as a way of restraining Germany

[5] See A. Silj, *Europe's Political Puzzle* (Cambridge, Mass.: Harvard Center for International Affairs, 1967), *passim*.

and of maximizing their own influence as a small state. But the Netherlands counted on British membership and the enlargement of the Community as soon as the British saw the error of their original decision to stay out. For the Dutch, the Community was fundamentally changed when early British membership became an impossibility. Finally, the historical record shows that the Dutch and the others signed the Rome Treaty in March 1957, more than a year before de Gaulle returned to power and began to transform French policy.

The subsequent clash between French and Dutch policy, no better illustrated than by the Fouchet negotiations, is probably based on the fact that these two nations have clearly defined policy objectives that do not coincide. Don't the other Common Market members have such fixed objectives? Although the other members of the Common Market have relatively coherent foreign policies, each of them makes an effort to find compromises between France and its antagonists or indeed between France and their own desires. Belgium, with a French-speaking population, Luxembourg, economically linked with France, West Germany, anxious for full reconciliation with France and Italy, in France's shadow and desirous of exerting greater power on the French model, all have reasons for seeking compromises with France. The Netherlands does not. To General de Gaulle, the Dutch are not, for this reason, a continental people; they are "Atlanticists."

In the Fouchet talks, the Dutch stood virtually alone in opposition to France. Belgium and Luxembourg were essentially in the camp of the compromisers, although Spaak, by typical exuberance, brought his country into line with the Dutch. It should not be forgotten that neither the West Germans nor the Italians were able to push on with the talks after Belgian and Dutch rejection of the French plans. It remains a matter of conjecture whether they chose to let the others act for them or whether Belgian and Dutch rejection was in itself sufficient to end the talks.

The first French veto of British membership

The second crisis, the French veto of the British application for membership in January 1963, was an outgrowth of the first.

The argument about the amount of progress the negotiations had made prior to the veto remains unsettled, but few doubt that the abrupt manner of the veto, announced at a de Gaulle press conference, was an affront to the other countries of the Community.

De Gaulle's veto was based in large measure on his accurate appraisal of the fundamental differences in French and British policy. And many of the objections he could apply to Britain would apply equally well to the Netherlands. The French President gave considerable weight to Britain's "Trojan horse" role. He insinuated that Britain, as a firm NATO ally of the United States, would defend the American approach within the European Community. Even if he were overstating the case, he clearly did oppose the presence of another nation that, like the Netherlands and Belgium, placed as great an emphasis on its Atlantic role as on its participation in the Community.

What de Gaulle failed to mention was nonetheless quite obvious. He feared Britain as a potential rival for the political leadership of the Community. And despite British reluctance to endorse far-reaching supranationalism, de Gaulle seemed to be concerned about the effect of British policy on political and economic integration after Britain had joined.

The Dutch and Belgians favored British membership for the very reason that it would provide potential new leadership within the Community. More disabused than de Gaulle, they realized that the British were unenthusiastic about supranationalism, but they accorded this secondary importance. The Benelux countries laid great stress on the democratic tradition in Britain and assumed that with Britain in the Community, increased emphasis would be placed on consulting the European Parliament, which France had opposed.

To a certain degree, Belgian and Dutch acceptance of elements of the common farm policy, beneficial to France, had been predicated on the assumption that later they would receive satisfaction in the form of British acceptance into the Community. When this prospect was swept aside, the Benelux nations, like Germany and Italy, groped for an alternative procedure. The solution was "synchronization," proposed by the Germans, and calling for each Common Market agreement to give satisfaction to each of the Six, without the need for a future payoff, such as the prospect of British entry had been. This method of operation was accepted without joy, and many Dutch subjected their continued membership in the Community to a searching if inconclusive examination. Benelux discontent with the Community grew, because they felt themselves trapped in an organization that was failing to fulfill their expectations and hopes.

Democratic control of the community

One of the major Dutch objections to the European Community is the lack of democratic control of Common Market decisions. Based on the relatively strong position of the States General, the Netherlands argues that powers formerly under the control of the legislature should not be transferred to the Community's Council of Ministers, where only governments are represented, but also in part to a European parliamentary group. To a lesser extent this sentiment is shared by all other Common Market countries except France, where the legislature has been reduced to a subordinate role.

The Dutch have been particularly insistent that as increased financial resources are placed at the disposal of the Community, steps should be taken to expand the budgetary powers of the European Parliament, a consultative assembly composed of members of national parliaments. In 1965 the independent Common Market Commission at last submitted a proposal, aimed at giving the Dutch some satisfaction in their demands for greater democratization. As part of a proposal concerning the financing of the common farm policy, which might well involve over $1.5 billion a year, the commission suggested an elaborate system of budgetary control that would enhance the influence of both the European Parliament and the commission itself. Commission officials expressly stated that while the financial proposals were aimed at meeting France's demands, the budgetary procedure was designed to balance the "package" by making a concession to the Dutch and, in fact, to greater integration.

The French, however, insisted that the Council of Ministers adopt only the financing provisions in 1965, deferring indefinitely any increase in the powers of the European Parliament over the budget. When they failed to obtain agreement on this approach by July 1, the date when the new financial regulation was to come into effect, they walked out of the Common Market Council.

The ultimate effect of this manuever was to end Dutch isolation in opposition to French Common Market policy. Although at first the Belgians wavered, all Five wormed a solid front of opposition to the French boycott as the crisis wore on. By January 1966 the French were forced to return to the Common Market, although the crisis clouds continued to hang over the Community concerning both the powers of the European Parliament and majority voting procedures in the Council of Ministers.

The 1965–1966 crisis did not in fact bring any fundamental changes in the European Community, and to that extent the French were unsuccessful. But by their walkout, they also stimulated joint action among the Five, on the basis of a defense of stronger Community institutions. Thus without altering its basic position, the Netherlands found itself with new allies. Although the alliance was temporary, it indicated that when the Community was threatened, it would have its defenders. Thus the Dutch succeeded in their policy of keeping at least a spark of the "Community spirit" alive after the first French veto of British membership.

The second French veto of British membership

The second British attempt to gain entry into the European Community had its origins during the 1965–1966 crisis. During this crisis the British Labour government, which had originally opposed membership, altered its attitude. Much of the impetus appears to have come from the Netherlands. Despite claims by Foreign Minister Luns that Europe would be no more complete without France than without Britain, rumors circulated in The Hague during the French boycott that the Dutch were considering inviting Britain to join the Common Market in place of France. As the boycott dragged on, many began to doubt that the French would ever agree to return to the Council of Ministers, particularly because of de Gaulle's well-known antipathy to the Common Market. This prospect caused concern in the Netherlands, for without France, the European Community was almost certain to be dominated by West Germany. In order to avert such a development, some Dutch gave serious consideration to an immediate invitation to Britain to join.

Although these plans never reached fruition, they did encourage the British to make a second attempt at membership. By the time that the British application was submitted in 1967, the British had also become aware of the attachment of their supporters within the Community to political as well as economic integration. Thus, in contrast to the first application, the second was an even clearer warning to France that Britain, once in the Community, would be a natural ally of the Benelux nations.

By the end of 1967 the second French veto of British membership had become unavoidable. French statements hardly veiled their concern that British entry would mean a new balance of power within the Community. Although this response stung all of the Five, the Benelux nations alone reacted.

Early in 1968 they announced the so-called Benelux Plan. If the French could not be moved, cooperation would be sought with Britain outside the Common Market framework and principally on technological problems. In addition, they announced that the Benelux countries would begin consultations on foreign policy questions—including relations with eastern Europe—and other countries were free to join. The tactic implicit in the Benelux initiative was to create a parallel enterprise to the Community with the participation of the Five, Britain, and possibly other nations. To make such a proposal represented a feat of unity for the Benelux countries and of political courage within the Community. The Benelux nations opened themselves to charges that they were willing to undermine the Community through the creation of outside organs having activities overlapping the Common Market. Obviously, their disillusionment with a Community hamstrung by French opposition to supranationalism and enlargement had led them to this point.

To be successful, the Benelux plan required the support not only of Britain, but of Italy and West Germany. But the

Germans were determined not to force a break with France, mainly because they believed that French support was needed in their policy of improved relations with eastern Europe. The Italians seemed unable to generate sufficient conviction that the correct moment had come for action.[6] Thus, the Benelux plan was not translated into action.

But, in the Western European Union, which groups Britain and the Six, foreign policy consultations were begun in 1969. Just as the French had been seriously worried that the Five would adopt the Benelux plan, they were concerned about where the WEU consultations might lead. Because they could not block these talks, and in the face of unusual solidarity among the Five, the French boycotted these discussions.

Faced with the apparent failure of their attempt to infuse some political vigor into the European Community, the three decided to devote renewed efforts to the strengthening of their own Benelux organization. Although it was no substitute for an enlarged Community, Benelux represented a method of increasing their joint economic strength and hence their bargaining power within the Common Market.

This survey has covered only the major political questions that have arisen during the history of the Common Market. The Benelux nations, of course, have a direct interest in many of the economic issues that have come before the Six. Indeed, because of its inability to advance toward political unification the European Community has concentrated upon these economic questions.

Economic issues: the Netherlands

For the Netherlands, the creation of the customs union, transportation policy, and agriculture have been the most important economic issues. The Dutch, as a traditional free-trading nation, urged the rapid removal of trade barriers among the Six and the adoption of a common external tariff at as low a level as possible. They supported Community participation in the Kennedy Round and were willing to sacrifice Community pro-

---

[6] The Germans submitted a more modest suggestion for reducing trade barriers between the Six and Britain, and the Italians gave general support to all suggestions.

tection in return for substantial concessions from other nations. In this effort, the Dutch found themselves in conflict with France and Italy, high-tariff countries. The results of the Kennedy Round, as far as the Common Market is concerned, indicates a substantial, although incomplete, victory for the Dutch position.

Yet one aspect of the common external tariff creates problems for the Netherlands. Because Rotterdam serves as a major port of entry for goods shipped from outside the Community to other Common Market countries, the Dutch collect customs duties far in excess of those accruing from purely Dutch imports. The Common Market Commission has proposed that a procedure be developed to distribute part of the Dutch customs proceeds to other countries. The Netherlands has been reluctant to accept this sizeable loss of tax revenues, but has indicated a willingness to study modifications in the present system if a new Community budget procedure is adopted.

The port of Rotterdam also provides the Netherlands with a special interest in the development of a Community transportation policy. An intense transportation network—roads, canals, and railroads—links Rotterdam with other parts of the Common Market. Dutch truckers have carried a considerable part of the freight transported by road in the Six. Now the Dutch fear that a Community quota system, under which carriage by Dutch truckers between two other Common Market countries would be limited, would be a severe blow to the transportation sector and perhaps to Rotterdam itself. The Dutch have thus been extremely cautious in supporting a common approach to transportation policy.

Finally, as a nation with efficient farm production, the Netherlands has favored a common agricultural policy with low price supports, particularly for dairy products. In the field of farm policy, the Dutch and the French, the Community's most efficient producers, often find themselves in agreement.

Economic issues: Belgium

Belgium shares relatively few of the basic Dutch economic concerns within the Common Market, with the exception of a liberal trade policy. In the field of agriculture, for example, the Belgians have been instrumental in the adoption of high price supports and large quotas for sugar. As a result, the Common Market has gone from a net importer to a surplus area for sugar production. Much the same is true for dairy products.

The most serious economic problem Belgium has faced within the framework of the European Community has been the phasing out of its inefficient coal production. Operating from outmoded and relatively poor mines, Belgium has been unable to maintain price competition with other areas of the Community and with imports from the United States. Through the European Coal and Steel Community, aid was pumped into Belgium to encourage mine closures, the establishment of new industries at mine sites, and the retraining of workers. Without this aid, Belgium would have suffered a severe economic crisis. But even with European Community aid, the Belgian government was faced with stern opposition from many miners to mine closings and has been forced to subsidize some inefficient operations.

Economic issues: Luxembourg

For Luxembourg, the development of a common market for steel has been of prime importance. But this small country has seen others in the Six, principally Italy, establish efficient and modern production that challenges Luxembourg for markets. In addition, the world excess of supply over demand has hurt Luxembourg producers. Thus the early years of the Coal and Steel Community provided Luxembourg with an economic advantage that has since been fading. In an effort to stimulate research in new uses of steel, the Coal and Steel Community has sponsored a series of world steel conferences in Luxembourg.

The transfer of many Coal and Steel Community officials to Brussels in 1967 also posed a threat to the Luxembourg economy, for the staff members had been an important source of revenue. The Luxembourg government fought with considerable success for the reassignment of certain personnel from Brussels in compensation. Luxembourg plans to become the financial and judicial seat of the European Community.

Through favorable tax laws, Luxembourg has become a principal European money market. In an effort to encourage greater activity on stock markets elsewhere and to stimulate the incorporation of foreign firms in other cities, the French have called for an end to the privileged tax position of the Grand Duchy. But the Luxembourg government appears reluctant to cede its advantageous position.

Despite their differing interests in the economic sector, the Benelux countries have been drawing together in their defense of the ideal of European integration. In effect, this means greater unity in support of the position consistently adopted by the Dutch government.

Commitment to Europe

The Dutch commitment to greater political integration and enlargement of the Community is due in large measure to Foreign Minister Joseph Luns, in office for more than fifteen years. By virtue of his tenure, he has been able to pursue a consistent approach, buttressed by a broad consensus among the major Dutch political parties in favor of extensive integration. A sentiment has, however, developed in recent years, critical of Luns's efforts in favor of British membership. Because of increased Dutch economic integration with the other Common Market countries, particularly with Germany, the need for British inclusion within the Common Market trade zone appears to have lessened.

The major turning point in the Belgian policy toward the European Community came with the accession in 1966 of Pierre Harmel to the Foreign Ministry. Paul-Henri Spaak, his predecessor, was considered one of the strongest advocates of European integration, but his policy lacked the Dutch coherence and tenacity. In part this was due to Spaak's desire that Belgium play its traditional role as mediator and his wish not to affront France, which would have stirred discontent among Belgian Walloons. In addition, Spaak preferred an ad hoc European policy to one worked out carefully in advance. Harmel, on the other hand, found it easy to work with the Dutch, and he was meticulous in the preparation of his own moves. His staff worked closely with the Dutch Foreign Ministry. A Walloon himself, he could not be accused of being opposed to the French. Because of his calm yet forceful approach, leadership of the Benelux group in the Common Market often passed to him. The Luxembourgers seemed responsive to this new Belgian approach.

The European Community has provided an arena for maximizing the influence that small states such as the Benelux nations may exert. They have not been overruled by their larger partners. But, even with increased unity among them, it appears unlikely that they will be able to take over a role of leadership. Their best hope for a Community in line with their own goals apparently remains the admission of Britain and other nations that share their democratic outlook and their Atlantic orientation.

THE BENELUX NATIONS AND THE ATLANTIC ALLIANCE

The three Benelux countries are among the most faithful supporters of the North Atlantic Treaty Organization. Their policy of full support for Atlantic military cooperation results from a realistic appraisal of their military capabilities and their security needs.

As small countries, the Benelux states suffered the harsh experience of war and occupation, in part because they stood against the aggressor individually rather than as members of an international force. This approach was not limited to them, of course, for full allied cooperation came well after hostilities had begun in both world wars. By the end of the war in 1945, most European countries recognized that they had become small powers and could assure their self-defense only through joint action. In addition, the fear of continuing Communist expansion in Europe and the need for American protection led to the creation of NATO.

In the postwar period Europe made a single attempt to provide for its own joint defense, including a rearmed Germany, through the creation of a European Defense Community. But this effort failed when it was rejected by the French parliament in 1954, and West Germany was subsequently accepted as a full member of NATO.

With the growing East-West *détente*, beginning in the late 1950s, NATO was subjected to new stresses. France pressed first for the creation of a NATO directorate that would give it, together with Britain and the United States, an overall responsibility for major questions facing the alliance. The smaller members, including the Benelux states, were reluctant to see the joint decision making by all fifteen members swept away. Eventually, because of American opposition, the French proposal was rejected.

In the second phase of its attack on NATO, France questioned the need for Europe to remain under the "hegemony" of the United States. While the United States provided much of the defense forces and the nuclear deterrent, it could in effect control the states of western Europe. But the alternative France seemed to be offering—a European force under French leadership—did not appear a valid substitute to the Europeans. They admitted that their sovereignty was limited by NATO, but they preferred to make sacrifices of sovereignty to an extra-European power that could provide the greatest protection.

This attitude represented the NATO orthodoxy and received the full support of the Benelux nations. Indeed, they played a leading role in NATO, with the Netherlands' Dirk U. Stikker and Belgium's Paul-Henri Spaak serving the organization as secretary general during much of the 1950s and 1960s.

In an effort to give Europe a measure of control over nuclear weapons used in its defense, the United States proposed a multilateral force in which all NATO members could participate. In the traditional NATO framework, only military commands were integrated in time of peace; military forces remained national units. The proposed MLF did not, however, come into existence. Europeans, including the Benelux nations, were concerned that someday its existence might serve to discourage the creation of an integrated European force, and in the interim they saw no real need for it.

Despite the MLF episode, France maintained its pressure on NATO, announcing finally in 1966 that it was withdrawing from joint military planning and operations and wanted NATO military headquarters off French territory by 1967. France also raised the specter of its possible withdrawal from NATO as a whole when this action became possible in 1969. These French moves raised doubts in Europe and the United States about the willingness of other states to remain in the alliance if France walked out.

Belgium and the Netherlands took the lead in 1966 and 1967 in providing a solution to the NATO crisis that had been provoked by France. NATO military commands were transferred from France to the Benelux area. In addition, Brussels was offered as the new site for NATO political headquarters, which were to follow the military staff out of Paris. Working with phenomenal speed, Belgium prepared new headquarters for both civil and military personnel.

The most important new political initiative came in the form of the Harmel Plan, submitted in 1966 and adopted in 1967. In his proposals, the Belgian foreign minister sought to begin the transformation of NATO from a purely defensive alliance into an instrument that could be used to promote an East-West *détente*. The plan had a two fold purpose. First, Harmel sought to stem left-wing opposition at home to the installation of NATO headquarters in Belgium. At the same time, he hoped to hold out the promise of a fundamental modification in NATO's purpose and thus encourage some members, especially Norway and Denmark, to continue in the alliance even if France withdrew. The plan itself called for increased consultations on subjects including relations with eastern Europe and the developing countries. But far more important than the substance of the proposal was the fact that it came from one of the smaller NATO members and indicated a commitment to the future of the alliance. The effect was lost neither on doubting members nor on France itself; all agreed to the plan.[7]

The Benelux nations have demonstrated a continuing commitment to the alliance, based on acute recognition of their own weaknesses as small nations. But they do not appear to favor a status quo. They are taking part in the gradual reduction of military forces that has been discernible throughout NATO. And should the prospects for political unification in Europe improve, they could be expected to support the creation of a European military force.

Benelux reliance on NATO implies a willingness to follow

[7] Undoubtedly, there would be less question about the need for NATO after the Soviet invasion of Czechoslovakia in August 1968.

the American lead on many of the major political questions facing these small nations. With memories of United States intervention during both world wars, the citizens of Benelux have a basically favorable disposition to American leadership.

At the same time, most people in all three countries believe that the United States has undermined the growing East-West *détente* through its action in Vietnam. In fact, the Vietnamese war has been the most important single factor since 1945 in weakening support for the United States in these countries.

The Benelux countries, although cautious about the pitfalls, are strong supporters of measures—particularly in the fields of trade and phased, bilateral disarmament—for improving relations between East and West. Although the Dutch have long recognized Communist China in an attempt to promote trade, none of the three nourishes illusions that they can make much headway acting alone. They remain partisans of an East-West *détente* in which the United States and a uniting Europe can work together in negotiations with the Communist nations.

CONCLUSIONS

Politics in the Benelux nations present sharp contrasts under a veneer of similitude. Each of the three is a constitutional monarchy with a parliamentary form of government. Each has demonstrated remarkable political stability and an acceptance of a gradual evolution in its governmental system.

But in the realm of domestic policy the differences are striking. The Netherlands is a political society including a great number of parties and groups, which hold specific and not always compatible ideas on how that society should be organized. These groups represent relatively homogeneous families, organized along religious or class lines, with relatively little overlapping. Yet they have never pushed their differences of opinion to the point of an open conflict that would endanger the system. In fact, they appear to prefer to seek compromises and ignore differences to the extent necessary to maintain the political system.

In part this is due to some underlying similarities, which the groups themselves do not openly admit. For example, if one party favors increased morality in public life or an increase in foreign aid, there can be and is no fundamental opposition. Although the religious parties would appear to be those where ideology would matter the most, in fact with them it probably matters the least. These are the parties of the center, and adherence to any one of them results from membership in a given church or from "feeling comfortable" with other members; neither of these situations today has much political relevance.

The Dutch approach is highly pragmatic, based upon the need to maintain a viable government that can deal with the most pressing national problems. By choosing to deal with political issues in a problem-solving manner, the government tends to shed much of its identification with ideologically oriented party programs. Only in the States General can the parties maintain their individual programs and seek to influence the course of government policy. This results in a breach between the party representatives in the cabinet and its members of parliament. This distinction between duties of members of a single party has been an accepted feature of Dutch political life.

The coalition is thus a full step removed from the will of the voter. A Dutchman knows in advance that the cabinet arising from any national elections will not reflect the views of even a single voter. He does not vote to choose a cabinet; he votes in an effort to influence the cabinet by increasing the percentage of votes given to one of its potential participants. And, if a single party receives too few votes, it may be excluded from the cabinet and have little influence at all.

A trend of manifest discontent with the political system has been discernible in the Netherlands in recent years. Much of the opposition comes from the younger voters, who seek to throw off their assigned subordinate role in the nation's political life and who demand a closer link between the voter and his government. Yet this dissent, represented by the D '66 party, has not hesitated to operate through the very traditional political system that it seeks to change. In this way, it is able to have an immediate effect on the traditional parties, afraid of losing seats.

The immediate problem for the Dutch political system is reform. Partly because of the threat of D '66 and partly because of increasing awareness of the sterility of hardened philosophical views in modern politics, most Dutch political leaders accept the need for a realignment in the party system. But neither the reform demanded by D '66 nor the refashioning of the parties will come unless the voters show greater discontent with the present system. In the late 1960s, protest does not seem to have reached a sufficiently high pitch to bring this change.

One virtually unique element of the Dutch political system appears to remain unchanged in any political reform: the States General. Through a combination of political factors—including the gap between party and government, the possibility of forming splinter parties, and the Dutch spirit—the States General has maintained its position in a meaningful parliamentary system. The powers of the national legislature have, of course, been eroded away in favor of the government, as in other countries. But the extent to which the parliament has been overshadowed by the cabinet has been limited. The Dutch not only take pride in their democratic system, they recognize the continuing need to maintain the legislature as a distinct branch of government, with its own prerogatives. For the politically aware of the Netherlands, support of the States General is an act of faith, performed in common by those of virtually all political persuasions.

Unlike the Dutch political system, which faces the prospect of a gradual reform in an attempt to improve it, the Belgian system is confronted with challenges that threaten a radical transformation without promising a more effective form of government.

Belgian political life, as in the Netherlands, is characterized by the presence of a number of groups based on religion, class, and language. In Belgium it may be posited that a higher degree of overlapping among groups has existed than in the Netherlands. But this situation has been gradually changing as the nation's division along language lines becomes more pronounced.

The principal problem facing not only the Belgian political system but the Belgian state itself is whether any conceivable political solution can enable the two language communities to continue to coexist in a constructive national atmosphere. The total dismemberment of the state does not appear to be a realistic possibility, but political chaos with a consequent internal and external weakening of the state is a real danger.

The solutions to Belgium's political problems will be reached through direct interaction between the nation's political leaders and the people. The Belgian Parliament has faded in political importance because of its members' inability to compromise their differences in the search for a solution to major national issues in general and the language question in particular. But Belgium has come to accept the need for agreements, made by the cabinet in accord with the leaders of the principal political and interest groups, to patch over differences that threaten the existence of the state.

Whether this system, often based on a public payoff to the two antagonistic sides, can endure depends on the willingness of linguistic extremists to accept a financial settlement of their demands. If these groups retain their strength, which now seems probable, and insist on fundamental changes in the status quo, no cabinet will be able to maintain a national consensus, even on the form of the state. It is generally accepted that a direct confrontation between Dutch- and French-speaking Belgians either in Parliament or in the cabinet itself is inconceivable. In such a situation, the numerical superiority of the Flemings would ensure their complete domination. This in turn would lead to open physical conflict. With the exception of occasional outbreaks of violence, Belgium appears certain to avoid this course. The alternative is federalism.

Many responsible Belgian political leaders doubt that a federal state can be created in a country where there are no true regional interests beyond those of the language groups. The two language families, with the Brussels bone of contention between them, are probably not the appropriate units for the formation of a federation. With these doubts about the chances for federalism, political leaders are attempting to find some form of decentralization that will meet many of the demands of the language groups while maintaining a functioning national government.

Almost any political solution in Belgium can be expected to do no more than patch over the fundamental fissures in Belgian society. The intransigence of the linguistic extremist groups reflects the attitudes of the people. Belgians of one language family have come increasingly to regard members of the other with mistrust bordering on hate. Such attitudes cannot be changed by political action. Many observers believe that only if the Belgian people attain a greater awareness of the economic challenges facing a nation excessively dependent on foreign technology and investment will they sublimate their differences for the good of the nation. But no cabinet has yet been able to influence the Belgians in this direction.

The marked contrasts in domestic political life in the Netherlands and Belgium are much less evident in their international behavior. Naturally, domestic considerations do influence their foreign policies. For example, the strength of the Dutch parliament leads the government to demand greater parliamentary control of the European Community, and the existence of two language groups in Belgium encourages successive Belgian foreign ministers to seek compromises between French and Dutch positions.

But perhaps more than any other countries in western Europe, the Benelux nations have accepted the need for European integration. It is no exaggeration to say that virtually all citizens of these three nations see the future of Benelux in a larger Europe. Although their reasons may differ, the Benelux peoples appear convinced that domestic and international strife can best be met by a fusion of their own political and economic life into a larger European Community. Until this objective becomes attainable, Benelux political development can be expected to follow the traditional pattern discussed here.

ANNOTATED BIBLIOGRAPHY

Not many works exist in English on the politics of the Benelux nations, and only a few more that are helpful have been published in other languages, notably French and Dutch. Useful publications are available from the information services of the three countries. Listed below are the leading works, useful for a basic understanding of the political structures of the Benelux nations.

Benelux

Dahl, Robert A., ed. *Political Oppositions in Western Democracies.* New Haven, Conn.: Yale University Press, 1966. See Hans Daalder, "The Netherlands: Opposition in a Segmented Society," pp. 188–236, and Val R. Lorwin, "Belgium: Religion, Class, and Language in National Politics," pp. 147–187.

De Mayer, J., *et al. Elections in the Countries of the European Communities and in the United Kingdom 1957–1959.* Bruges: De Tempel, 1967. Useful, with excellent electoral maps, although somewhat out of date.

Mast, André. *Les Pays du Benelux.* Paris: Pichon et Durand-Auzias, 1960. The best one-volume work on the three countries.

Benelux—Organization

Publications distributed by the General Secretariat of the Benelux Economic Union, 39, rue de la Régence, Brussels 1, Belgium, including:

Treaty Establishing the Benelux Economic Union (official text in Dutch and French).

Meade, James E. *Negotiations for Benelux: An Annotated Chronicle 1943–1956.* Princeton, N.J.: Princeton University Press, 1957.

Benelux—European Community

Numerous references are made to the Benelux nations in the rich bibliography of works on European integration. Considerable attention is devoted to them in:

Silj, A. *Europe's Political Puzzle.* Cambridge, Mass.: Harvard University Center for International Affairs, 1967.

The Netherlands

The Netherlands Government, The Hague, distributes occasional mimeographed papers on a wide variety of subjects and the following publications:

Digest of the Kingdom of the Netherlands, 1966. Five volumes covering constitutional organization, history and politics, social services, education, arts and sciences, and economy.

Constitution of the Kingdom of the Netherlands.

The Union of Netherlands Muncipalities, The Hague, mimeographed papers on Dutch local government.

Second Report on Physical Planning in the Netherlands. The Hague: Government Printing Office, 1966.

Nonofficial publications:

Daalder, Hans. "Parties and Politics in the Netherlands," *Political Studies,* 3 (1955), pp. 1–16.

———. *The Relation between Cabinet and Parliament in the Netherlands* (paper delivered before the International Political Science Association, 1958).

Goudsblom, Johan. *Dutch Society*. New York: Random House, 1967. The footnotes in this comprehensive study contain useful bibliographical indications.

Lijphart, Arend. *The Politics of Accommodation: Pluralism and Democracy in the Netherlands*. Berkeley and Los Angeles: University of California Press, 1968. The footnotes in this excellent work contain additional bibliography.

———. *The Trauma of Decolonization: The Dutch and West New Guinea*. New Haven, Conn.: Yale University Press, 1966. Useful bibliography in footnotes, esp. p. 86.

Meier, Henk J. *Politiek Zakboek 1967*. Amsterdam: Bekking, 1967. Survey of Dutch political parties.

Organization for Economic Cooperation and Development, Paris. Occasional studies of Netherlands economy in *Economic Surveys* series.

Palmier, Leslie. *Indonesia and the Dutch*. New York: Oxford, 1962.

Sociologica Netherlandica. A semiannual publication of the Netherlands Sociological Society with articles in English on many aspects of Dutch life.

Van den Berg, J. *De Anatomie van Nederland*. Amsterdam: De Bezige Bij, 1967. The first of two planned volumes on Dutch government and the national power structure. A most useful work.

Vandenbosch, Amry. *Dutch Foreign Policy since 1815*. The Hague: Nijhoff, 1959.

Belgium

The Belgian Ministry of Foreign Affairs and External Trade, Brussels, publishes occasional papers on Belgian government and the monthly series:

Memo from Belgium. An excellent and up-to-date survey of domestic Belgian politics. See especially:

Senelle, Robert. *The Political and Economic Structure of Belgium*, Feb.–April 1966. Includes text of *Belgian Constitution*.

The Belgian Information and Documentation Institute, 3, rue Montoyer, Brussels 4, Belgium, publishes excellent occasional papers on Belgium including:

Belgium at Work, 1966.

Belgium Basic Statistics, 1967.

The Language Problem in Belgium, 1967. A comprehensive and dispassionate survey of the problem.

Nonofficial publications:

Anstey, Roger. *King Leopold's Legacy*. London: Oxford, 1966.

Centre de Recherche et d'Information Socio-Politiques (CRISP), Brussels, publishes a *Courrier Hebdomadaire* containing detailed analyses of Belgian political problems.

Debuyst, F. *La Fonction Parlementaire en Belgique: Mecanismes d'Accés et Images*. Brussels: CRISP, 1967. An outstanding political study with an extensive bibliography on Belgian politics.

Meynaud, Jean, *et al. La Décision Politique en Belgique*. Paris: Armand Colin, 1965. The definitive work on Belgian decision making.

Organization for Economic Cooperation and Development, Paris. Occasional studies of Belgium-Luxembourg economy in *Economic Surveys* series.

Waleffe, Bernard. *Some Constitutional Aspects of Recent Cabinet Development in Great Britain and Belgium*. Brussels: Emile Bruylant, 1968.

Luxembourg

The Ministry of State publishes occasional papers, often relating to the national economy and government, and documents including:

The Constitution of the Grand-Duchy of Luxembourg (in French).

Bulletin de Documentation. A periodical.

The Ministry of National Economy and Energy has published:

La Politique Gouvernementale de Reconversion et de Diversification Industrielles, 1967.

Quasi-official publications:

Herchen, Arthur. *History of the Grand-Duchy of Luxembourg*, trans. A. H. Cooper-Prichard. Luxembourg: Linden, 1950.

Majeurs, Pierre. *Principes Élémentaires de Droit Public Luxembourgeois*. Luxembourg, 1967. A teacher's manual.

Pescatore, Pierre. *Conclusion et Effet des Traités Internationaux*. Luxembourg: Government Printing Office, 1964.

INDEX [1]

Accra Pan-African Conference, 221
administration, Belgium, 162–164;
  Netherlands, 134–136
Agenda Committee (B), 124
agriculture (N), 116–117
Albert I, 28, 57
Albert and Isabelle of Austria, 15
Albert, Prince of Liège, 109
aldermen (B), 77
Algemeen Handelsblad, 46
Amsterdam, 9, 49, 79
annexation, of Belgium by France,
  17; of Luxembourg by France, 17
Anti-Revolutionaries (N), 134
Anti-Revolutionary party (N), 88–89
Antwerp, 15, 27, 36, 107
Argentina, 27
Asser, T. M. V., 23
authority, Netherlands, 48–49

Batavian Republic, 14
Battle of the Bulge, 33
Baudouin, 29, 157–158
Beatrix, 40, 129
Belgium, colonial policy, 219–224;
  commune, 75–80; constitution, 25,
  192–195; economy, 33–35, 175–177;
  in European Community, 242–243;
  elections, 108–113; executive branch,
  156–164; geography, 7–9; history,
  15–20, 24–28; independence, 20; interest groups, 120–127; investment
  laws, 35; legal system, 191–198;
  legislature, 164–183; neutrality, 28;
  Parliament, 25, 112–113, 164–183,
  Chamber of Representatives, 108–
  109, Senate, 108–109; political
  parties, 98–108; society, 53–62
Belgium-Luxembourg Economic Union, 32, 34, 224
Benelux countries, and the Atlantic
  Alliance, 245–248; early unity, 10–
  11; European integration, 231–245;
  international role, 17–20

Benelux organization, 3, 224–231
Benelux Plan, 240–241
Binnenhof, 143
Boerenbond (B), 123
Boerenpartij, 51, 91, 94, 153
Borinage, 124
Brabantine Revolution, 16
Britain, 152, 235, 236–238, 239–241
Brussels, 9, 78, 79–80, 107, 108, 169,
  247
Brussels World's Fair, 48, 221
burgomaster, Belgium, 77–78; Nether-
  lands, 70–72, 75
Burundi, 223

cabinet, Belgium, 159–161, 181–183;
  Netherlands, 131–132, 141–147
Calvinism, 41, 49
Calvinist Political party (N), 91
Calvinist Political Union (N), 91–92
Catholic party (B), 99
Catholic People's party (N), 86–87,
  94, 130, 140–141, 151–152
Charles II, 15
Charles V, 10
Charles VI of Austria, 16
Charlotte, 30
China, 27
Christian Historical Union (N), 89–
  90, 151–152
Christian Social party (B), 29, 99,
  101–103, 110, 112, 122, 124, 125,
  169, 171–173, 175–176, 179
Christian Workers' Movement (B),
  125
class, Belgium, 55; Netherlands, 39
College of Burgomaster and Alder-
  men (N), 70
colonial policy, Belgium, 219–224;
  Netherlands, 215–219
Comité d'Arrondissement, 102
Common Action (B), 125
Common Market (*see* European Com-
  munity)

[1] B = Belgium, L = Luxembourg, and N = Netherlands in the case of
institutions peculiar to each country.

Political Science

Modern Comparative Politics Series
General Editor, Peter H. Merkl

Modern Comparative Politics
Peter H. Merkl

France
The Politics of Continuity in Change
Lowell G. Noonan

The Benelux Nations
The Politics of Small-Country Democracies
Gordon L. Weil

Comparative Federalism
The Territorial Dimension of Politics
Ivo D. Duchacek

Forthcoming titles to be announced.

Holt, Rinehart and Winston, Inc.
383 Madison Avenue, New York 10017